JULIUS CAESAR:
The Pursuit of Power

Other Books by Ernle Bradford

The Story of the *Mary Rose*
The Mighty *Hood*
The Great Siege
Ulysses Found
Three Centuries of Sailing
The Companion Guide to the Greek Islands
The Mediterranean: Portrait of a Sea
The Sword and the Scimitar: the Saga of the Crusades
The Year of Thermopylae

Biographies

Southward the Caravels: the story of Henry the Navigator
Drake
The Sultan's Admiral: the life of Barbarossa
Christopher Columbus
Nelson
Hannibal

JULIUS CAESAR:

The Pursuit of Power

by

Ernle Bradford

Hamish Hamilton · London

First published in Great Britain 1984
by Hamish Hamilton Ltd
Garden House 57–59 Long Acre London WC2E 9JZ

Copyright © 1984 Ernle Bradford

British Library Cataloguing in Publication Data

Bradford, Ernle
　Julius Caesar.
　1. Caesar, Julius, 100 B.C.–44 B.C.
　2. Heads of state—Rome—Biography
　3. Generals—Rome—Biography
　I. Title
　937'.05'0924　　　DG261

　ISBN 0-241-11198-6

Photoset by Rowland Phototypesetting Ltd
Bury St Edmunds, Suffolk
Printed in Great Britain by
St Edmundsbury Press,
Bury St Edmunds, Suffolk

Contents

Acknowledgements

I should like first of all to express my particular thanks to Mr A. R. Burn who has helped and advised me on this book, as on others before it, both during its preparation and on the subsequent revision of the completed manuscript. I am very indebted for his assistance on matters of fact, while on matters of emphasis or faults and omissions all errors remain mine.

I would also like to record my thanks, as so often over the years, to the London Library. I have used throughout for the translations from Plutarch the one usually known as Dryden's version, since I find that its sonorous English seems to me better to reflect the original than a modern translation would do. I would like to thank Penguin Books Limited for extracts from Suetonius, *Lives of the Caesars*, trans. Robert Graves; and Juvenal, *The Sixteen Satires*, trans. Peter Green.

Ernle Bradford
September, 1983

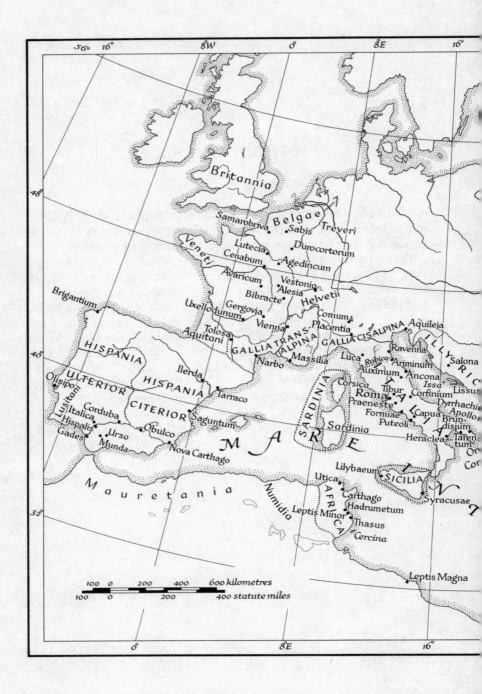

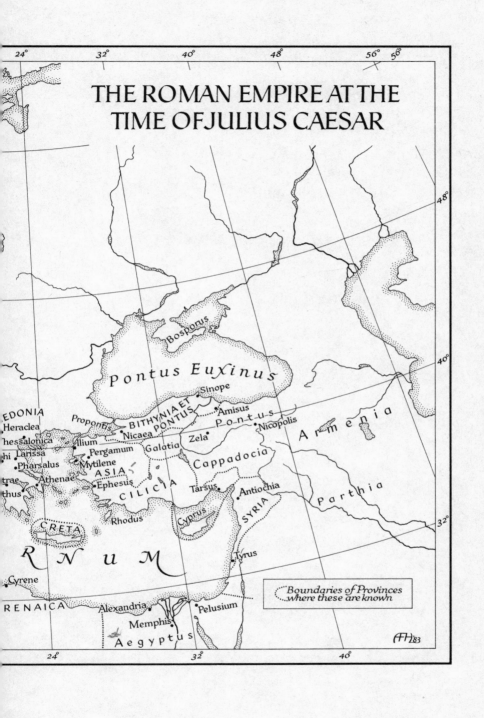

THE ROMAN EMPIRE AT THE TIME OF JULIUS CAESAR

Bosporus

Pontus Euxinus

EDONIA
Heraclea
hessalonica
hi Larissa
Pharsalus
trae Athenae
thus

Proponti
Nicaea
Ilium
Pergamum
Galatia
Mytilene
ASIA
Ephesus
CILICIA

BITHYNIA ET
PONTUS

Sinope

Amisus
Pontus
Zela
Nicopolis

Cappadocia

Tarsus

Cyprus

Antiochia
SYRIA

Armenia

Parthia

Rhodus

CRETA

R   N   U   M

Tyrus

Cyrene

RENAICA

Alexandria
Memphis
Aegyptus

Pelusium

Boundaries of Provinces
where these are known

(FH)83

To the memory of Zachary Macaulay Booth

Immortalia ne speres, monet annus et almum
Quae rapit hora diem.

'Let the dice fly high'.

'Luck is the greatest power in all things and especially in war.'

'If things do not always fall right, luck can be given a helping hand.'

Caius Julius Caesar

CHAPTER ONE
Ancestry and Antecedents

Caesar was an aristocrat. He was an aristocrat by birth and by nature: two things that are far from synonymous. To be born into the so-called aristocracy of a country or an age means little in itself. Some, by their abilities and conduct, earn the right to be called aristocrats. But few over all the centuries are 'born to the purple', more than earn their title, and so distinguish themselves that they establish a new standard for 'the best'. Caesar was one of these: although it must always be accepted that morality (in the sense of moral conduct) played no part in his distinction.

Caius Julius Caesar was born in July 100 BC. He was the only son of Caius Julius and Aurelia and, more important, nephew of the then consul Marius. The Julii were one of Rome's original patrician families, but one that had left relatively little mark upon history. His mother, also of noble birth, seems to have been cast in the mould of the old type of Roman matron: women unaffected by the new fashions from Greece and the East which were so profoundly changing the manners and morals of Rome. It was an old-fashioned family, in fact. His father became a praetor (one of the chief officers of the senate) but never rose to the dignity of consul.

The family was neither rich nor poor, well-born but comparatively undistinguished, and conservative in the real sense of being moderate, cautious and averse to change.

The month in which Caesar was born was formerly called *Quintilis* but was subsequently renamed July in his honour. His personal name or praenomen was Caius. The first Caius in the clan had been born some seventy years before and had married a certain Marcia of the patrician family which claimed descent from the legendary kings of Rome. Caesar himself laid claim to an ancestry so ancient that it could not be disputed since there were no records except that on both sides his family had been noble from time immemorial. In one public speech he was to declare that his family were descended in direct line from

I

Venus/Aphrodite. Since, according to Homer, the goddess was the mother of Aeneas, the Trojan hero, and since, according to later legend, Aeneas was the founder of the Roman race, Caesar was laying claim to an ancestry that could not be challenged. His admirers seem to have accepted this explanation of his lineage, although how much Caesar himself believed it must remain doubtful. Certainly a hallmark of his character was always a strange insouciance, as if – perhaps because of the supposedly divine origin of the Julian line – he felt that nothing could touch him unless decreed by the fates. The name Caesar is connected by tradition with an ancestor who is said to have killed an elephant of the Carthaginian army, the sobriquet deriving from the Punic word for an 'elephant'.

As was customary at that time among the upper classes Caesar was taught Greek. His tutor was an educated Gaul, most probably from northern Italy, who was said to have been as well versed in Latin as in Greek literature and in later years to have established a school of rhetoric which was attended by Caesar during his praetorship in 66 BC. It might at first seem strange that an aristocratic family should employ a Gaul as a tutor, especially in Greek, when Italy swarmed with Greeks and almost every household of any importance could point to a Greek tutor, secretary or librarian, but it is perhaps an indication of the innate conservatism of the family: Greeks were reputed to be effeminate in their manners, often homosexual, and were considered degenerate by old-fashioned Romans. A Gaul on the other hand, and an educated Gaul, was a very different man to have about the house. In the early days when Rome had been gradually subjugating Italy they had proved the most troublesome, freedom-loving, and bravest of all the tribes whom the Romans had encountered. When Hannibal had swept over the Alps in 218 BC, the Gauls had risen with him and, throughout the fifteen years he had spent in Italy, had proved the backbone of the Carthaginian's army. The Romans accordingly had a great respect for the Gauls: not only for their fighting qualities but, now that they had become settlers and farmers, for their diligence, endurance and faithfulness. It was true that in 'Gaul-across-the-Alps' their related tribes still swarmed as wild, fearsome and untamed – except in Romanized Narbonese Gaul – as when they had harried Italy. But now among the rich and noble Romans the big-boned, fair-haired Gauls were a familiar sight and respected for their many qualities, not least for their attachment to the family they served much as once they had been attached to their own clan. In somewhat similar fashion, many centuries later, the rulers of Britain's empire would find in Egypt their trustworthy servants among the Sudanese, and in India and the Far East the amah, or devoted native nurse to care for their children.

Of Caesar's early years nothing is recorded except that he is said to have written a poem in praise of Hercules and a tragedy based on the story of Oedipus. Certainly he was to write poetry until late in his life (though almost nothing has survived), and of course the muscular, limpid prose which distinguishes his seven books of commentaries on the wars in Gaul remains an eternal monument. The subject of Hercules might have been invented for the future hero and cleanser of Augean stables, but Oedipus seems a curious choice although a Freudian might make too much of the fact that, as a child, his relationship with his mother Aurelia had always been very affectionate and happy, and in later years he was passionately attached to her. His father, having been praetor and then propraetor in Asia, died at Pisa in 85 BC so that Caesar – with two sisters but no brother – became the man of the family in his sixteenth year. His mother, throughout the storm of his life, remained a steadfast image of the Roman hearthside and of values that everywhere else were collapsing. If Caesar's political, financial, and sexual morals were a far call from those of old Rome, at least in his conduct as a soldier – in his toughness, endurance, and tenacity – he invariably displayed the same qualities which had given the Romans of an earlier century the final victory over Hannibal.

In 84 BC, at the age of sixteen, Caesar put on the toga of manhood. He was at this time in his life, Suetonius tell us, 'tall, fair and well-built', while Plutarch adds that 'he had a fine white skin' but contradicts Suetonius by saying that he was 'slightly built'. He had a rather broad face and keen, dark-brown eyes. Since both biographers lived long after Caesar was dead they were relying on busts and statues, hearsay and the memories of old men, themselves recounting tales told them as children. Suetonius, however, had access to the imperial and senatorial archives as well as to a large body of contemporary memoirs, while Plutarch cites lists of authorities for his *Lives* and was clearly a diligent researcher.

Caesar's marriage had been arranged before his father's death; indeed a formal engagement, as was not uncustomary, had taken place while he was still a boy. The bride whom his father had proposed was Cossutia who, although rich, came only from an equestrian family and therefore, would be of no particular asset to one who was both patrician and noble, patrician signifying the inner circle of the old aristocracy and noble those who belonged to the *political* inner circle. One thing is clear: after the death of Caesar's father, the engagement with Cossutia was broken off. It is possible that Caesar listened to the voice of his own ambition in this as well as to his mother and, especially perhaps, to her sister, Julia.

The widow of the famous Marius, who had been seven times consul and leader of the 'popular' party, was a woman who still exerted considerable influence upon the government of the time. Rome was a republic, and had been so ever since the expulsion of the kings in the distant past. Power was held by the senate, composed of three hundred members, although in theory this was a democratic state since every Roman citizen was a member of the Assembly, the executive and legislative body. Out of the senate were annually elected the chief officers of the state, the two consuls, the six praetors, and others. In a time of emergency a dictator might be elected, who took precedence over all the officials, but his position had to be ratified every six months. This had happened during the terrible invasion of Italy by Hannibal, when the old aristocrat Quintus Fabius Maximus had been elected dictator at a time when the divided command of the consuls had almost delivered Italy into the Carthaginian's hands.

In the years since then, with the conquest of Carthage and the absorption of its African and Spanish empire, and then of nearly all the eastern Mediterranean states deriving from the conquests of Alexander the Great, Rome had become an imperial nation with conquered or otherwise submissive territories all round the Mediterranean shores. The republican framework, which had well suited Italy after the subjugation of the native tribes and the Gauls to the north, was not adequate to deal with the new responsibilities or organizing a multitude of countries, nations and races – with different languages, customs and religions. Even before Caesar was born, and certainly during his early life, the system that had evolved over centuries was collapsing through the pressure of circumstances for which it had never been designed. Historians and scholars, looking back with hindsight, have been quick to point out that the republic would have disintegrated even if Caesar had never lived. The fact is that Caesar in his struggle for power threw down the old building and laid the foundations for the Imperial one that would be its successor whether inadvertently or by design.

The acquisition of empire, and particularly the riches of the East, had effected an immense change on the Roman scene, both externally and internally. Externally the principal change was from an army which had formerly been composed of Roman citizens, summoned from their farms and small-holdings in time of national emergency, to a number of large armies situated in the various provinces, and composed of paid professional soldiers, not only of Italian but of many other nationalities. Internally, the accessibility of great wealth – especially for the powerful families who could occupy the offices that led to it – had transformed the Roman scene. The Rome of the citizen/farmer/soldier had given way to the Rome of the capitalist, the entrepreneur and the absentee landlord, whose broad acres were farmed by hundreds of slaves from the many subjugated nations within the empire. At the same time the city itself had filled with the dispossessed, the peasants and small farmers, rural villagers whose hamlets had lost their purpose with the

4

advent of slave labour, and all the scourings of the Mediterranean ports and littorals. As Peter Green has written in his introduction to Juvenal's *Satires*: 'Collapsing social standards are as sure a sign of eventual upheaval as the ominous drying up of springs and wells which heralds a volcanic eruption.' Although he was writing over a century after Caesar's birth, his was the Rome described by the great satirist:

> The wagons thundering past
> Through those narrow twisting streets, the oaths of draymen
> Caught in a traffic jam . . .

If a business appointment

> Summons the tycoon, he gets there fast, by litter,
> Tacking above the crowd. There's plenty of room inside:
> He can read, or take notes, or snooze as he jogs along –
> Those drawn blinds are most soporific. Even so
> He outstrips us: however fast we pedestrians hurry
> We're blocked by the crowds ahead, while those behind us
> Tread on our heels. Sharp elbows buffet my ribs,
> Poles poke into me; one lout swings a crossbeam
> Down on my skull, another scores with a barrel.
> My legs are mud-encrusted, big feet kick me, a hobnailed
> Soldier's boot lands squarely on my toe. Do you see
> All that steam and bustle? The great man's hangers-on
> Are getting their free dinner, each with his own
> Kitchen-boy in attendance. Those outsize dixies,
> And all the rest of the gear one poor little slave
> Must balance on his head, while he trots along
> To keep the charcoal glowing, would tax the strength
> Of a muscle-bound general. Here's the great trunk of a fir-tree
> Swaying along its wagon, and look, another dray
> Behind it, stacked high with pine-logs, a nodding threat
> Over the heads of the crowd.
>
> Juvenal (*Trans Peter Green*)

Politically the peninsula was torn apart during Caesar's boyhood by what was called the Social War – the war in which many of the allies of Rome (*socii*) rebelled against the city. They were tired of paying taxes and being sacrificed for Rome while denied the vote by the old reactionaries of the senate, as well as the privileges of Roman citizenship. It was the cry (later to become familiar) of 'No taxation without representation!' The war lasted from 91–87 BC, while Caesar was a boy, and cost on a rough estimate 300,000 lives, but by its end some 80,000

5

new citizens were enfranchised. Its hero was the great soldier Marius, a man of obscure origins but one of the outstanding Roman soldiers: victor in Spain and in Gaul, his life was almost as tumultuous as his nephew Caesar's was to be. Then, hard on the heels of the social war, came a power conflict between what had gradually become the two main political 'parties' in Italy. No parties as such existed in name but distinctions, as between Conservative and Labour, Republican and Democrat, have been in evidence since man became a social and city-dwelling animal. They were very evident in ancient Athens, and since the Romans took almost all their thought, art, political science, science itself, poetry, drama, and philosophy from Greece, it would hardly be surprising if they took their political groupings from the same source.

Although not clearly distinguished by simple names, the two main groups were the *Populares* (*Demos*) and the *Optimates* (*Aristoi*). These were not organized political parties as are understood today in the western world, but somewhat vague groupings impelled by somewhat dissimilar aims and objectives. Of course, as always with human beings, their principal aim was the same: power and the control of power by their own group. Wealth and all that it brought with it would automatically follow. In the civil strife between the *Populares* and the *Optimates* the *Populares* were headed by Caesar's uncle by marriage, Marius, and the *Optimates* by the patrician Sulla. During Marius' absence in the East and after his death in 86 BC the *Populares* were led by L. Cornelius Cinna.

It was almost certainly Caesar's widowed aunt Julia who now took a hand in the first major development in his life, for, after breaking off his engagement to Cossutia, he immediately married Cornelia, the daughter of the now all-powerful Cinna. Marriages were very much matters of politics in the Roman world, and the patrician Julian clan had doubly allied itself with the popular party. Caesar, now in his seventeenth year, was young to marry but no doubt his aunt Julia saw the opportunity as too good to miss. In any case, as events would show, he seems to have been genuinely fond of Cornelia. She bore him a daughter in the following year who was called Julia after her clan. She too was to play an important part in the politics of his life.

Six years older than Caesar was a man who embraced the policies of the *Optimates* as zealously as Caesar did those of the *Populares*. This was the great orator and politician, Marcus Tullius Cicero. As a man, a citizen and politician, Cicero was vain and weak; politically he in many respects resembled the celebrated 'Vicar of Bray' in the old English ballad. His real genius was with language; in his letters, his oratorical works, his speculative philosophy, he raised the Latin tongue to the peak of its perfection. His political stand is most clearly seen in a speech written in defence of a man called Sextius, who had been arrested for his involvement in one of the innumerable brawls that disfigured the political face of Rome. The orator paints a dream picture of the party he favoured, which never existed in the Rome that he knew and can only have existed in his head:

In the Commonwealth there have always been two parties – the *Populares* and the *Optimates*. The *Populares* say and do what will please the mob. The *Optimates* say and do what will please the best men. And who are the best men? They are of all ranks and infinite in number – senators, municipal citizens, farmers, men of business, even freedmen. The type is distinct. They are the well-to-do, the sound, the honest who do no wrong to any man. The object at which they aim is quiet with honour. They are the conservatives of the State. Religion and good government, the Senate's authority, the laws and customs of our ancestors, public faith, integrity, sound administration – these are the principles on which they rest, and these they will maintain with their lives. Their path is perilous. The enemies of the State are stronger than its defenders; they are bold and desperate, and go with a will to the work of destruction . . . The people are conservative at heart; the demagogues cannot rouse them, and are forced to pack the Assembly with hired gangs. Take away these gangs, stop corruption at the elections, and we shall all be of one mind. The people will be on our side. The citizens of Rome are not *Populares*. They hate the *Populares*, and prefer honourable men.

But the patricians who supported the *Optimates* had forgotten nothing, learned nothing, and were every whit as violent and unscrupulous as the party that Cicero castigated. If one conceives of Rome as resembling one of the more notorious South American 'Republics' of today, it is possible to gain some idea of the world in which Caesar was born and grew up.

CHAPTER TWO

Beginnings

During the seventh and last consulship of Marius, Caesar had been observed by the great man (he was a friend of his uncle's adopted son) and had been marked out for future advancement.

One of the many victims of the civil war between the *Populares* and the *Optimates* had been the noble L. Cornelius Merula, the *flamen dialis* or priest of Jupiter, who had committed suicide on the victory of the popular party four years before. One of the requirements for filling this office, one of the highest priestly positions in Rome, was patrician birth and the priest must also only marry a patrician; so the decision that Caesar should be *flamen dialis* may have been part reason for the breaking of his engagement to Cossutia, for Cinna's daughter was patrician. However, the office of priest of Jupiter was very ancient, and hedged around by so many traditions and taboos that the man who accepted it was very much a prisoner of his priestly status. He had to wear traditional old-fashioned heavy garments, be 'the man of only one woman', never be absent for more than two consecutive nights from Rome, and, most important of all, never hold any other public office. It is highly unlikely that the austere, peaceful life of a priest would have suited Caesar, and to be debarred from all forms of political or military activity would have effectively castrated his whole career.

He was saved from this by a *volte-face* in Roman affairs, when his father-in-law Cinna was murdered by his own soldiers and the *Optimates* under the leadership of Sulla swept to power after a decisive victory in further civil war. Immediately everything was changed. From being the nephew of the dead Marius, and the son-in-law of the all-powerful Cinna with the expectation of considerable honour, Caesar was now seen as intimately connected with the party that was disgraced and out of power – and Sulla was determined to restore all favours to the aristocrats and the senate. A terrible proscription was organized not only in Rome but throughout Italy. The popular party was to be extirpated, its leading members killed and their property

8

seized. No one, in fact, was safe, as Sulla's friends were quick to place on the lists of the proscribed the names of their personal enemies. Sulla, appointed dictator so long as he judged necessary, held the whole Roman world in his grasp.

Caesar was soon acquainted with the change of circumstances. His cousin, the young Marius, who had had himself unconstitutionally elected to the consulship in the year of Sulla's triumph, committed suicide. Caesar, however, had taken no part in politics or the war, being groomed for his future priestly office. But he remained immensely vulnerable, being in the very heart of the Marian-Cinnan network of blood relationships. His youth, his political and military non-involvement, and the very holiness of the office for which he had been intended, may have been the reasons why he was spared when so many others, with no equivalent entanglements, were daily being murdered. Instead of sending orders for Caesar's execution, the dictator summoned him for an interview, and there seems little doubt that Sulla wished to draw this young patrician into his own party. But there was a condition required for this act of conciliation. He must put away his wife Cornelia and, though this is only guesswork, presumably marry somebody chosen by Sulla.

Few men in Caesar's position in the Rome of that time would have done anything but renounce their wife and marry any woman that Sulla designated. Caesar's certainly unexpected reply was to refuse to divorce Cornelia. This may be considered a very brave or a very foolish action, but in any case the effect was the same – he was forced to flee into hiding. At the same time, all the dowry that his wife had brought him and other legacies due to her from her family were confiscated. Caesar became a fugitive in the Sabine country of central Italy. It can hardly have been political wisdom that led to his refusal of the dictator's offer, and it certainly seems that a young man's love for his wife put him in such peril. Some evidence of this is that Cornelia was to remain his wife until her death in 69.

Caesar now learned to live as a fugitive. For the first time, in the life of a comfortable, even spoiled young aristocrat, he knew hardship and fear. Suffering from malaria, carried from one hiding place to another, he was captured in the end by one of Sulla's proscription police, who were combing every district of Italy for those who had been put on the lists of wanted men. As must have happened so many times during that tortured period, he was forced to buy his life from the leader of the patrol who had discovered him with a large bribe. Had he been a poorer man his head would have secured for his captor the bounty hunter's reward. But Caesar was able to offer more, and resumed his life as a fugitive. No doubt he would have been caught yet again, and this time with no possible redress, but the intercession of his noble relatives at

9

the court of the dictator, and even of the Vestal Virgins, finally prevailed on Sulla to remove him from the death list – although perhaps it was intimated that he would do well to leave Italy. Sulla revealed that he had observed Caesar closely and had disapproved of much that he saw. As Dio Cassius records it, he remarked: 'Beware of this youth who wears his girdle so loosely fastened.' This was a comment on the fact that Caesar affected what was considered a rather effeminate style of dressing with a loose belt, and fringed sleeves to his wrists. Then, as always, he paid a great deal of attention to his appearance, having superfluous hair removed with tweezers and the hair on his head elaborately arranged. Possibly apocryphal is Suetonius' story that Sulla, granting his pardon, remarked to the suppliants: 'Keep him since you so wish, but I would have you know that this young man who is so precious to you will one day overthrow the aristocratic party, which you and I have fought so hard to defend. There are many Mariuses in him.'

It was clearly prudent for Caesar to remove himself as far as possible from Rome, and an appointment was found for him on the staff of M. Minucius Thermus, the propraetor of Asia. At that time it was customary for Roman generals stationed away from Italy to have on their staff a number of well-bred young men, without any special military knowledge, who could provide some cultured company while at the same time seeing for themselves something of the world, of action, and the governance of foreign provinces. They were also sometimes used on diplomatic and other missions in connection with the work of Empire. In 81, when Caesar joined his staff, the propraetor was engaged on the task of punishing the citizens of Mitylene, capital of the island of Lesbos, for their rebellion against the Romans in the wars inspired by Mithridates the Great. The aim of this famous king of Pontus, the north-eastern district of Asia Minor, was – and was to remain for many years – the expulsion of the Romans from all Asia. (Mithridates was to remain a thorn in the Roman side for much of Caesar's life.) The young man's first mission from his general was to travel to the kingdom of Bithynia, part of which bordered on the Black Sea, and ask its ruler to expedite the despatch of his fleet, which he had promised for the Mitylene blockade.

Nicomedes IV of Bithynia had given his allegiance to Rome when he came to power and remained faithful to his masters during all the intrigues and power struggles initiated by Mithridates. Since his kingdom controlled the Asiatic shores of the Bosphorus, Nicomedes with his powerful fleet had a tight hold on all the traffic and shipping in the Dardanelles. His court was one of extreme luxury, and since he profited by the protection of Rome he had no desire to see any trouble in Asia. He may have poisoned his father, not an uncommon practice in the East when heirs felt they had waited too long for the throne, and he was renowned as a sodomite, again not uncommon in the East.

The propraetor's aristocratic young messenger was naturally given an effusive welcome by Nicomedes, sensible that he had been dilatory in despatching the promised fleet and eager to curry favour with his Roman protectors. On learning Caesar's mission, the King immediately offered him his own sleeping quarters so that he could refresh himself after his tiring journey. There was nothing to this in itself – but Caesar's enemies were to make much of it in the years to come. 'The King's guards,' Cicero was to say, 'escorted him there, and he slept on a bed of gold with a purple covering.' On the following day, while the fleet was being rapidly readied for despatch southward, an elaborate feast was given in the King's palace to do honour to the propraetor's emissary, as well as to a delegation of Roman merchants who happened to be in Bithynia. Caesar, forgetful perhaps of the dignity of his mission, joined in the mood of the moment and performed the role of cup-bearer to Nicomedes during the banquet. In doing so he put himself in the same company as a number of elegant and effeminate youths who formed part of the well-known seraglio of the King. Cicero was later to maintain in several letters that Caesar, 'descendant of Venus, lost his virginity in Bithynia'. This accusation was widely repeated by his opponents in years to come, although why so much importance was given to the imputation it is hard to see since homosexuality was hardly unknown in the Rome of that day. It was, however, loosely associated by the old conservative aristocrats (such as Caesar's own parents), with the degeneracy of Greece and with the effeminacy of the rich and indolent East.

The incident became widely known in Rome, having presumably been reported by the merchants who were present at the banquet, and certainly had a damaging effect on Caesar's reputation. Years later, on the occasion of his Gallic triumph, his soldiers following his decorated chariot through the city chanted ribald songs, as they were privileged to do on such occasions. One of them, as will be seen, referring to Nicomedes and Caesar, was enough to make him lose his temper.

On this occasion Caesar protested vigorously and swore that the whole story was false, but he was never allowed to forget it even though he later became known as one of the most notorious womanizers in Rome. Cornelius Dolabella, who had every reason to hate Caesar since the latter had, unsuccessfully, prosecuted him for maladministration in Macedonia, called him 'the female rival of Bithynia's queen,' and 'the bottom half of the royal bed'. C. Scribonius Curio, who was consul in 77, called him 'Nicomedes' bride', 'the brothel of Bithynia', and 'every woman's husband and every man's wife'. Years later, when Nicomedes was dead, Caesar, speaking in the senate in defence of some dependents of the late King, reminded his audience that he was obligated to Nicomedes 'for numerous favours'. Cicero interrupted him with 'Let us pass over that, I pray you, since there is no one who is unaware of what he gave you and what he received in return.' Suetonius quotes two lines from a satirical poem by Licinius Calvus, a well known orator and poet of the time:

> The riches of Bithynia's King
> Who Caesar on his couch abused.

The truth of the matter will never be known, and it seems of small relevance in the light of Caesar's life. Like many a young man he may have passed through a homosexual phase. It bothered nineteenth-century historians but need not trouble us today, although Caesar himself was to suffer from the scandal. He did in fact compound the error that gave rise to it, by returning to Bithynia after seeing the fleet safely to the blockade of Mitylene; 'on the pretext of having to deliver a sum to some client of his,' Suetonius writes.

It is clear though that Caesar, unlike many of the young nobles who hung around the courts of generals and propraetors, took his military duties seriously. After the successful storming of Mitylene in 80 he was decorated with the civic crown by Minucius Thermus. The *corona civica* was a wreath of oak leaves awarded to those who had saved the life of a fellow soldier in battle, and although some commanders gave them away too freely, it is doubtful if Caesar's was anything other than a genuine award, since Minucius Thermus was a supporter of Sulla and the *Optimates*. The holder of this highly-honoured decoration, which might be worn on all festive occasions, was entitled to sit next to the senators at the public games, and when he appeared on the scene all the spectators, senators included, rose to their feet. It had long been established that the award in the case of senators' sons gave them a preferential position in the 'Honours List', which may explain (something which has puzzled many commentators) why Caesar was able to become consul in 59 at the age of forty, when forty-two was usually the minimum age for the consulate.

The Mitylene campaign was soon over and the troops of Minucius Thermus were to be dismissed. Hearing that the governor of Cilicia, the south-easternmost corner of Asia Minor, was about to embark on a campaign against the pirates who haunted the creeks and river-mouths of the area, Caesar went to offer him his services. He was already with the Governor's forces when, in 78, the news reached him that Sulla was dead and Caesar left immediately for Italy. He hoped no doubt to take advantage of the confusion that would follow the dictator's death, but he arrived to find that, as Suetonius puts it, 'the political atmosphere was less favourable then he had been led to believe'. An insurrection had begun, led by one of the consuls, Marcus Aemilius Lepidus, who had assumed the leadership of the *Populares*. This might have seemed to appeal to Caesar, especially when he was earnestly asked to join it and 'magnificent offers' were made to him. However, with remarkably cool judgement for a young man of twenty-two, he appraised the situation carefully – and correctly. The Sullans still had a large majority in the senate while Lepidus did not have the strength of character or capabilities to achieve success. When the whole enterprise collapsed in ruins Caesar's judgement was confirmed and he himself emerged completely unscathed.

Caesar had been away from Rome for three years and now was his first chance to renew his acquaintanceship with public affairs and to cast around for the direction in which his ambitions might find fulfilment. It is clear that he had no desire for the career for which he had early been trained, the priesthood, and he was neither rich enough, nor temperamentally inclined, to idle away his days as did many young upper-class Romans. He needed first of all to get himself known, and inevitably turned towards the Forum. One path to a political career, the one which Cicero adopted, was that of rhetoric and the law. Caesar had received an excellent education, and his acute mind, coupled with his training in Greek and Latin rhetoric, made him look for a cause where he could acquire the most publicity, as well as laying the foundation of a solid reputation. He made his start by prosecuting Gnaeus Cornelius Dolabella (the same who, inflamed with hatred, would accuse him of homosexual relations with Nicomedes). Dolabella was one of the leading Sullans – the dictator had nominated him for the consulship in 81 – and had recently been accorded a triumph in Rome for some rather obscure military exploits. Subsequently he had been governor of Macedonia where he had exceeded in his rapacity even the limits normally extended to governors of provinces, who were expected to make their fortunes during this summer period of their lives. The only action that could be taken to redress the complaints of the governed and overtaxed (robbed, would be more accurate) was for a Roman citizen to come forward as prosecutor. A complaint was formally laid before the tribunal outlining the intended form of the indictment and backed by evidence from the complainants. In the event, the wealthy Dolabella secured the services of two of the greatest lawyers of the day, one of whom, Aurelius Cotta, was a kinsman of Caesar, and managed with their help to get acquitted. Caesar had lost his first case, but he had achieved his main object: he had won great credit as an orator, and the very fact that the accused had felt himself in need of such eminent men to secure his acquittal added lustre to Caesar's reputation.

It is clear that his Greek clients were also impressed by his performance (his speeches survived in document and were regarded in Rome as a literary masterpiece), and the following year he was entrusted with the case against another Sullan. This was Gaius Antonius Hybrida, who, during Sulla's campaign in Greece, had looted and pillaged a great number of Greek cities. So skilfully did Caesar work up his case and deliver his indictment that Antonius was forced to appeal to the people's tribunes over the head of the judging praetors who had considered the complaint well-founded. He was acquitted, but the acquittal in itself caused a scandal. Again, Caesar had not won, but his reputation was now made and he became recognized as one of the greatest orators of his time and second only to Cicero. He had won many friends in Greece, many friends in Rome (as well as enemies), and he had established his position, by his attacks on two notorious Sullans, as a follower of his uncle Marius and an up-and-coming man in the popular party. By these two actions Caesar had laid the foundations of his political career.

CHAPTER THREE

A Greek Adventure

After two years in Rome Caesar suddenly travelled to the East again. It has often been said by historians that this was because he feared reprisals from Dolabella and the other Sullans, but this is somewhat doubtful. In the days of the dictator he had merely gone into hiding – and there was no equal to Sulla now. According to Suetonius – 'he decided to visit Rhodes until the ill-feeling against him [in Rome] had died down and take a course in rhetoric from Apollonius Molon, the greatest exponent of the art'. Plutarch, although somewhat weak about this period of his life, gives an important clue: 'In his pleadings at Rome, his eloquence soon obtained him great credit and favour, and he won no less upon the affections of the people by the affability of his manners and address, in which he showed a tact and consideration beyond what could have been considered at his age; and the open house he kept, the entertainments he gave, and the general splendour of his manner of life contributed little by little to create and increase his political influence. His enemies slighted the growth of it at first, presuming it would soon fail when his money was gone . . .' The probability is that Caesar's money had indeed gone. The Julii, as has been said, were not rich, while Sulla had confiscated his wife's dowry and other personal moneys and there is no evidence that they had been returned. Historians basing their conclusions on Suetonius, that he sailed for Rhodes to take lessons from Apollonius Molon, have ignored a very salient point in the story of Caesar's voyage through the Aegean. This is that 'winter had already set in when he sailed for Rhodes and was captured by pirates off the island of Pharmacussa'. But there were regular sailings between Italian ports and the important Aegean island of Rhodes, while the small island of Pharmacussa was off the Asian coast hard by the city of Miletus – a long way to the north of Rhodes. It is inconceivable, even in the wintry Aegean, that any vessel could have strayed so far off its course, and suggests that Caesar had not adopted the normal course of taking a Rhodes-bound ship from Italy, but had embarked from Greece on a Miletus-bound vessel. He could almost certainly have gone from Brundisium to Dyrrachium (Brindisi-Durazzo), the usual route for visitors to Greece. After the prosecutions, unsuccessful though they were, of Dolabella over his embezzlement in Macedonia and Antonius for his shameless plundering of Greek cities, Caesar had many indebted clients in Greece who may have owed him money; certainly they owed him hospitality, for his two actions had brought to light the conduct of important Romans in Greece and had almost certainly had a restraining effect upon the activities of other Roman soldiers and governors. Caesar was a Graecophile, in any case, and it would have been natural for him to visit a country where he was certain of hospitality even if not financial reward. Wherever he embarked on the Aegean coast for his second sea journey, possibly Athens, he could again have sailed direct for Rhodes through the Cyclades; instead his ship was clearly destined for Miletus, which, as Gérard Walter has pointed out in his *Caesar*, was 'on the way which leads via Pergamos straight to the kingdom of Nicomedes IV'.

There was a very good reason for Caesar to go to Bithynia: the King had recently died and being childless, and mindful of the protection that Rome had afforded him as well as of his country's fate at the hands of Mithridates if the succession was disputed, he had bequeathed Bithynia to the Romans. Marcus Juncus, the governor of Asia Minor, was about to take over Bithynia's affairs and make an inventory of the whole estate. It is more than likely, though no correspondence exists between Caesar and Nicomedes, that the attractive young Roman aristocrat expected to be mentioned in the King's will. There was every reason then for Caesar, after his visit to Greece, to make his way to the court of this prosperous and important kingdom; far more than to visit the renowned Greek rhetorician in Rhodes, who in any case could be included later during his visit to the Aegean.

While on its way towards Miletus, however, Caesar's vessel was captured by some of the pirates who infested the sea coast of Asia Minor, and who would continue to prove a curse on the imperial shipping routes until removed by the great Pompey. The crew probably went overboard but the obviously important young Roman – travelling with a staff of a physician and two personal servants – was taken as a hostage. Although it has been constantly quoted in nearly all biographies, the account by Plutarch is so revealing of Caesar's character that some of it must be given here: 'When these men at first demanded of him twenty talents for his ransom, he laughed at them for not understanding the value of their prisoner, and voluntarily engaged to give them fifty.'

Caesar was quite happy to do this, for he did not have to produce the money himself. Since they appeared not to be able to keep order in their territories, and since the pirates were obviously drawn from their own people and their cities flourished from this very piracy, the inhabitants of coastal Asia Minor were under a strict obligation to Rome to secure the release of any Roman citizen captured in their vicinity and, where necessary, to provide the ransom money.

Having sent off messengers to inform the local governors of the capture of so important a Roman citizen, Caesar, his doctor and their two servants, settled down to wait. The accounts that we have of this period are usually believed to derive from a report written by his physician, which was later used by both Plutarch and Suetonius and by the earlier historian Velleius Paterculus. According to Plutarch 'he was left among some of the most bloodthirsty people in the world . . . yet he made so little of them that, when he had a mind to sleep, he would send for them, and order them to make no noise.' Paterculus, our earliest authority, has it that he induced among them 'as much fear as respect', but also mentions how careful Ceasar was not to do anything that might make his jailers suspect him of plotting to escape. It was unlikely in any case that he could have done so: it was winter and any small boats would have been hauled up ashore under the pirates' watchful eyes. 'For thirty-eight days,' writes Plutarch, 'with time on his hands, he played and exercised with them, wrote verses and speeches which he read to them, and if they did not admire them sufficiently would call them ignorant barbarians. Apparently in jest, he would threaten to hang them.'

When the ransom finally arrived Caesar and his fellow-prisoners embarked and returned to Miletus. The pirates thought no doubt that that was the last they would hear of this seemingly rich young Roman: people who had escaped from such a dangerous situation hardly, if ever, ventured into that area again. But they had reckoned without Caesar. What they had taken for a jest was more than earnest. On arrival at Miletus – only a short sail or 'pull' away – Caesar at once raised several ships, their crews (possibly pirates themselves), no doubt on the basis of 'no cure, no pay'. Despite his pretence of relaxed geniality, he had clearly been infuriated by his detention. It was winter; the island (probably the larger of two in this area, and one which has a good harbour) would have been barren and bone-chilling. Also, and he was to remain so all his life, he was an authoritarian, a strict believer that civilization could only be maintained by the exercise of discipline over all the anarchic forces which would destroy it.

While the pirates were still engaged upon their 'Treasure Island', Caesar returned. The lean, apparently soft and somewhat effeminate young man was transformed into an eagle of vengeance. In what appears to have been a miniature sea-battle – the pirates attempting to escape as soon as the other vessels were sighted – several of their boats were sunk and the crews of the others all surrendered. Both ashore, and in the vessels that remained afloat, Caesar had re-captured not only the money that had been advanced by the neighbouring cities for his ransom but everything else that the pirates had stored away on Pharmacussa. His visit to Bithynia had – temporarily – been postponed, but he had acquired a small fortune which, even after the expenses of the expedition had been met and the ransom money returned to the cities from which it had come, should still yield a handsome profit to the man who had initiated the destruction of the pirates' nest and the capture of their loot and their leaders.

The captured pirates were taken to Pergamos, where the governor of Asia Minor, Marcus Juncus, normally resided. Finding that he was away settling the affairs of Bithynia, Caesar followed him there. To his disgust he found that the governor, 'having an eye to their wealth, which was considerable', was unwilling to give an immediate decision on the fate of the prisoners. Indeed, he said that he would rather sell them than execute them as this would be of benefit to the treasury. Velleius Paterculus refers to the governor as 'no less envious than cowardly'. He was envious perhaps because of the wealth which would accrue to Caesar, but 'cowardly' is difficult to explain. It seems unlikely that the governor feared that friends of the captured men might take revenge upon him if they were executed, unless, of course, he had been working hand in glove with the pirates operating off his coastline. Such a thing is not impossible, for the behaviour of many Roman governors and generals at this stage in the empire was often far more reprehensible than simple collusion.

Caesar took matters into his own hands and returned at once to Pergamos. Before the governor's instructions to proceed with the sale of the pirates had arrived, he, acting on his own initiative, had fulfilled his promise to the pirates and had them crucified.

Having settled his affairs in Bithynia, and enriched by his share of the pirates' plunder, Caesar now proceeded to pay that visit to Rhodes which is usually given as his reason for being in the East at all. But he can have had little time to benefit from his stay with the eloquent Apollonius Molon, for almost immediately the third war initiated by King Mithridates broke out, this time brought about by the fact that Mithridates refused to accept the will of Nicomedes bequeathing Bithynia to Rome. Hearing that some of the King's forces had broken into the province of Asia, Caesar immediately – acting on his own account and without any orders – crossed over from Rhodes to the mainland and either raised his own forces or took charge of the local militia. With these troops under his command he drove the enemy out of the province: a remarkable action for so young a man and one which once again showed his dash and initiative.

Caesar's time in Greece and the Aegean and Asia Minor, as a young man in his middle twenties, showed all the hallmarks of his later career. He was first and foremost a politician, had a natural bent for the military life, was financially unscrupulous, and would tolerate no man standing in his way or threatening his path to power.

CHAPTER FOUR

Politics and Money

In the year 73, while Caesar was a staff officer in Asia Minor with the congenial duty of helping to remove the pirate menace from the eastern Mediterranean, he learned that his uncle, Gaius Cotta, had died. This left a vacancy in the College of Pontiffs, and Caesar, aged only twenty-six, had been nominated to fill it. It was an important step forward in his career, and it is not surprising that he immediately set out for Italy. Once again it is noticeable that, although he thrived on the active military life, he was always willing to abandon it the moment that some political advantage beckoned from Rome. The College of Pontiffs, which had been established very early in Roman history to watch over the preservation of religious observance and orthodoxy, had none of the disadvantages of his previous dalliance with the priesthood and all the advantages of one of the most exclusive clubs in the capital city. While non-political, it offered a privileged position in ruling circles and, to the right man at the right time, the ultimate and attractive prospect of aspiring to the office of *Pontifex Maximus*, the pagan Pope of Rome. There can be no doubt that Caesar's family connections had been more than helpful in securing him this nomination, while his winning the civic crown at Mitylene and the commendation of his commander also probably played their part.

Having made the crossing from Asia Minor, or Rhodes, to Greece, Caesar then crossed the Adriatic in a small boat of only four oars, manned by ten slaves and accompanied by two friends. Years later, in 49, at the height of his battle for the Roman world, he was to attempt to repeat the journey in somewhat similar fashion – only to be defeated by the weather. On this occasion, however, the crossing was successful, although at one moment there was an alarm.

> On the way over he thought he saw pirate ships and immediately took off his clothes presumably to swim for it rather than be captured yet again and fastened a dagger to his side. He soon realised he was

mistaken and that what he had taken for the masts of ships was a row
of trees coming up on the horizon.

(A nice touch by Velleius Paterculus)

On arrival in Rome, confirmed in his office in the College of Pontiffs,
his ambition spurred him to make use of his military service and his
civic crown to apply for the office of military tribune, twenty-four of
whom were nominated annually. He was elected in 73 but did not
assume his rank until the year after his return to Italy. The office did
not necessarily imply active service in the field, but was often concerned solely with military organization and staff work at home, and the
engagement only lasted for six months. But the holder was entitled to
be called 'Military Tribune of the People' for life, and the office was
often an early step on the political ladder for young men of good family.

The significance of the office of the tribunes had been largely
abolished by the dictator Sulla, who had forbidden them from publicly
addressing meetings of the people, one of their ancient rights. Caesar
was foremost among those who sought to restore these privileges, once
again openly demonstrating that he took his stand with the popular
party. (Three years later all restrictions on the tribunate were lifted.)
All our Latin sources mention Caesar's election to military tribune
because this post was filled by popular vote. It was the first office in
which the people had shown their favour towards Caesar. In the year
70, Plautius, one of the tribunes, laid a bill before the people to grant an
amnesty to all those followers of Marius and Cinna who had been
exiled during the Sullan regime. Again the *Populares* were seen to be in
the ascendant, and Caesar himself spoke out – for the first time – to the
Roman people, advocating the amnesty and mentioning his brother-
in-law Lucius Cinna who was among those who had been banished.
The return of all these exiled followers of Marius immeasurably
strengthened the popular party, and marked the turn of the political
tide.

But Caesar's life in Rome was far from being that of a totally
dedicated politician. Indeed many of his future opponents assumed
that he was a political lightweight because of his luxurious style of living
and his constant pursuit of women. One of the reasons for his
popularity with women was undoubtedly his elegance and charm –
something which, one suspects, was singularly lacking in most Roman
husbands. (Cicero has a scathing reference to the meticulous arrangement of Caesar's hair and his habit of adjusting his parting with one
finger.) But his womanizing, though it may have infuriated some
members of his own class (for obvious reasons), can only have amused
the masses while he endeared himself to them by his extravagant
expenditure.

Plutarch writes on this score:

He was so profuse in his expenses, that before he had any public employment, he was in debt thirteen hundred talents. [Impossible to calculate in the shifting values of modern currencies, but many thousands of pounds sterling.] Many thought that by incurring such expense to be popular, he changed a solid good for what would prove but a short and uncertain return; but in truth he was purchasing what was of the greatest value at an inconsiderable rate. When he was made surveyor of the Appian way, he disbursed, besides the public money, a great sum out of his private purse; and when he was aedile (magistrates superintending trade, money, streets and buildings, the games etc.) he provided such a number of gladiators, that he entertained the people with three hundred and twenty single combats, and by his great liberality and magnificence in theatrical shows, in processions, and public feastings, he threw into the shade all the attempts that had been made before him, and gained so much upon the people, that every one was eager to find out new offices and new honours for him in return for his munificence.

Between the years 72–70 Caesar disappears from the view of his ancient biographers. Some of his subsequent biographers have found it impossible to believe that during this period he was inactive, for these were the years of the great revolt of the slaves under Spartacus, when this former Thracian bandit was leading an army which ravaged Italy and two consuls and one Roman army after another were defeated. Yet we can be very sure that his biographers would have been quick to tell us if he had been in any way involved, since they detail much more trivial parts of his life. It would seem that Caesar, now rising thirty, was absorbed by indolence and luxury, only disturbed by a passion for internal politics and in laying the foundations for his future career by what amounted to bribing the masses. It may well be that at this time in his life he was making amends to himself for his hard years under Sulla and his self-exile in the eastern empire at a time when most young men of his class were enjoying the pleasures of Rome.

Certainly, he did not stint himself now, and tales of his wild extravagance lulled to rest any fears there may ever have been among the *Optimates* that Caesar was another Marius. Abstemious with regard to drink, he also seems to have been more or less indifferent to the quality of food, but he was a passionate collector of every form of art: gems, statues, carvings, and paintings by the masters. Suetonius writes that, 'so high were the prices he paid for slaves of attainments and good character that he was ashamed of his extravagance and would not have the sums put down in his accounts.' He was a connoisseur of pearls, particularly of the fresh water variety (later given as one of his reasons for invading Britain where they were said to be plentiful). He gave Servilia, the mother of Marcus Brutus so prominent among his murderers, a pearl of almost inestimable value – 60,000 gold pieces – and she is described as 'the woman whom Caesar loved best'. (It is possible that he was Brutus' father.) But he loved many, and Suetonius lists a number of the wives of the nobility whom he seduced at one time or another, among them those of most of his friends, including Pompey, Crassus and Gabinius – and that at a time when they were the leaders of the party to which he subscribed and whose goodwill he needed. This 'descendant of Venus' seems to have had a nature as passionate as the goddess herself, though even more contradictory. Sir Charles Oman summed up this aspect of his life: 'He was the inevitable co-respondent in every fashionable divorce, and when we look at the list of the ladies whose names are linked with his, we can only wonder at the state of society in Rome which permitted him to survive unscathed to middle age. The marvel is that he did not end in some dark corner, with a dagger between his ribs long before he attained the age of thirty.'

In the year 68 Caesar emerges again into history, and the year was marked by three important events. First of all his aunt Julia died. The death of the widow of the great Marius could not be allowed to pass without public notice, and Caesar made the very most of it. He had recently been appointed a quaestor (one of the state treasurers and paymasters), an office which brought with it membership of the senate. As a member of the College of Pontiffs and now as a senator, he was in a position to ask for a ritual eulogy of his aunt, a public procession which included musicians, a choir of mourners, an effigy of the dead on a state hearse and then further mourners and relatives. The procession much resembled a modern state funeral. On this occasion, however, Caesar with his instinct for showmanship did something for which there was no precedent, and which was at the same time a deliberately provoca-tive gesture to the *Optimates*. In the procession, occasioning gasps among the citizens thronging the route, was borne the family statue of the great Marius, which it had been forbidden to show in public ever since Sulla had declared him an enemy of the state. When the procession stopped and the image of his dead aunt was placed as was customary in front of the orator's platform, Caesar mounted it and pronounced the eulogy on the woman who had been Marius' wife. It was now that he also saw fit to extol the virtues of his own family, laying claim to their descent from the kings of ancient Rome and the goddess Venus. The interesting point was not so much Caesar's extravagant claims for his family but that he made them in the context of Julia's marriage to Marius, a man of humble birth. Many of the aristocracy in a similar position, just as today, would have been happy to conceal such a *mésalliance*, but Caesar, it seems, was eager to stress that the noble blood from which he was descended was also allied with one who had, as it were, 'risen from the ranks'. It was yet another statement of his membership of the popular party, and also perhaps a first claim to the leadership of it.

The third major event of this year was the death of Caesar's wife Cornelia. She was probably only in her late twenties and she remains a shadowy figure, although Caesar's action in refusing to divorce her at the orders of the dictator Sulla does indeed seem to suggest that he had really loved her. But apart from bearing his daughter Julia we know nothing of her and can only surmise, in view of Caesar's long list of known mistresses, that her marriage can hardly have been a happy one – unless one accepts what is probably true, that a Roman wife did not expect a faithful husband.

Perhaps Caesar felt some qualms about his treatment of Cinna's daughter – some uneasiness about the years that he had left her when he was abroad, and his constant absence with other women when at home. At any rate, she was accorded a funeral somewhat like the one he had arranged for his aunt Julia. This was most unusual, since normally such obsequies were only offered to older women, and those who had been the wives of famous or distinguished men. Plutarch observes: 'This also procured him some favour, and by this show of affection he won upon the feelings of the people, who looked upon him as a man of great tenderness and kindness of heart.' Yes, even here he achieved some political capital.

CHAPTER FIVE

The Shape of Ambition

Caesar was now appointed as quaestor to a post in Farther Spain. This cannot have suited him at all. Farther Spain was as far west as anyone could then be sent, and a quaestorship there was far from influential: all the important posts were in Rome. It seems very probable the ruling party had decided that Caesar had gone quite far enough in his recent activities, and the greater the distance which separated him from Rome the better.

His duties were onerous, for he had to be entirely at the service of the controlling magistrate and undertake whatever tasks he was given. For a whole year, under the propraetor (a kind of governor-general) he was sent on what amounted to an assize-circuit, visiting the four main cities of this western province – Gades (Cadiz), Corduba (Cordova), Hispalis (Seville) and Astigi (Ecija) – as well as many of the other lesser towns. Becoming a quaestor had suited Caesar in so far as it admitted him to the senate, but service so far away from the capital was certainly not to his taste. Clearly he neither liked the job, nor possibly the place, for it is noticeable that he left Spain ahead of the official termination of his appointment. There was nothing to keep him in the area as there had been in Asia Minor, where he seems to have enjoyed himself.

Suetonius relates a suspect story relating to Cadiz which can hardly be omitted from any biography:

> Being at Gades he saw a statue of Alexander the Great in the temple of Hercules and was heard to give a great sigh. It would seem that he was despondent because, at an age when Alexander had already conquered the whole world, he himself had done nothing of any importance.

Spain was still a somewhat barbarous province, but Caesar must constantly have been reminded of its importance – particularly in view of its mineral wealth – and that it was the riches of Spain which had enabled the Carthaginian Hannibal to mount his famous campaign against Rome. There was a more recent instance of the strength that was latent in Spain: this was the revolt begun by Sertorius, a former lieutenant of Marius, which had aroused the Spanish desire for freedom and had raged almost uncontrollably for eight years. It was only extinguished in 72. Throughout his future career Caesar never forgot Spain in the context of Mediterranean power. After his time as quaestor there he was possessed by a fury of ambition, driving him into open action that threatened the state – or the *status quo* in Rome. Those who had once suspected that he might aim like Marius at a dictatorship – and then had dismissed him as a pleasure-loving philanderer – found their earlier suspicions reinforced.

Leaving the province in 68 he did not go, as might reasonably have been expected, straight to Rome, but made his way to the Latin colonies north of the Po which were agitating for full civic rights such as were enjoyed by their fellows south of the river. This area, long dominated by the Gauls who had settled there, had become increasingly Romanized and the aspirations of the citizens of towns such as Milan and Cremona could no longer be limited by the old framework. Caesar knew this well, knew too that it would be a 'popular' move to secure city rights for them and would make them in the future beholden to him if he could achieve this aim. The oligarchy dominating the senate, the *Optimates*, opposed any extension of citizenship, since it might weaken their position. Now Caesar seemed prepared even to incite the cities north of the Po to civil war (something which he had refused to be party to in the days of Lepidus). His gambler's nature stood clearly revealed, and the throw might well have come off but for the fact that there were two legions available in Italy which had been readied for transport to the East for the war against Mithridates. Seeing the danger, the senate held them back and Caesar's aim was thwarted. He had, however, secured many new friends in the north – a potential power base upon which he would one day draw.

A year after the death of his wife Caesar married again. This time there could be no question of sentiment, since he married Pompeia whose mother was the daughter of Sulla and whose father was the son of one of the pro-Sulla consuls who had done so much to reduce the power of the tribunes in 88. He had, then, married right into the heart of the *Optimates*. Moreover his new wife's family were extremely wealthy and Caesar still required money to pursue his ambitions.

The prime political consideration in Rome at this moment was the appointment of someone to take over command of the Mediterranean sea and rid it once and for all of piracy. Caesar, as we have seen, had personal knowledge of this scourge, which had now reached such proportions that the whole trade of the empire was at risk. The pirates,

as was quite clear, often worked hand in glove with Roman administrators and by contributing agreed percentages to the administrators
were treating the Mediterranean as their private lake. The only way to
rid the sea-lanes of this intolerable mischief was to appoint a supreme
commander at the head of a national fleet. The man proposed for this
position by one of the tribunes was Cnaeus Pompeius Magnus,
Pompey the Great.

Six years older than Caesar, he was a leading figure among the
Optimates: the man who had marched with Sulla and become one of the
dictator's greatest generals, had been accorded the surname of Magnus
in consequence of his victories in Africa over the Marian party. Pompey
the Great should by all accounts have been the one man that Caesar
would dislike more than all the other supporters of the conservative
party. But Caesar, in the grip of the ambition that he seems to have
brought back with him from Spain, had decided that Pompey was the
man to ally himself with if he himself was to reach the upper echelons of
power. When the proposition to give Pompey overall command of a
fleet of two hundred vessels and all the soldiers and sailors he needed
for the campaign was put to the people's assembly it was immediately
passed. The senators, however, were alarmed at the idea of giving such
a command to one man, particularly perhaps because it seemed to be so
popular with the masses. They saw the threat of a dictatorship and also,
one suspects, there were those among them who had financial interests
in the piracy. The entire senate, with one notable exception, informed
the people's assembly of their rejection of the plan. The exception was
Caesar, who spoke out in its favour, thus aligning himself with Pompey
and at the same time showing himself to the people in a favourable light
as a popularist in agreement with their wishes. In the event, there was
no way in which those who opposed the proposition could prevent its
being carried out, and Pompey was duly given this independent
command – with almost double the amount of ships and men that had
first been proposed.

As it turned out, the Romans could not have done better than to give
this far-ranging command to Pompey, for it completely suited his
talents. In the turmoil caused by the Mithridatic wars the coasts of Asia
Minor had become infested with pirates because the Romans were too
involved on land to be able to devote their energies to the sea-lanes, but
many of the rebels against whom he was to conduct his campaign were
far from being the rough and undisciplined murderers and rogues that
the word pirate nowadays tends to conjure up. As Plutarch writes:

> whilst the Romans were embroiled in their civil wars, being engaged
> against one another even before the very gates of Rome, the seas lay
> waste and unguarded, and by degrees enticed and drew them on not

only to seize upon and spoil the merchants and ships upon the seas, but also to lay waste the islands and seaport towns. So that now there embarked with these pirates men of wealth and noble birth and superior abilities, as if it had been a natural occupation to gain distinction in. They had divers arsenals, or piratic harbours, as likewise watchtowers and beacons, all along the sea-coast; and fleets were received that were well manned with the finest mariners, and well served with the most expert pilots, and composed of swift-sailing and light-built vessels adapted for their special purpose . . . There were of these corsairs above one thousand sail and they had taken no less than four hundred cities . . .

Pompey was not only a great soldier but a great organizer and administrator. He divided the Mediterranean into thirteen sections, allotted a squadron of his ships to each, and systematically combed the sea from one end to another. This disciplined and organized operation was something that the pirates had never met with before and, since they operated as individuals or small groups, they fell easy prey to the Roman squadrons. By the end of 67 (Plutarch with, one suspects, some exaggeration says 'within forty days') Pompey had systematically swept the western sea and completely cleared the trade routes of the empire. The corn ships moved freely again, the price of bread fell in Rome, imports and exports flowed normally and the people of Rome hailed Pompey as their deliverer. He was the hero of the hour.

It was in this atmosphere that, early in the following year, Manilius, one of the tribunes, proposed that Pompey be given an even more important task – the overall command in the Mithridatic War. There was even further consternation among the aristocratic oligarchy, for whom Pompey in the past had seemed only a tool to be used. He was not of the nobility but only from the class of the knights, and he now seemed to be getting beyond their control. Caesar once again supported the proposal, knowing as well as the senators who opposed it that – since the restoration of the power of the tribunes – it could not ultimately be gainsaid. As Dio Cassius puts it: 'Caesar wanted to flatter the people, *who seemed to him far more powerful than the senate* [my italics], and to prepare the way for a similar decree in his own favour at some time in the future.' He had seen that Pompey's star was in the ascendant. He may have calculated too that there was a chance Pompey would be killed in the East (as so many Romans had been), and that in any case his long absence from Rome would remove him from the political field. And Caesar never at any time forgot that, however great a commander's achievements in foreign fields and even if he was awarded a triumph upon his return, the man who was away missed the shifts and nuances in the political heart of empire. Even as a young man he had always ensured a regular flow of information from the capital city. Pompey, as his life shows, was an admirable soldier and an honest administrator, but the cunning cat's cradle of politics was not his forte.

Besides, the absence of Pompey from the city would leave Caesar free to cultivate the friendship of Licinius Crassus – whose surname has become synonymous with exorbitant wealth – and as always Caesar needed money to endear himself to the populace, as well as to indulge his own luxurious tastes. 'Nobody,' Crassus is reported as saying, 'can afford to become a force in politics unless he can support a private army.' It may have been about this time that Caesar became the lover of Tertulla, Crassus' wife; there are references in Suetonius, Plutarch and Cicero to the fact that Tertulla was well-known for her infidelities and she is known to have been one of Caesar's mistresses. Apart from his wealth, Crassus came from an ancient and distinguished family and had been consul with Pompey prior to a recent rift between them – something which Caesar was in due course to heal. In the meantime the millionaire found it convenient to have an active and able young man from his own class to act as his adviser and helper in his numerous concerns, which ranged from silver mines to slave farms and property dealing. In Pompey and Crassus Caesar had deliberately sought – and found – two different aspects of power, both of which he intended to turn to his advantage.

CHAPTER SIX

From Conspirator to Chief Priest

Crassus was determined to buy his way into power and, in the course of doing so, was happy to help along others who would owe their growing ascendancy to him. As client-states to Rome itself, so clients were essential to any rich Roman. Caesar, as his now intimate friend and adviser, was naturally one of those to be assisted, and Crassus, who had been elected in 65 to the censorship, was able to exercise both his position and his money to help promote his protégé.

The censors held the highest office of all Roman magistrates; they were responsible not only for the conduct and morals of citizens (an irony in view of the lives of some of them) but also superintended the five-yearly census. It was this that gave the censor much of his power, and Crassus (like Caesar) had his eye on the people who lived north of the Po: he wished to include them in the roll of citizens. He had a further ambition, and this was to make Egypt into a Roman province. It had long been ruled by the Greek Ptolemies but the last king, Ptolemy XI, had been murdered shortly after his accession to the throne and was said to have bequeathed his rich kingdom to Rome, just as Nicomedes of Bithynia had done. If Crassus could achieve either or both of these ambitions he would add immeasurably to the number of clients who would give him their support in the jungle of Roman politics. He was as pleased as Caesar to see the departure of Pompey to the East – and for the same reasons. He was also happy to help along his younger associate, and he – like then many another – saw no threat to his own position from the dandified, art-loving philanderer.

Crassus now provided the funds to support Caesar in his campaign for the office of *curule aedile*. This was yet a further rung on the ladder of any ambitious senator, being an urban magistracy with the function of superintending trade, the money-market, streets and buildings, the sanitation of the city, and the games. It was, as we know, in this latter department that Caesar was to shine, buying himself goodwill with borrowed money. Although money from the treasury was available for the games, it was a recognized fact in political life that it was only by spending an immense amount over and above this that higher offices of state could be attained through the enthusiastic approval of the people. Needless to say, Caesar was elected and with him as his colleague was a certain Marcus Calpurnius Bibulus, a man who was later to feature largely in Caesar's life. Bibulus was an honest, stubborn old-fashioned type of Roman, an aristocrat of the opposite party to Caesar's, the type of staid conservative with whom history has made us familiar, and certainly no match for the mercurial Caesar. The latter, as Suetonius tells us, laid on wild-beast hunts and stage-plays, sometimes at his own expense but at other times in co-operation with his colleague. Yet even when Bibulus was involved in the production of some entertainment it made no difference – it was Caesar who got the praise. As Bibulus himself wrily remarked: 'In the Forum the Temple of the Heavenly Twins is always just known as 'Castor's', so I always fare like Pollux to Caesar's Castor whenever it comes to giving a public entertainment together.'

In Pompey's absence Crassus was making a great play for most powerful man in the Roman world. Caesar's aedileship was a comparatively small move upon this chessboard, for Crassus almost certainly had a hand in financing the election of the two consuls, P. Cornelius Sulla and P. Autronius Paetus for the year 65. However the senate took alarm at the spectacle of Rome's wealthiest man now aspiring to manipulate the consulship, and the two men were condemned for electoral corruption.

The senate's action in revoking the consulships and appointing in their place the two senators (and fellow-candidates) who had been their accusers was to provoke a storm which shook the fabric of Rome, rotten though that was. But before detailing this old scandal, in which Caesar very probably played a part, it is worth noticing another act of his during his year of office. This was to put on a special series of gladiatorial games, entirely at his own expense and unconnected with the normal city festivals, to commemorate the death of his father twenty years before. The significance of this was obvious enough – the celebration of the Julian clan – and, rather than immortalizing the memory of a man who had lived a comparatively undistinguished life, to call the public's attention to the munificence and glory of his son. Being responsible for the public places as aedile, Caesar also had the statues and memorials of Marius, which had been banished from the Forum and streets during Sulla's dictatorship, cleaned and gilded and restored to their former places. The people, for whom Marius, the man of common stock, had ever remained a hero, were delighted and showed their approval, but the *Optimates* very naturally took exception to this celebration of the man they regarded as the enemy of the conservative tradition. Catulus, the leader of the *Optimates* in the senate, and one of the most distinguished Romans of the time, made a speech against Caesar, ending with the ominous and perspicacious words: 'Caesar is no longer trying to undermine the republic, he is now using battering-rams.'

There remains some doubt about Caesar's part in the other major event of that stormy year: the conspiracy to assassinate the two consuls, Cotta and Torquatus, who had been elected in place of the two favoured by Crassus. At the same time as this proposed double murder, a revolt was supposed to take place among the cities north of the Po (where Caesar had already shown himself active) and, during the confusion following the death of the consuls, Crassus, it was said, was to seize the dictatorship with Caesar as his Master of the Horse (Second-in-Command of the Army). Suetonius, who reports this affair giving his earlier authorities, is the only source we have, but he is somewhat suspect all the same since Cicero, who disliked intensely what Caesar stood for, makes no mention of his having had any connection with this abortive plot although he does mention the projected role of Crassus. Since Caesar was now so intimate a friend and adviser to the millionaire it seems likely that he was aware of the plot and may even, as Suetonius suggests, have been intended to play a major role in it. Nevertheless, the verdict must be 'Not Proven'.

In Egypt Ptolemy Auletes, the Fluteplayer, and father of the Cleopatra who was to play so large a part on the Roman scene in the years to come, having murdered his predecessor, had just been driven from the throne by his subjects in Alexandria. The burning question was – had the murdered king already bequeathed Egypt to the Roman State? If so, then a Governor-General with special powers should be appointed to look into the affairs of Egypt and take over the administration of the kingdom. This was the role for which Caesar, with the help of Crassus, had cast himself. Egypt, that prosperous and powerful lynchpin of the Mediterranean, would give the two men a great power base to counterbalance the one that Pompey was establishing for himself in Asia. Crassus probably felt that Caesar would be happy to act as a lieutenant in such an office, but Caesar was undoubtedly looking beyond the ambitions of his 'master'. It is not surprising that the conservative senators, who had been closely watching the activities of the two men, were determined to block any such move – even at the cost of not acquiring such an important territory for Rome. The man who effectively destroyed the arguments of the Crassus-Caesar party was Cicero, who acted as spokesman for the *Optimates* and succeeded in having the whole proposal thrown out. One thing is clear – in every direction the once indolent aristocrat was now, at the age of thirty-six, manoeuvring legally or illegally to grasp the reins of power.

Shortly after their defeat over the Egyptian affair Crassus and Caesar learned that the very man who had swayed the tide against them was standing for consul in the following year. It was natural that they should wish to block Cicero, Caesar out of irritation over Egypt and Crassus, in addition, because Cicero was one of the few men eligible for the consulship who owed no obligations, financial or otherwise, to the millionaire. Lucius Sergius Catilina, (known to history as Catiline) a formidable and sinister figure who had been heavily involved in the plot to kill the two consuls, was himself proposed to stand as a candidate – with the backing of Crassus – as well as another creature of his, Caius Antonius. Yet despite the formidable power of money brought against him and despite the determined opposition of all those who were of the Crassus/Caesar faction, Cicero was triumphantly elected to the office. The *Optimates* had again succeeded in preventing a mockery being made of the consulship, even though Crassus managed to get one of his chosen candidates, Caius Antonius, elected as the second consul, with Catiline not far distant in the running – and therefore a possible hopeful for the following year.

The next move of the two conspirators (for such one must by now call them) was to support a bill of great importance and complexity about the redistribution of land – outside as well as in Italy, including Egypt, of all unlikely places since the senate had just firmly declared it to be no concern of the Roman people. One of the recently elected tribunes of the people (always of use to Caesar) P. Servilius Rullus proposed the new agrarian law, which, although it had good social aims, would have given Crassus and Caesar a power base that would have counter-balanced that of Pompey (who had now conquered Mithridates and annexed his large estates). For under the new law the land of the Ptolemies could have been annexed and ten special commissioners elected by the people. But only those who were present in Rome at the time could be eligible; Pompey, absent in the East, would not have been able to stand.

Cicero, as consul, had indicated that he would support the law if he felt that it was useful for the people, but when he attempted to attend one of the meetings of the tribunes he was received in such a violently hostile manner that he had to withdraw. Even if he had not already scented trouble in something in which Crassus and Caesar were so evidently involved, this would have been enough to convince him that the agrarian law was designed to increase the power of the two men whom he saw as the greatest threat to the republic. Cicero, although not a man of strong character, did possess some moral fibre. He genuinely believed in the republican institutions which most of the *Optimates* feebly upheld, but which he knew the popular party, with men like Caesar in it, were certain to destroy. He opposed Rullus' bill in four

33

speeches and, despite Caesar's oratory and the wealth of Crassus against him, he managed to get it defeated. He was the greatest magistrate of the Roman Republic and a formidable adversary.

Caesar had lost, but he had made a great number of friends who would one day be useful to him, and he now set about yet another move on the political chessboard. At the beginning of 63 Metellus Pius, the *pontifex maximus*, died from illness. This highest religious office in the state normally went only to the most distinguished men, former consuls or great generals who had deserved well of the state. In this case it was widely believed that either Lutatius Catulus, that senior figure in the senate and leader of the *Optimates*, or Servilius Isauricus, who had been Caesar's former chief in Asia Minor, would secure the office. To the general astonishment of the senate Caesar put himself forward as a candidate.

He was only thirty-seven, he had no great record as a general or a statesman behind him and he was known to be massively in debt. But, apart from his influence with Pompey and Crassus, he was popular in plebeian circles. It was just here that the power now lay, and Caesar had long been aware of it. In the past the law had entitled the people to vote for this great office, but Sulla had repealed this and given the power back to the College of Pontiffs. If the election had depended on this small group Caesar knew that he would have no chance of success, so his aim for a long time had been to get the power of election restored to the people. Now one of Caesar's collaborators in his many machinations at this time was the tribune Titus Labienus, who had served with Caesar in the East. Labienus and a fellow tribune had recently put forward a bill according new honours to Pompey for his outstanding services. This had been easily carried, and in its wake Labienus had proposed that the law regarding the election to the priesthoods (which included the pontifex maximus) should be restored. The senate, which clearly had not seen the potential dangers of the issue, agreed to this.

It was common knowledge that Caesar was in debt on a vast scale, so when he made his almost impudent bid for the office Catulus himself approached Caesar and made him an offer on condition of his withdrawing his candidacy. This was a blunder, for he had now let Caesar know how much money he and his supporters had to spend, and Caesar's answer was to borrow even more and continue his steady bribery of the electorate. On the day of the elections the story goes that, as his mother was seeing him out of the house, he said to her: 'Today you will either see me as High Priest or an exile.' (There is no doubt that had he failed his creditors would have made sure that prison awaited him unless he had first of all managed to escape to some safe and distant land.) He carried the day – and to such an extent that even

34

in the political wards of his two rivals he secured more votes than they did.

The office which he now held had, before the founding of the republic, been reserved for the kings of Rome and was now tenable for life by the elected candidate. It carried immense prestige and influence. Caesar had gained not only the base from which he could begin to restore his financial position but immeasurably expand it, the patronage that could be extended by the holder of this once-regal office being practically unlimited. By cunning use of the tribune Labienus and by the lavish expenditure of money (much of it, no doubt, from Crassus) Caesar had moved to a dominant position on the centre of the board.

"Today you will either see me a High Priest or an exile"

CHAPTER SEVEN

A State of Crisis

It was with some surprise that people heard that an aged senator Gaius Rabirius, a staunch *Optimate*, was to be tried for high treason at the instigation of the same Labienus who had helped Caesar to his new position. The surprise arose principally because the murder of which he was accused had taken place thirty-seven years before, when a tribune of the people, Saturninus, a noted radical, had been killed. This had been done under an emergency decree of the senate, which could be invoked whenever the senate saw fit to say that the state was in danger. These vague but sweeping powers were naturally anathema to Caesar and those of his persuasion, for they could one day be used against them.

To prosecute Rabirius was in effect to attack the power of the senate and in particular of the Sullan oligarchy. Caesar managed to get himself nominated as one of the judges in the case and passionately sought the condemnation of the old man. The death sentence was actually pronounced and might even have been carried out but for the intervention of Cicero. He had perceived Caesar's real purpose – the attempt to weaken senatorial powers – and the assembly broke up. Caesar, acting through Labienus, tried yet again to have Rabirius brought to trial, although this time with the penalty reduced from death to a large fine. Once more Cicero moved to his defence and Caesar was thwarted. He had however clearly declared war on the old days of massive senatorial power. No one could doubt that the intention of the popular party was to see the authority of the senate significantly reduced.

The strange figure of Lucius Sergius Catilina – Catiline – now threatened to take over the forefront of the Roman stage. This debt-ridden aristocrat, who had already been defeated in the consular elections, once more put himself forward for the office. He had a considerable following among the many who had been ruined in the tumultuous wars of previous years, great charm and no scruples (the latter not so unusual in the Rome of the period). His social programme drew many to him since he envisaged a cancellation of debts – something which would have been attractive to Caesar though not to Crassus, although there seems little doubt that he was in touch with both of them. Nothing, however, so serves to bring together in unity the moneyed and propertied classes as a programme of social revolution such as was being outlined by Catiline and his followers, and both the principal orders of society, the senators and the knights, now closed ranks. Cicero, as consul and as leading spokesman for law and order, often proudly referred to this amalgamation of interests as the 'Concord of the Orders'. Certainly Catiline soon realized that his quest for the consulship would make no headway against so powerful a block and he decided on revolutionary means.

In July 63 there took place the election for the offices of state for the following year. Caesar, pursuing the normal course on the rungs of power, was elected a *praetor*. This was the post of a magistrate performing some of the duties of a consul, and second only to the consulship itself in the offices of state. It carried the advantage that a provincial governorship usually followed the year of office, and it was in the great provinces that reputations could be made and fortunes acquired. At the same time Catiline was defeated in his election for the consulship. There can be little doubt that up until now both Crassus and Caesar had been in support of Catiline: he was their type of man. But a Catiline defeated in his second attempt could have no interest to them and, in any case, once his determination to seize power illegally was known, he became a liability. Crassus had his wealth to safeguard him against most things, but Caesar had little more than the positions he had won for himself and, as High Priest and praetor; he was now well established on the formal route to the top. It seems most likely that at this point both men withdrew their support from the man who was already recruiting an army of revolution.

A conspiracy on this scale could hardly escape detection, especially in a city that swarmed with spies and informers, and Cicero as consul was naturally soon made aware of it. At the same time Caesar and Crassus, eager to exculpate themselves from any association with Catiline, hastened to tell the consul all they knew. It was not a worthy action, and Cicero himself can hardly have been in any doubt that these two men, whom he had long mistrusted, were potentially as ill-disposed towards the republic as any of the conspirators. Cicero had already taken the precaution of calling up a large number of trusted armed followers, thus issuing an open warning to any who intended to use violence against the state. But Catiline by now was too far advanced on the path of revolution to turn back. The grand design was for the revolution to start in Etruria, where an army was being mustered, and to

37

be heralded by outbreaks of arson in Rome – designed to confuse the ordinary citizens – while at the same time those leading citizens and senators who were clearly law-abiding and hostile to the overthrow of the republic would be murdered. First among these, of course, was Cicero. He had singled himself out in all his speeches and actions as a man who resolutely upheld law and order and was the staunchest known defendant of the old institutions.

It is largely from Cicero's own magnificent orations against Catiline that we know so much about the plot. These were subsequently published so as to be read and remembered by the Roman people and they constitute one of the landmarks of their literature. Catiline now fled from Rome and made his way to Etruria, where the insurrection broke out in late October. The planned assassinations, however, did not take place, probably largely due to Cicero's vigilance and the maintenance of an impressive guard on himself and all others who had been placed on the death list. It was now the turn of the senate to declare a state of war. An attempt was made on Cicero's life and Catiline was branded as a public enemy, while the consuls mustered the troops for the defence of the state. During all this time, it would appear, Caesar and Crassus were lying very low. Caesar's feelings were no doubt ambivalent. He had much to gain by the cancellation of all debts, while in the confusion of a civil war, with the consuls engaged with the armies and the senate in a state of disorder, an opportunist could only benefit.

Then the conspirators within the city unwittingly betrayed themselves. They made approaches to a delegation of Gauls who were visiting Rome, with the object of securing their assistance by a rebellion in their own country, thus furthering the chaos and making the aims of the Catilinarians easier to attain. The Gauls for whatever reason (perhaps they had more sense of dignity and responsibility than many Romans) passed the incriminating letters to the consular authorities. Five of the leading conspirators, who included members of the senate, were immediately seized and placed under arrest. Arrest warrants were also made out for four others who were clearly implicated.

On 5 December the senate met to decide the fate of the arrested conspirators. It was one of the most dramatic meetings on record, for Crassus failed to attend while Caesar, whose position as praetor called on him to speak, did so in such a way that scholars and historians have been arguing about the interpretation of his speech ever since. The rules demanded that one of the consuls-elect for the following year should speak first and this was a certain D. Junius Silanus. He proposed that the arrested conspirators should pay 'the ultimate' penalty and the fourteen consulars present concurred in this judgement. Our authorities, including Cicero when he was later reviewing

38

the whole affair, all agree that death was meant by this – 'they should not for a moment enjoy the light or breathe the air of which they had sought to deprive their fellow citizens'. It was now the duty of Caesar to speak and, in a long and involved speech, which seems to suggest some embarrassment, he made a case for the conspirators to be condemned to imprisonment for life in the towns which were best fitted to ensure their security (these to be selected by Cicero), and all their property to be confiscated. It was certainly an ambiguous speech, but silence would only have confirmed some of the ugly rumours that were already in circulation.

Caesar's position was an awkward one since it was known that he had been well-acquainted with Catiline, and he had no wish to give offence to the people, who felt that the conspirators represented their real interests far better than the well-entrenched aristocrats who now condemned them. Also there was the important point that Caesar himself had made, condemning the use of emergency decrees by the senate to bring about the deaths of Roman citizens. In his speech, designed to save the lives of the accused, he made the point that life imprisonment was far worse for a man than death, for death could only mean a release from the burdens and miseries of life itself. In these words spoke the _Pontifex maximus_, the high priest of the Roman state religion. Had he forgotten his demand of the death sentence for the old man Rabirius, or his insistence on the crucifixion of the pirates in his youth?

The ominous suggestion that really influenced the senate was Caesar's statement that the people in general did not recall the deeds that had led to a punishment, but only the punishment itself. 'The crime would be forgotten, but the end remembered.' Second only to Cicero, Caesar was the greatest orator in the Roman world and his speech had a profound effect. The senators understood the implication that the people of Rome might one day avenge themselves for the death of the conspirators (because their aims coincided more nearly with those of the people themselves). The response of the consul-elect Silanus was to prevaricate and to maintain that by 'the ultimate penalty' he had meant no more than imprisonment for life. Cicero's riposte was to suggest that 'such a wise and merciful man' as Caesar had contrived, by his own statement, to suggest a penalty for the accused that was far worse than death. If such was the case, then Caesar was proposing a torture far worse than he, Cicero, had suggested. Nevertheless, Caesar had won, and the 'conversion' of the respected consul-elect Silanus (whose wife Servilia was one of Caesar's mistresses) seemed to sway the senate in favour of imprisonment rather than death. Only Catulus could be found among the consulars ready to approve the death sentence. But there did remain one Roman of the antique breed to stand up and vehemently disagree with the acquiescence of his seniors. This was the redoubtable Marcus Porcius Cato, a descendant of the famous Cato the Censor who had distinguished himself in the third war against Carthage and had largely been responsible, in the last and final war against Rome's major rival in the Mediterranean, for the destruction of that city. This young Cato was of the same opinion as Cicero. Traitors to the Republic must die.

An unusual character, the direct antithesis to Caesar in almost every way, he has been portrayed by Sir Ronald Syme in *The Roman Revolution*:

> Aged thirty-three and only quaestorian in rank, this man prevailed by force of character. Cato extolled the virtues that won empire for Rome in ancient days, denouncing the undeserving rich, and strove to recall the aristocracy to the duties of their station. This was not convention, pretence or delusion. Upright and austere, a ferocious defender of his own class, a hard drinker and an astute politician, the authentic Cato, so far from being a visionary, claimed to be a realist of traditional Roman temper and tenacity.

He hated Caesar and everything he stood for, and he also had personal reasons for this hatred. Servilia, Silanus' wife was his sister, and Caesar to him was therefore the corrupter not only of public but of private morals. He lashed out at Caesar in a way that Cicero would not have dared, accusing him of wishing to destroy the state and of attempting to frighten the senate with a vision of what might happen if they did what they should. Caesar, he maintained, was lucky to have got clear of implication in the whole matter himself, and that was the reason why he was trying to prevent the malefactors from paying the just penalty. Not only should these criminals be condemned to death but their properties should also be confiscated for the benefit of the very state against which they had conspired.

This passion and directness, reflecting no doubt what many senators felt but dared not say, swept away the assembly. Caesar spoke yet again against the imposition of the death sentence, but by now the mood had radically altered and there was a growing animosity against him. The senators had remembered their duty and had been recalled by Cato to an old Roman sense of what was right. Caesar appealed to the tribunes of the people to use their *veto*, but none would support him, and there was a riot. Hearing the uproar, some of Cicero's armed guards who were stationed outside rushed in to see if their master was in danger. 'They unsheathed their swords,' says Suetonius, 'and threatened Caesar with death unless he ceased his opposition [to the motion].' Most of the senators near him fled from the scene; only a few of his friends huddled round him and covered him protectively with their togas. For the first time in his life Caesar came near to death in the Roman senate, and he was sufficiently impressed by the experience to stay away from the senate house for the rest of the year. He, whose rise had been occasioned by preying on the passions of the Romans, now had a first-hand knowledge of them. It was not an experience any man would ever be likely to forget – unless over a long period of time he had become possessed by overweening arrogance.

CHAPTER EIGHT

The Praetor and a Scandal

Despite the tumult with which the senate meeting had ended, Caesar had nevertheless achieved a great deal by his speech urging a life sentence, rather than death, for the conspirators. The people now had him firmly fixed in their minds as a merciful man and, despite his breeding, not one of the hard and implacable aristocrats of the senate. Besides, hardly had the arrested conspirators been executed than some of the senators began to have qualms about what had been done and, after the elections, two of the new tribunes began to speak out against the death sentences. It was as Caesar had foreseen; whatever his motives had been, he had better understood the feelings of the Roman people than such diehards as Cato. The two men would hate each other all their lives; indeed, Caesar would continue to hate Cato even after the latter's death. The whole Catiline conspiracy came to an end when Catiline himself fell fighting against the government troops early in 62. His story has been told by the historian Sallust, and he appears in Roman history as a dark and malevolent figure. Whether he was any worse than those who had once supported him and then abandoned him is a matter for doubt.

Caesar showed his long memory early in January that year when he mounted an attack in the senate on the 'most venerated of Romans', Catulus, for the latter's neglect in failing to restore the temple of Jupiter on the Capitol. The whole story need not concern us here, but it reveals something more of Caesar's nature: he made a bad enemy. Cato was the next to feel his animosity and, in what seems from this distance in time a storm in the political teacup, Caesar managed to see that he was humiliated and had to take refuge in one of the temples for safety. As praetor, Caesar was always conscious not only of his *dignitas*, that essential ingredient of the Roman aristocrat's life, but of the powers that he now enjoyed, and would act sharply in defence of his position. A Roman knight Vettius, who may at one time have been part of the Catiline conspiracy, but who had certainly turned informer and may even have been in the pay of Cicero, produced a long list of others who had been involved in the plot. He gave this to the president of the special court which dealt with such matters, adding that he had other names yet to furnish – and among them was Caesar's. Another one of the known friends of Cicero, a senator Quintus Curius, said publicly that he had had information from Catiline that Caesar was involved. Against Vettius Caesar had fairly easy redress, denying the accusation in the senate and calling Cicero as a witness that he, Caesar, had early passed on to him all the information that he had acquired about the conspiracy. It was easy, because of Caesar's distinguished position, to deal with a man like Vettius: 'his goods were seized, he was man-handled', and Caesar 'had him thrown into prison'.

As for Curius, he was deprived of the honours that he had hoped to gain by a denouncement of conspirators. Nor did Caesar stop there, but immediately used his rank and position against a man called Novius Niger who had been president of the court which had heard the charge against him. Novius had overstepped himself, for Caesar was a magis-trate of higher rank. In the protection of his dignity and rank Caesar was as fierce as a wildcat and determined to be treated with respect.

In that same year of plot and violence and intrigue there occurred an even stranger affair. This was the matter of Publius Clodius, an aristocrat of old family who has been described as 'one of the most profligate characters of a profligate age'. His fierce opposition to Cicero and his 'rake-hell' character may well have endeared him to Caesar but he stepped beyond the acceptable mark – even in Rome – at the festival of the *Bona Dea*. The Good Goddess was above all the goddess of women, and was one of those many manifestations of the Great Earth Mother who had once dominated much of the Mediter-ranean for millennia. She had re-emerged disguised in many forms but her chief characteristics were always the same: she represented the female principle, those areas of the female cycle, of childbirth, of all that side of life from which men were automatically debarred. She was described by Cicero as 'a goddess whose very name is a mystery beyond the power of man to know', and her worship was conducted by the Vestal Virgins. Every year on the occasion of her festival, which was always held in the house of a magistrate, all the men of the house were compelled to leave and the mysteries attaching to the Good Goddess were conducted by the women.

In the year 62 the house chosen for this celebration was that of Caesar, and his wife Pompeia was, as it were, the hostess. Now Pompeia herself – and who can blame her knowing Caesar's sexual conduct – was not noted for her faithfulness, while Clodius had a reputation that even in Rome was considered scandalous: he was believed among much else to have had incestuous relations with his

43

sister Clodia whom the poet Catullus loved. On this occasion, possibly because he wished to prosecute a love affair with Pompeia or, equally likely, because it seemed amusing to invade a sacred festival, Clodius had himself disguised as a woman and slipped into the house of Caesar. The story, based on Plutarch's account, has often been told but it seems worth including since it gives so much of the atmosphere of the Rome that Caesar knew:

> As Pompeia was at that time celebrating this feast, Clodius, who as yet had no beard, and so thought to pass undiscovered, took upon him the dress and ornaments of a singing woman, and so came thither, having the air of a young girl. Finding the doors open, he was without any stop introduced by the maid, who was in the intrigue. She presently went to tell Pompeia, but as she was away a long time, he grew uneasy in waiting for her, and left his post and traversed the house from one room to another, still taking care to avoid the lights, till at last Aurelia's woman met him, and invited him to play with her, as the women did among themselves. He refused to comply, and she presently pulled him forward, and asked him who he was, and whence he came. Clodius told her he was waiting for Pompeia's own maid, Abra, being in fact her own name also, and as he said so, betrayed himself by his voice. Upon which the woman shrieking, ran into the company where there were lights, and cried out, she had discovered a man. The women were all in fright. Aurelia covered up the sacred things and stopped the proceedings, and having ordered the doors to be shut, went about with lights to find Clodius, who was got into the maid's room that he had come in with, and was seized there. The women knew him, and drove him out of doors, and at once, that same night, went home and told their husbands the story.

The scandal, which rocked Rome (inured to scandal as that city was), became transformed into a matter of politics, revolving around the question as to which court should be responsible for trying Clodius. Caesar's position was an awkward one, and if Clodius (as some have suggested) had been acting at the instigation of Caesar's enemies he could hardly have embarrassed him more. It was not the matter of his being perhaps the cuckolded husband – such were common enough, and Caesar often responsible – but the fact that the attempted adultery and the sacrilegious intrusion into the rites of the Bona Dea had taken place in the house of the Pontifex Maximus. Because of his position Caesar's wife was herself playing the role of a priestess at this gathering.

What would Caesar do? The answer was, curiously enough as it then seemed, relatively nothing. True, he divorced his wife Pompeia, on the grounds that members of his household must be above suspicion: a remark that has often laughingly been quoted against him, but which was completely justified because of his status as the high priest of Roman religion. At the trial of Clodius, Cicero, as defendant of Roman morality, very naturally spoke vehemently against the accused. Caesar, the injured husband – to most people's astonishment – said that he had no knowledge of the affair. The fact was that he and Crassus had come to the conclusion that the rake Clodius was exactly the kind of man they needed to replace Catiline in working upon the passions of the Roman mob. Where Catiline had failed them, Clodius might succeed. Crassus, in fact, seems to have advanced Clodius enough money to bribe the majority of the jurors so that, despite his own feeble defence (which Cicero demolished), thirty-one of the jurors voted for his acquittal as against twenty-five who, true to their consciences or responding to Cicero's oratory, pronounced him guilty. Despite the scandal, Caesar came out of the affair quite well, for he had probably long wanted to divorce Pompeia since she was childless. Also Clodius was now beholden to both Crassus and Caesar, Crassus for money and Caesar for his denial of any knowledge of the background for the charge.

For some reason or other – perhaps because of the trial of Clodius – the allotment of the praetorial provinces was delayed until March that year. Caesar could now look forward to the rewards of his position, for he had drawn the governorship of Farther Spain – where he had served before as quaestor. His troubles were far from over, however, for his creditors in Rome began to press him so hard that it was even doubtful whether he would be able to get away to the province where he hoped to restore his finances. Once again Crassus came to his rescue, enabling Caesar to escape his most urgent creditors and assume his command. The province comprised Baetica, the Romanized and peaceful southern part of the peninsula, and Lusitania, western Spain and the mountainous spine of Portugal. The latter was scarcely settled and was a constant source of trouble to both the governors and the governed in the south. Caesar looked to it with anticipation as possibly providing him with the type of military success that could make a governor's fame and fortune. He badly needed some military glory to counterbalance the great sun of Pompey that had risen in the East.

Spain
Egypt
Portugal

45

CHAPTER NINE

Pompey and Caesar

Overshadowing all these events in Rome, dwarfing the intrigues of Crassus and Caesar and the Clodius scandal, loomed the immense figure of Pompey the Great. Pompeius Magnus seemed at that time so much more distinguished than any other Roman. Yet, in fact, as any study of his life reveals, his career was hardly different from that of any conspicious Roman of the time. It was only his outstanding successes, first in Africa against the last of the Marians, then against Sertorius in Spain and next in his sweeping command of the sea against the pirates, which gave this impression. In all other respects he had shown himself as unrepresentative of the old conception of republican virtues as any other who wished to overturn Cicero's dream of the republic. As Sir Ronald Syme puts it: 'The career of Pompeius opened in fraud and violence. It was prosecuted, in war and in peace, through illegality and treachery.'

Now, early in 61, before Caesar had left for Spain, Pompey returned to Italy triumphant with his 40,000 legionaries. He had not only settled all the troubles of Asia Minor, thus enriching Rome with immense and increasing wealth, but he brought back – a gift, as it were, to the empire – the rich and important province of Syria. Mithridates was dead, Roman influence extended as far as the Caucasus, and the sea was pirate-free. In the course of the past three years and more he had not only enriched his country immeasurably but, of course, himself as well. Such was to be expected, for the rewards enjoyed by victorious Roman generals were not just the medals, titles and retirement pensions that their successors in our century may consider their simple due. Pompey the Great was now almost certainly richer than Crassus: what is more he had hundreds of indebted clients in the territories that he had subdued and thousands of devoted legionaries whom he had also benefited, and to whom he had promised land on a very large scale. On arriving in Italy he had dismissed his soldiers, though many senators had feared he might use them to impose a dictatorship, and advanced on Rome in total confidence. Caesar was among the first to propose massive new honours to the returning conqueror, for he saw that Pompey as well as Crassus might make a more than useful ally.

J. A. Froude in his *Caesar – a Sketch* conveys the atmosphere of Pompey's reception as well as the subsequent disillusionment with him:

> He was received as he advanced with the shouts of applauding multitudes. He entered Rome in a galaxy of glory. A splendid column commemorated the cities which he had taken, the twelve million human beings whom he had slain or subjected. His triumph was the most magnificent which the Roman citizens had ever witnessed, and by special vote he was permitted to wear his triumphal robe in the senate as often and as long as might please him. The fireworks over, and with the aureole of glory about his brow, the great Pompey, like another Samson shorn of his locks, dropped into impotence and insignificance.

The fact was – and Caesar in the remaining weeks before he left for Spain will have had time to discern it – Pompey was no orator, and a poor politician. He might shine on distant fields of battle and in military organization but he did not distinguish himself in the senate. Like many another returning warrior who has been years away from home (MacArthur springs to mind), during his long residence in other climates and among his soldiers or the prostrate conquered he had lost touch with the seat of power and the tortuous maze of manipulation. Caesar, as has been observed, was always, even as a youth in the East, accustomed to hear regularly from correspondents in Rome and to return there whenever opportunity offered. He knew – as Pompey perhaps did not, or had forgotten – that it was in the capital that the alliances were made and the political manoeuvres engendered. Cicero, in a letter to his friend Atticus, reported with evident satisfaction, after listening to a speech by Pompey: 'He gave no pleasure to the wretched; to the bad he seemed vapid and spineless; he was not pleasing to the well-to-do; to the good he seemed without any weight; and so he was looked on coldly.' He had also made the grave error – in the eyes of the senate – of settling affairs abroad in a high-handed manner without bothering to consult them, and he had made extravagant promises of land to his soldiers which the senators were determined he should not keep.

But all this was in the future and Caesar, after first taking the measure of his man, had now set off for Spain. The journey from Rome to Corduba took him three weeks, the standard time for that day, but Caesar was never the man to relax on this or other similar rounds of travel. On one journey which took twenty-seven days from Rome to southern Spain he composed a long poem called 'The Journey', while during a crossing of the Alps he wrote, or dictated, a two-volume work *On Analogy*. The elder Pliny recorded that he had heard how 'Caesar was accustomed to write or dictate and read at the same time, simultaneously dictating to his secretaries four letters on the most important subjects or, if he had nothing else to do, as many as seven.' On this occasion Plutarch provides the somewhat unconvincing tale that, as they were passing through a squalid Alpine village, and the conversation turned jokingly to the question of what political offices were competed for there, Caesar remarked seriously: 'For my part I would rather be first among these wretches than second in Rome.'

His province at once engaged his attention and he clearly showed which part of it was of most concern to him, for, not content with the twenty cohorts at his disposal (about 10,000 men), he at once set about enlisting a further ten. It was clear that he intended action against the mountain tribes, who were constantly harassing the peaceful inhabitants in the south. As he was to do many times afterwards, he issued an ultimatum (which he knew would be ignored) telling them to leave their homes in the Herminius range and settle peacefully in the plain. Dio Cassius remarks that Caesar was perfectly well aware that they would refuse, but he now had his *casus belli*; the occasion for a war which he hoped would make him both rich and famous.

Compared with the campaigns which Pompey had been conducting in the East these military operations against mountain tribes were small indeed, but they nevertheless enabled Caesar and his soldiers to loot and despoil a number of cities – sometimes, so his critics maintained, ones which had offered no resistance or had previously submitted. This mattered little to Caesar and less to his troops, while as far as the distant senate in Rome was concerned he was taming and bringing within Roman control new areas of land and, therefore, new sources of wealth. He was careful also to see that the appropriate amount of money was sent back to Rome – and to the right people – so that any critics would be silenced. His despatches (which we do not have) were almost certainly couched in the same exhilarating style as his famous later ones from Gaul. He had early discovered in himself a talent for soldiering, but now he showed that he was born to generalship. As an administrator he also displayed all his notable powers and he managed to secure for himself many grateful clients and followers among the peaceful inhabitants of Spain. His troops hailed him as *Imperator*, Victorious Commander, while by cancelling a major part of outstanding debts he secured many supporters who would be useful in the future. But all the time he had his eye on Rome.

In the elections of 60 Caesar was entitled to stand for the consulship of 59. He was entitled to a triumph and, with this in mind, returned to Rome before the expiry of his office. However, all hinged on a legal technicality which forced him to choose between standing as a candidate for the consulship or being accorded a triumph. If the senate had been well-disposed towards him, and if Cato had not ensured that the law remained unchanged, he might have enjoyed both. As it was, and it shows as always Caesar's choice of options when it came to military or political matters, he forewent the triumph and chose to stand for the consulship. In this he was wise, for many triumphs would fall his way in later years. It was a gamble, but at this moment he needed a consulship more than anything else. And Caesar was always a gambler.

Another candidate for the consulship was the same Marcus Calpurnius Bibulus who had been Caesar's more-than-uneasy colleague as praetor and who took almost the same view of Caesar as did Cato. These two old aristocrats, as well as many others, regarded the profligate Caesar as a man who had used his birth – and the advantages which it gave him – as a means of attaining power by joining the Left. (Modern examples are not uncommon.) True conservatives viewed such men not only with suspicion but considerable dislike, which could easily turn to hatred.

Many in the senate believed Caesar might well become one of the next consuls, but whether his fellow consul would be Bibulus or a third candidate, one Lucius Lucceius (not even a member of the nobility), was in some doubt. Caesar, finding the idea of Lucceius as a colleague slightly less distasteful than his known enemy Bibulus, cultivated him, but the dominant junto in the senate, anxious that at least one of the future consuls should be acceptable to them, put their shoulders behind Bibulus and his campaign (and this meant money). Caesar now had even deeper grievances against the 'old brigade': they had managed to prevent him from securing a triumph and they were to go even farther. The rewards of a consulship were to be found in the year after it terminated, when the consuls were given the great provincial commands that secured wealth, prestige and often fame. The senators, recognizing the danger of Caesar and the ineffectiveness of Bibulus, gave them instead the insulting reward of something comparable to boundary and forestry commissions in areas belonging to the state. This not only deprived them of the expected profits of office but was an open humiliation. Bibulus might accept the position, being a wealthy conservative, but they had sadly misjudged their man if they thought that Caesar would take such an insult lying down.

The old caucus who had so offended Caesar had made an even bigger mistake (and one which shows only too clearly that the aristocratic so-called *Optimates* were quite unfit to rule an empire) by infuriating Pompey. They had long despised him for his comparatively humble origins and they now envied and feared him because he had made for himself a power base of immense proportions in the East. If Pompey had not been so unwise as to disband his army he might indeed have set himself up as a dictator, from which position he could have ensured that his soldiers received all that he had promised. But he had been foolish – or arrogant enough – to think he was a prince among men and above any of the senators. Now he was to be humiliated. The land-law which Pompey sought to enable his troops to be rewarded for their services was blocked. Pompey, who had ruled like an emperor in the East, who had held almost limitless power, organizing and apportioning territories as he thought fit, was to have his promises to his troops made null and void – as if he was just any other citizen who had promised more than he could perform. The senators who had feared his power when he had his army behind him had decided to remind him that, now that he was in Rome, and without his troops, he was no more than any other senator. For the moment the conservative *Optimates* seemed to have enjoyed great success by demeaning Caesar and injuring Pompey, but in the long run they had ensured their ultimate ruin. It was these actions of the senate that brought about the partnership of two powerful and embittered men, and the unlikely alliance of Caesar and Pompey dates from shortly after that time.

It seems that either before or after Caesar's election as consul in the summer of 60 (and opinions differ among ancient authorities as well as subsequent historians) he and Pompey engaged in some kind of contract to support each other politically. Caesar promised that he would do all he could to ensure the distribution of land promised to Pompey's troops. At a slightly later date, although all within the same year, the two men were joined in their agreement by yet a third – and this was Crassus. This was somewhat unexpected, for Crassus had made no secret of his dislike of Pompey. He feared and envied him for his victories, and he had clearly shown his feelings by opposing the land-bill. But Crassus had now also suffered at the hands of the senate (which seems to have been almost determined on its own overthrow). He had tried to introduce a measure which would mean that the tax-farmers would enjoy a certain financial rebate, his interest in this being solely that they were dependents of the knights. (Crassus' policy was always to favour the knightly class since he was a business man as were many of them.) His opponents in the senate, the same type of men who had frustrated Caesar and Pompey, were equally willing to wound Crassus for his constant backing of opponents of the *Optimates*. The concessions that Crassus asked for were refused and yet another powerful man was left discountenanced and angry.

It was Caesar, the youngest, the least distinguished, and certainly by far the poorest of the three, who took the necessary steps to reconcile

Crassus and Pompey. The two things Caesar did possess were political skill and sagacity. He saw that he needed both men at this stage in his career, for they represented in their different ways assets which he had not yet acquired. It was to his advantage, and theirs too, to bring them together into a united force.

There can have been no intention at this time of forming a triumvirate to dominate the Roman world, for an emissary of Caesar's actually approached Cicero and invited him to join a partnership. This was almost certainly an idea of Caesar's to disarm Cicero and have on their side – instead of against them – the clarity of his mind and the brilliance of his oratory. Cicero refused to join them, not perhaps so much out of ethical or republican scruples, but because he was even more jealous of Pompey than Crassus. This was largely because Pompey's triumphs in the East had overshadowed Cicero's year as consul, when he felt that he had been the man responsible for saving the Republic during the Catiline affair. It was a bad day for Rome when he declined the offer, for his influence and his respect for the law and for republican principles might have prevented the formation of what became known as the First Triumvirate. This was the agreement of Caesar, Crassus and Pompey to act in concert with one another and never oppose one another politically.

CHAPTER TEN

Caesar's Consulship

From the moment that these three men had decided to pool their resources – military power and fame, monetary power, and political genius – the end of the republic was in sight. Cicero, who disliked or envied them almost equally, although reserving his deepest dislike and, indeed, fear for Caesar, recognized that such an autocracy could nullify the Senate's power. Yet it cannot be overemphasized that Cicero's dream republic had never existed in his own lifetime, if indeed ever. As a 'new man', one who was born neither noble nor rich, Cicero often seems like any middle-class man of great ability who has made his way to the top and is then captured by the glamour of his new associates – the old aristocrats who were born into positions of power as were their ancestors before them. On the one hand he saw the old order, men descended from the great days of the Republic, and on the other cynical self-seekers determined on personal power to the detriment of everything fine and noble. But, as Michael Grant has pointed out, things were not so simple:

> The 'free' republic that was now being superseded was not a democracy, and never had been. It had long been run by tough, unprogressive and dishonest cliques, whose incompetence to govern the large empire was now painfully clear. These cliques were now replaced by a board of three, who were exceptionally able men, and for the time being were united in their aims. In the end, they were destined to fail, because their unity could not be maintained. Yet their noble enemies would have failed as well – and for the same reason, because they would inevitably have become divided among themselves.

At the beginning of 59 Caesar and Bibulus assumed office, and it was not long before the antagonism between these two irreconcilable men became evident for all to see. At first, however, Caesar made it appear as if there had never been any differences of opinion between them and spoke blandly of the need to act only for the general good and in agreement with the senate. If, as one must presume, this was designed to reassure Bibulus and, on the surface at any rate, to make it look as if the two consuls were reconciled then he seems at first to have succeeded. Each consul was normally required to take precedence over the other for alternate months (since they were equal), and Caesar was meticulous in conforming to this ritual and to the formal technicalities that went with it. Similarly he pleased the senate by having an official record made of their daily transactions – something which had only been done before on special occasions. This naturally gratified their vanity and reassured Bibulus and the *Optimates* whom he represented that Caesar, now that he was consul, would conform. But the leopard does not change his spots and, as Appian remarks, 'Caesar was very well versed in the art of hypocrisy.'

He needed to lull the suspicions of his opponents, for he knew that his first major action was certain to go completely against the grain of the old aristocrats. This was the land-bill for the resettlement of Pompey's veterans, one of the things that he had promised his fellow triumvir, as well as the ratification of the settlements that Pompey had made in the East. A new agrarian law was badly needed, in any case, for great areas of Italy were uncultivated while a city like Rome was full of idle hands living, as it were, on the dole. A commission was to be put in charge of the distribution of the land and the cost would be defrayed by Pompey's wealth from the East, as well as by the revenues from the new provinces that he had won. Realizing that such important an act as the redistribution of the state lands of Italy would cause a shudder to run through the ranks of the conservatives, Caesar wisely made a very necessary concession – that the rich southern lands of Campania should be excluded. Furthermore, not only would Pompey's veterans be satisfied, but the poor from the city would also be entitled to land-grants. All in all, it was a judicious piece of legislation and Caesar was very careful to treat the senate with formal deference, inviting every senator to make criticisms of or suggestions for the draft, even to the extent of cancelling anything that did not seem right. Most of the senators, who had been expecting Caesar to treat them in a high-handed, authoritarian way, were embarrassed by the scrupulosity with which the bill was presented.

They hated it of course, because it was contrary to their interests, but they had difficulty in finding arguments against something which was clearly to the benefit of the country (and all the time they must have been aware of the threat posed by Pompey's disbanded soldiers). Cato had the courage of his convictions, however, and stood out against the whole bill, maintaining that people should be content with the constitution of the republic as it was. He attempted to talk out the bill, but Caesar, using his consular powers, had him placed under arrest. This high-handed action, though it was quite legitimate, caused those senators who would have liked to speak against the redistribution of land to walk out of the senate, one of them shouting at Caesar: 'I would rather be in jail with Cato than here with you,' The consul realized that he had overstepped the mark and had Cato released; he did not want to create a martyr.

The upshot was that – as there was no senatorial decree – Caesar took the whole matter to the popular assembly. The senators who opposed him had offered no constructive proposals on land reform, and therefore the people must decide. But he was clever enough to give the old guard one last chance to define their objections to the bill as it stood and invited Bibulus, as his fellow consul, to the popular assembly to say what he had against it, entreating him to give his objections to the bill, or to state any changes he would like made. Everything depended on Bibulus, he told the people, to which the unwise consul replied: 'You are not going to get it – not even if you all want it!'

Caesar had trapped him into betraying the real position of the *Optimates*: total conservatism in their own interest, and the devil take the people! Having thus exposed his enemies in the senate, Caesar had yet a further trick up his sleeve. Both Crassus and Pompey addressed the popular assembly in the Forum and declared their complete assent to the land-bill as it stood. This was the moment of truth – especially for the senators. They were faced by an alliance of the three most powerful men in Rome. The point was emphasized when Caesar asked for Pompey's support against those who opposed the bill, and the latter replied: 'If anyone dares to draw a sword, I shall take up my shield as well.' (He emphasized that he meant what he said by summoning his veterans to Rome.) The velvet glove which Caesar had earlier displayed had been discarded. When it was suggested to Bibulus by the other *Optimates* that he should exercise his veto against his consular colleague he and Cato were attacked outside the temple of Castor by a crowd of people with armed men among them and forced to retreat to the safety of their homes. It was this open violence towards the senate which made it clear to all that the old days were indeed over. The rule of the three men – the First Triumvirate – had been established.

After this display of violence, Caesar put the bill to the people and it was immediately carried. A special clause laid down that within a given period all the senators had to take an oath to abide by it – thus preventing any further delaying tactics. All opposition was silenced and, although Cato and one or two others were still prepared to protest, it was pointed out to them by their friends and relatives that it would be not only political, but actual suicide to do so. Cicero indeed, who had

54

prudently withdrawn to the country during this time of upheaval, wrote to Cato that 'it would be foolish and indeed mad, to refuse to accept the accomplished fact'.

The hatred against Caesar was now manifest among all his opponents, for they had no doubt that it was his hand that lay behind not only the agrarian bill but also the violence with which leading members of the senate had been openly threatened. From this moment date nearly all the scurrilous attacks upon his private life and – if one doubts that he ever passed through a homosexual phase in his youth – it is clear that this was the worst that his enemies could impute against him. Bibulus, who now hated Caesar as much as anyone, after only four months of his term of office, now withdrew into his house for the rest of his consulship and became responsible for the widely-circulated and bitter jibe: 'Pompey is king of Rome, and Caesar is his queen.'

It mattered little what was said. The fact remained that the senate had been powerless in the face of the triumvirate. Caesar's dextrous handling of the situation – however sordid – was politically brilliant. He had right on his side, for the agrarian laws had long needed changing, and he had the people's support for his actions. Pompey was satisfied, as were his veterans, and Pompey's disposition of affairs in the East was now also ratified.

It remained to secure the concessions for the tax-farmers that Crassus had wanted and – despite fierce opposition from Cato – this was again achieved by taking the matter to the people. In the first six months of his consulship Caesar had succeeded in welding the triumvirate into an unbreakable chain against which the senate was powerless. He had also very naturally promoted his own interests, for he had endeared himself to the soldiers by his agrarian bill and, by his concessions to the tax-farmers, secured the approval of the knightly order (as well as almost certainly making money for himself). He now proceeded to extend the alliance by marrying Calpurnia, the daughter of a certain Piso. He was a friend of Clodius, had been involved in the Catiline conspiracy, and has been described as 'an unprincipled debauchee and a cruel and corrupt magistrate'. Certainly he had considerable wealth and was to amass even more during a governorship of Macedonia in which he plundered the province even beyond the limits that were normally considered tolerable in Rome.

Calpurnia was to be Caesar's last wife and, although he continued as openly unfaithful to her as to his previous wives, she seems to have genuinely cared for him: he remained irresistible to women. At almost the same time another marriage also took place – one that again was of the greatest advantage to Caesar. The forty-seven-year-old Pompey married Caesar's seventeen-year-old daughter, Julia, thus binding these two members of the triumvirate even closer together. Despite the considerable age difference, this too seems to have been a happy marriage. Indeed from now on the influence of Crassus, although only very slowly, seems to decline. Pompey had the money and power, Caesar's finances had improved through his own manipulations and by marriage, while Crassus could in no way match Caesar in political ability.

Further violence ensued when the agrarian law was extended to include Campania, but yet again there was little or nothing that those opposed to the triumvirate could do since Caesar had the backing of the people while the other consul, Bibulus, had more or less abandoned his duties. Meanwhile the triumvirs had their eyes on Egypt, particularly Caesar because of his previous interest and Pompey because he regarded the whole East as very much his concern. Earlier, the annexation of the kingdom had been urged on the grounds of the reported will of the late Ptolemy. The reigning king, Ptolemy Auletes, father of the famous Cleopatra, was eager enough to retain control of his wealthy kingdom but he found that the Romans demanded an enormous price for their support. Yet he needed official recognition and support from Rome to shore up his very shaky hold upon the throne. Caesar, as consul, was the man to secure this, and he spoke on the King's behalf before both senate and people urging an official confirmation of the royal title as well as an alliance of the republic with Egypt. The confirmation of Ptolemy's title meant little to the Romans, but all could see that to guarantee the King's position by an alliance was halfway to laying their hands on his country. The innocent (and one sometimes wonders how many there can have been in that city) might even see Caesar and Pompey as benefactors of Rome – as indeed they were. But they had not done it for nothing, and the sum they received from the King in return for their help was so vast that even the wealthy Ptolemy had to borrow from Roman financiers to meet it. Caesar was now certainly tasting the fruits of office, but still he needed to look ahead and make plans for the proconsulship that would follow the next year.

The only way to effect a change from the ignominious appointments was to secure one of the tribunes as an ally (well-compensated, of course) to introduce a motion before the people's assembly appointing Caesar to a real command for the following year in a province that was worthy of his attention. He found his man in a certain Publius Vatinius, a tribune who was prepared to take up the matter without consulting the senate. Now Caesar knew well that, with the East settled by Pompey, the major areas of the Roman world where there was plenty of money to be made, as well as fame and reputation, were to the north and west. The areas in which he was interested, he indicated to Vatinius, were Cisalpine Gaul (northern Italy) and Illyricum (the

Adriatic coast of what is now Yugoslavia). The reasons for his choice of Cisalpine Gaul were relatively simple. He had long shown an interest in its people and had tried to secure Roman citizenship for them, while the region was rich and its large population would make a good recruiting ground. Caesar would need troops, for in troops lay power. Illyricum, on the other hand, was Romanized only along the coast and Caesar no doubt had plans for campaigns which would extend far inland: an opportunity to gain fame, extend the empire, and loot without fear of consequences. Vatinius secured both of these provinces for him, and something more. The governorship of the two areas was to be extended from the usual one or two years to five, starting from the expiry of his consulship on 1 January 58.

CHAPTER ELEVEN

Proconsul

While 'Pompey was king, and Caesar was queen', his fellow consul Bibulus had not entirely given up the battle. True, he had withdrawn to his house, but from here he waged a propaganda war against Caesar that attracted the attention of Rome. Even the ordinary people of the city must have felt that there was something very curious about a year in which there appeared to be only one consul: 'The event occurred, as I recall, when *Caesar* governed Rome . . .'

And as early as this in Caesar's career Bibulus was able to circulate via gossip and graffiti the telling words: 'Caesar was once in love with a king, but now he is in love with kingship.' There can be little doubt that in the latter part of the consulship this constant slanderous activity managed to damage him, even in the eyes of some of those who had been his supporters. Moreover, once a politician is in power he becomes a different man from the one who has previously held out promises. Caesar on his own had not only possessed grace and charm and oratorical skills, but had displayed all the popular traits of caring for the masses – and indeed doing something for them. He had shown this already in his consulship, but the people in general did not take to his associates: Crassus the millionaire without the human touch, and Pompey, respected as a soldier yet somehow unable to show much warmth or communicate with his fellows. Cicero, who had returned to Rome now that the most dangerous troubles seemed to be over, was happy to be able to report to his friend Atticus that Caesar had been ill-received at a new play, and that among the lines which had caused the audience to applaud was one where the principal actor turned towards Caesar's seat and, pointing, said: 'It is our misery which has made you so great . . .'

It was a year of great bitterness on account of numerous actions initiated by Caesar in the senate, but in which nevertheless he overcame his opponents. Even Pompey and Crassus must occasionally have felt a twinge of concern at the superlative ease with which their fellow triumvir rode the horse of power. Caesar, with his almost feline prescience, must have sensed this – and have known that, as the year drew to an end, it was fortunate that he had to go to his commands where he would be far from Rome, yet able to lay his hands on the source of power as Pompey had done in his military career in the East. At the instigation of Vatinius he had been voted three legions for the task and, with a view to campaigning in Illyricum, he stationed them at Aquileia, one of the strongest of all Roman fortresses, standing at the head of the Adriatic.

As the year of Caesar's consulship drew to an end it was seen to have been, for those times, relatively moderate. Even those who had anticipated anarchy, revolution and terror, had to acknowledge that such had not been the case, although it was clear that the senate was cowed by the triumvirate. Cicero, who had gloomily foreseen the establishment of a dictatorship, was proved incorrect, while the rich found that their wealth had remained relatively unassailed. The people, on the other hand, had benefitted comparatively little from the new agrarian law, except some of the poor and, of course, Pompey's soldiers. On the one side there was probably a feeling of some relief, and on the other some disappointment, but it would take a very long time to improve the condition of the poor and Caesar seems to some extent to have adopted the motto that was to be dear to his successor Octavian/Augustus: 'Hasten slowly'. Now that he had held the consulship and could, as it were, proceed no farther in that direction of political power, he looked to the coming years to give him an unassailable power-base. Meanwhile Pompey and Crassus would remain in Rome to uphold the triumvirate. Then, almost as Caesar was about to leave for his province in the north and east, the appointee to the other Gallic province, Narbonese or Transalpine Gaul, suddenly died.

Named after its capital Narbo (Narbonne) this area of southern France had been Romanized for at least fifty years. The great port of Massilia (Marseilles), which had been an early Greek foundation, had been faithful to Rome right through the Hannibalic war and had disseminated Greco-Roman trade and culture for over a century. The Romans had taken it under their protection and using it as a base had gradually infiltrated most of the area of the Rhône valley. Beyond it lay the louring North: the lands of the untamed Gauls who threatened the Roman province, and beyond that the savage and almost unknown tribes of the Belgians and the Germans. Here was an area quite unlike the civilized regions of the East which Pompey had conquered, and it was here, Caesar felt, that immense gains might be won. (He had to counterbalance his fellow triumvir's triumphs with something distinctive, something quite new.) Illyricum could wait, while Cisalpine Gaul was quiet enough, and more than useful for manpower in the legions.

59

But north of Narbonese Gaul lay an area of unknown wealth which could provide a singular addition to the empire. It had never figured in history and had been seen by relatively few Romans – merchants and adventurous traders for the most part.

It is evidence of Pompey's political naïvety that, when his fellow triumvir suggested adding Narbonese Gaul to his other proconsular attachments, Pompey was prepared to stand up in the senate and propose that the responsibility for Transalpine Gaul should be added to Caesar's commands. The senators – even those among them who favoured the popular party – were amazed at the idea that this clearly dangerous man should be given even more power, but they were too cowed by the triumvirate to do anything save acquiesce. Only Cato, with his usual intransigence (and his true love of republican principles), was man enough to speak out against the proposal, denouncing Caesar for trading his daughter for the support of Pompey and a further province. He spoke with the voice of an Old Rome that had died with the advent of Empire.

When he left Rome Caesar knew well that his actions both before and during his consulship would provide material for his open enemies – and others – to bring him to book for anything from high treason to graft at all levels. He had endeavoured to effect a reconciliation with Cicero by offering him a position as his legate and right-hand man, but Cicero had seen that this would be a betrayal of his principles and his friends and had wisely refused. He did not want to be contaminated, and he knew as well as Caesar that the latter was protected by law only so long as he remained in office. Already there were many signs that the three allies were in very deep trouble: the two consuls whom they had earmarked to represent their interests in the following year were prevented from campaigning for office by the worthy Bibulus, who, as was fully his right, had the consular elections postponed. Caesar could feel the hatred of his enemies closing around him like a net; the city was becoming unsafe for him, and he moved outside the walls where he spent three months engaged in the preparations for his coming campaigns. As the law stood, once outside the walls his future governorship had begun and until it was over he could not be prosecuted for anything that had happened within the city.

Before he left it was essential to deal with his major enemies, as well as to secure a 'friend' whose interests coincided with his own. This was the violent and profligate Clodius who was already indebted to him, and whom the triumvirate now managed to get elected as one of the tribunes for the following year. In this position he would serve them well, and he acted in their interests immediately by having Cicero indicted for the leading role he had played in the execution of the Catiline conspirators. Cicero knew well enough that this would mean banishment or worse, and he knew too that Clodius would stop at nothing. He fled abroad to distant Macedonia for safety. That was one great enemy of the triumvirate safely removed, and the next to go was Cato.

Clodius introduced a bill for the annexation of the kingdom of Cyprus to the empire, and Cato was the man chosen to deal with it. Although it is unlikely that he wanted to leave Rome at that moment, with Pompey and Crassus dominating the city and the senate and Clodius in a position of power, yet Cato could hardly refuse to go. It would have been an insult to the Roman people to reject such an offer, and so the crooked schemer had the upright man trapped. With these two enemies out of Rome, Caesar could leave.

His year as consul had enabled him to lay the foundations for his final rise, but he knew that only if he triumphed in Gaul and achieved so great a strength that he was almost unassailable could he ever return to the city. He also knew that he must keep in constant touch with friends in Rome, never making Pompey's mistake but always keeping a watch over his shoulder. During the years of campaigning that were to follow, years during which the readers of his accounts might think (and were supposed to) that Caesar was totally concerned with fighting the enemy for the greater glory of Rome it was for the greater glory of himself.

He was now forty-three years old and ahead lay eight years of such harsh campaigning as would have taxed the strength of any young man. The youth who had appeared slight and almost delicate had evolved into an adult of such intense energy that he would wear out men far younger than himself, and was capable of an endurance that few in history can match. It is clear too that at the time he himself had no conception of how long he would be away in the field, nor of the extent of the territory into which his campaigns would lead him. After all, Narbonese Gaul had only come under his command as almost an afterthought and there was only one legion stationed in the province, plus the three legions that waited at Aquileia.

Transalpine Gaul had long been an area of concern to the Romans, for the danger to Italy from violent warrior tribes crossing the Alps was real and constant. Those famous opening words of the *Gallic War* which have haunted or reduced to tears generations of European schoolboys – 'All Gaul is divided into three parts' – refer to the three main races who inhabited the area. These were the Gauls themselves, the Belgae and the Aquitani.

J. A. Froude has summarized the areas involved and the people that inhabited them:

The Transalpine Gaul of Caesar was the country included between the Rhine, the Ocean, the Pyrenees, the Mediterranean, and the

Alps. Within these limits, including Switzerland, there was at this time a population vaguely estimated at six or seven millions. The Roman Province [Narbonese Gaul] stretched along the coast to the Spanish border; it was bounded on the north by the Cevennes mountains, and for some generations by the Isère; but it had been found necessary lately to annex the territory of the Allobroges (Dauphiné and Savoy), and the proconsular authority was now extended to within a few miles of Geneva. The rest was divided into three sections, inhabited by races which, if allied, were distinctly different in language, laws, and institutions. The Aquitani, who were connected with the Spaniards, or perhaps the Basques, held the country between the Pyrenees and the Garonne. The Belgae, whom Caesar believed to have been originally Germans, extended from the mouth of the Seine to the mouth of the Rhine, and inland to the Marne and the Moselle. The people whom the Romans meant especially when they spoke of Gauls occupied all the remainder. At one time the Celts had probably been master of the whole of France, but had gradually yielded to encroachment.

To this it should be added that there were some 200 different tribes of Celtic Gaul.

The news that had reached Rome and which will have alerted Caesar was that a Celtic people, the Helvetii, who had settled in Switzerland had decided, under duress from their German neighbours, to leave their homeland and travel west with a view to settling beyond the Rhône. This was a mass migration, men, women and children, well over 300,000 of them, and the direction in which they were moving seemed to indicate that they would pass through the Roman province. It was clear that this massive locust-like movement must be halted, or the province's security would be put in jeopardy. The Allobroges, who inhabited what is now Savoy, were probably on their chosen route, but since they had recently been in revolt against Rome it was unlikely that they would do anything to oppose the Helvetii.

Caesar took eight days to reach Geneva, the legionaries making about 35 miles a day. That was where their strength lay, all over the world, against enemies who had no conception of their endurance and discipline. The fourth legion was sent up to join him, along with the allies or provincial auxiliaries. Even so, a legion at maximum strength had no more than 6,000 men and the Helvetii are credited with having had 92,000 men of military age. Caesar, for so long absent from the military world, totally absorbed in the almost equally dangerous one of Roman politics, and whose previous experiences in Spain, and earlier in Asia Minor, had been relatively small, showed from the very start that he remained a master here too. He immediately had the bridge over the Rhône at Geneva demolished.

Seeing that they could not expect an unopposed passage, the Helvetian chiefs came to him in a delegation. They said that they had no wish to make war against the Romans, and only asked for a peaceful passage through the province so that they could reach the lands where they wanted to settle – far in the west. Caesar prevaricated and told them he would give them a reply on 13 April (he had arrived at Geneva on the 2nd). This gave him eight days – eight days in which he intended to block the other routes by which the Helvetii could move on to the west. When they returned, still hopeful that everything could be arranged without recourse to arms, they found an implacable Caesar who told them that he could not allow them any passage through the province and that he would oppose any attempt to force one. It is clear throughout, reading between the lines, that the Helvetii were only on the move in search of new lands and, burdened with their families, and carts and baggage, had no wish for battle. They made one or two attempts to cross the Rhône, but in vain, and so they decided to take another and more difficult passage whereby they would not come in conflict with the Romans. This northern route passed through territory to the north of the Narbonese province and so would be of no concern to the province or its governor.

The threat, then, seemed over and another man might have congratulated himself on having achieved a considerable victory without recourse to arms, a brilliant piece of defensive generalship. Only a proconsul intent on conquest and military glory, as Caesar was, would have done anything more than check on the withdrawal of the Helvetii before returning with a feeling of considerable triumph to home base. But Caesar was after another kind of triumph altogether.

CHAPTER TWELVE

The Tools of the Trade

Caesar had other plans for the 'peaceful' withdrawal of the Helvetii. But, before considering this first of his Gallic campaigns, it is important to take a look at the men, the units and the arms with which Rome had built up her empire and with which Caesar was about to expand it. Naturally, in view of his Roman audience, Caesar does not bother to elaborate upon the equipment of his troops, but specialists in many countries have since made studies of Roman arms and armour, much helped by the activities of archaeologists. Enough is now known to throw some light upon almost all the basic activities of the legions.

The army of Rome had started out originally as a purely citizen army called out from their homes and farms whenever the republic was threatened and, as soon as the emergency was over, discharged. As for the legionary's arms and armour, they were whatever he himself could provide. All men between seventeen and forty-six were considered available as soldiers of the state and were given a minimal payment to cover their time spent in the national service. It can readily be seen that such a system could work when these were no more than citizen-soldiers and peasant-farmers defending their small republic, but it began to break down the moment that Rome acquired an empire and overseas entanglements. The man who changed the old military system was Caesar's uncle, the great Marius, who realized during a lengthy war in North Africa – where there was naturally a great shortage of recruits – that the whole system must be radically altered to meet the new circumstances.

Previously, a property-qualification as well as Roman citizenship had been required of a legionary, but Marius now discarded the former and threw the army open to every Roman citizen. This meant that the urban poor, who were steadily increasing in numbers, flocked to the legions. They looked to their general to provide for them, and consequently a successful general, who could furnish plenty of opportunities for plunder, was always sure of a following. It was plunder, not pay, that rewarded these soldiers. Caesar changed this somewhat by giving his soldiers adequate pay, but this remained the basic ration, as it were, and the looting of a great town and the plundering of foreign land and settlements was what the soldier hoped for. At the same time, being now a professional, he was landless and, when it came to his retirement, looked to his general to provide him with a big enough plot for him to settle and engage those other talents inherited from his peasant forebears.

Another great change that Marius made was to give each soldier an identification with his own particular legion. Whereas previously the legions had been disbanded at the end of every campaign – so that continuity was lost – the legions were now given numbers and a distinctive standard, the eagle. These were to Roman troops what the Colours became to British infantry in later centuries. The loss of an eagle was a disgrace to a legion which would one day have to be redeemed by blood. Another of Marius' major changes was to cut down the size of the baggage trains, which had previously both held up the pace of the army and provided a desirable object for plunder. Marius saw to it that these were both better organized and reduced, thus increasing mobility. At the same time he had to compensate for this loss of immediate provisions by turning each soldier into his own food carrier. So, in addition to his sword, his spear, his entrenching tool, stakes for palisades and so on, the Roman soldier now also carried his own essential supplies. Jokingly, they referred to themselves as 'Marius' mules'.

The eagle was the standard of the whole legion and, by Caesar's time, it was made of silver and gold. When the legion marched, it was carried by the senior centurion and guarded by the first cohort of the troops: otherwise it never left camp. There were also special standards for each cohort (a gold hand, for instance, or a series of silver discs) and special banners or flags which bore the name of the legion. All these trappings of war had the same intention – of inspiring regimental spirit, a dedication to one's own legion, and rivalry with others. Eagles, standards and flags were attached to long poles, ending in an iron-shod point so that they could be stuck in the earth. The poles were fitted with hand-grips so that, when planted in muddy or awkward ground, the bearer could quickly hoist them free whenever the order came to move.

By the time of Caesar the arms of the legionary had been streamlined from an earlier complexity into two only – the sword and the spear. Swords were basically of a type that the Roman had first encountered in Spain. They had a double-cutting edge and a stabbing-point, were sheathed in a metal-bound leather scabbard, and hung on the legionary's right hand side. The blade-length of a standard sword was 50–56 cm. The spears came in two main types; both were throwing spears, known as a *pilum*, and one was a light-weight and the other a heavy-weight. Both were constructed on the same principle: a long metal shaft which ended in a spear point was attached to a wooden shaft. It was thus quite unlike the simple spears of antiquity and, when sunk deep into a man or a horse, instead of simply standing proud as a wooden spear would have done, the *pilum* with its soft iron neck would bend at the point where it joined the wooden stock. A horse thus struck would very likely be brought to the ground, and a man transfixed would be unable to run away but held on the spot by the curve that the *pilum* had now become.

The Caesarian legionary was protected by a mail shirt that hung about halfway down his thighs, under which he wore a leather jerkin, and on his head what is called a Montefortino helmet (so-called after the cemetery where an example was found). This type of helmet had protective cheek pieces and was pear-shaped, rising to a lead-filled topknot which held a horsehair crest. A rim ran around the bottom of the helmet, swept out farther at the back to protect the neck against glancing blows. The shield was oval-shaped and, to judge from one example found in Egypt, was made from laminated strips of wood – in this case birch which had then been covered with lamb's wool felt. Shields were often leather covered, and were metal-rimmed and carried a metal boss in the centre. Greaves were rarely worn by the ordinary legionary, and his equipment ended in his heavy leather sandals, leather-laced over the foot and up round the ankles, the soles studded with iron nails.

The famed centurion was undoubtedly the backbone of the Roman army. Senior officers might come and go, but centurions were the only lifetime officers. In Caesar's time they were usually men who had started in the ranks (although in later days so highly valued had the rank become that even monied men sought to buy a centurionate). As regulars they would serve twenty-five years or even more, usually with the same legion. As his name suggests, the commander of a century, the centurion was expected to be a 'hard case', for on him largely rested the discipline of the legions. His badge of office was the vine cane – often laid across the soldier's back – and he was distinguished from the legionary by wearing the crest on his helmet transversely and his sword on the left, while on his right he had a dagger. They were expected to be Spartans, to stand and fight and die. There were fifty-nine centurions to a legion.

Each legion was commanded by six tribunes, usually young men aspiring to become senators, or others who had tried the military life, developed a taste for it, and would stay there for years. Senior to them were the prefects, who might become aides to generals or be put in command of cavalry, or even become a prefect of the fleet – for the

Romans made no real distinction between military service ashore or afloat. Above them in the chain of command came the legate (under Caesar, of a legion), usually a senator, and therefore one who must at some time previously have been a magistrate, or quaestor. These were the men who, under great captains like Caesar or Pompey, formed an experienced group of commanders, a general staff as it were.

The whole legion, if at its full strength – which was rare enough – consisted of 6,000 men divided into ten cohorts. Further subdivisions within the cohort were each commanded by a centurion, and each with its individual standard bearer and hornblower (the group's signalman). In the old legions of pre-Marian days each had also had attached to it its own cavalry, light infantry or skirmishers, engineers and artillerymen. In the new army these departments had become quite separate units on their own. If the siege of a town was to be undertaken, then the corps of engineers and artillery had to be brought up, similarly whenever cavalry was needed. The latter largely came from Spain, although Caesar was to conscript useful cavalry from Gaul and Germany at various times in his campaigns. The new legion, was, therefore, not a self-contained structure as it had been in the past, but what it had lost in one sense it had gained in another. Its flexibility as a unit of disciplined, highly-trained professionals made it a formidable instrument of war in the hands of a man of genius. The legionary's training was rigorous: weapons drill, long runs in full armour, practice fighting with swords which had a button on the point, javelin-throwing and, throughout their training, constant attention to the condition of arms and armour, with on-the-spot checks by eagle-eyed centurions. All this attention to detail, so familiar to armies of later centuries (if of any quality), was what gave the Roman legionary his permanent edge over the brave barbarian.

For there can be no doubt about the bravery and the fighting qualities of the warriors of Gallic and Germanic stock with whom the legionaries were soon to come in conflict. Long-moustached, shaggy-haired, despising the protective armour of their enemies, the peoples of the north inhabited a Homeric world. Boastful, deep-drinking, prone to fits of berserker rage, wearing great torques and massive armbands of gold, whether Gauls or Germans, all had one thing in common – they lived for war. Unlike the Romans and the Greeks, they went trousered through the world – such clothing being more suitable for their climate, but setting them apart as 'barbarians' in the eyes of Mediterranean peoples. The Greek historian Diodorus wrote of them: 'They enlarge the bronze helmets that they wear with horns, to give an appearance of great size. They carry shields as long as their bodies, embossed with the head of some beast. They speak in riddles, hinting darkly at their meaning, while always extolling themselves. Terrible in aspect, they appear very threatening; yet they have sharp wits and are often clever in learning.' Since, under the influence of their Druidic religion, they were confident of an afterlife, they had no fear of death, and the ambition of the warrior was to die in battle.

CHAPTER THIRTEEN

The First Planned Victories

Caesar refused to accept the fact that the withdrawal of the Helvetii to the north meant that the threat to the province was over. He intended that the danger should at least appear to remain. When he later came to publish his commentaries on his campaigns, he took care that they should show him as a Roman provincial governor doing no more than his duty by protecting the interests of the state.

Although the Helvetii had made it clear that they did not want to fight the Romans, and that they only wished to migrate to other lands where they would be free from harassment by the Germans, they had in the past – seven years before Caesar was born – defeated a Roman consul and enforced the subjection of his entire army ('passing under the yoke'). This gave good grounds for wishing to humiliate them, but better were now provided by the pro-Roman tribe of the Aedui and their neighbours, who appealed for military assistance against this great migratory wave which threatened their peace and their lands. It is more than probable that this appeal was made at Caesar's instigation, for he had already summoned a further two legions from Cisalpine Gaul – as if anticipating trouble.

He made his base at Lyons where the gentle river Saône joins the turbulent Rhône. Here he regrouped his forces: he now had nearly 50,000 men under his command, the legionaries from Italy, the Tenth Legion under Labienus, his legate, a detachment of cavalry provided by the Aedui and a number of auxiliaries recruited from the province. This should have been more than enough to deal with the Helvetii, who, although they had many more fighting men, were hampered by their immense baggage train and by the fact that, since the whole tribe was on the move, they had the encumbrance of their old men, women and children. Caesar could have fallen upon them even before they reached the Saône, but he deliberately waited until they had actually begun their crossing to the north bank. When more than half were across, he fell upon the remainder who were waiting. A considerable

69

number were killed and, in his own words: 'The others fled and hid in the forests nearby.' It was a cheap and easy victory.

Now an embassy came from the Helvetii under the leadership of the man who so long ago had inflicted that crushing defeat upon the Romans. The old chief, Divico, chosen perhaps for the very reason that the Romans would respect an adversary who had been so formidable when young, came to ask for peace with honour, and humbled himself sufficiently to say that his people would settle 'in whatever place should be assigned to them by the will of the Romans'. Unfortunately, the old man closed his speech with arrogance, reminding Caesar of the previous Roman defeat at his hands. It was enough: Caesar would entertain no thought of letting these people go forward in peace, citing the damage that they had done in their passage through the lands of the Aedui and their neighbours.

For a further two weeks the Romans hung on the heels of the Helvetii as they migrated northwards. Then, a savage defeat of his Aeduan horsemen by the Helvetii, coupled with a breakdown in his grain-supply, caused Caesar to make a long diversion to Bibracte (Mont Beuvray) to get further provisions. It is noticeable about the whole of this part of the campaign that Caesar, referring to himself as he habitually does in the third person (to give an air of objectivity to his account) is concealing the real situation – that the Aedui, who were supposed to have asked for his support, were far from wholeheartedly behind him. In fact, the tribe was split between those who accepted that the Romans were there to stay and those who maintained that, 'they would prefer to be dominated by other Gauls rather than the Romans'. It was clear that Dumnorix, the brother of Divitiacus, the leader of the Aedui, was the most powerful anti-Roman force in their politics while Divitiacus, a weaker man, would also have been happy to get rid of the Romans if he could. However, by inviting Caesar to protect his tribe against the Helvetii (almost certainly pressurized to do so) Divitiacus was made to appear a traitor to his people, while his brother Dumnorix stood out as the staunch patriot. Since a great deal of Gallic politics always revolved around the contest between brothers as to who was to be the chief of a tribe, it was clear that the star of Dumnorix was in the ascendant. It was to be much the same all through Caesar's Gallic campaigns: even those who professed friendship for the Romans, or acquiesced in their presence, were only too happy to get rid of them – if and when the opportunity presented itself. The Gauls, unlike many of those in the East whom Pompey had conquered, were a passionately freedom-loving people. What betrayed them ultimately into Roman hands was their equally passionate internecine feuds. (Not unlike the Scottish clans many centuries later, they hated each other almost as much as the over-all enemy.)

The Helvetii, having observed the Romans turn back towards Bibracte, and probably informed by some of the Aedui that they were short of provisions, were unwise enough to presume that they could repeat their old success and inflict a crushing defeat upon these invaders of the Gallic world. If the Helvetii had managed to do so, there can be little doubt that they would have been welcomed everywhere and that their passage through the territories of other tribes would have been made easy for them. They were foolish, however, in not pursuing their course away to the north. Even hampered as they were by their baggage trains and their non-combatant civilians, they should have been able to get far enough away before Caesar's forces had re-provisioned to make it a waste of time for the Romans to follow them. As it was, they prepared to attack.

Caesar moved his legions to a hill, sent out his cavalry to harass the advancing Helvetii, and calmly awaited them. To show the young officers who had accompanied him (and who probably had no experience of warfare) that there was no question of retreat, he had all the horses – including his own – sent away from the immediate vicinity. The Helvetii, full of the usual courage to be expected among the 'barbarians', but quite lacking in tactical expertise, advanced up the hill in the face of the well-entrenched and disciplined Roman troops. The result could easily be foreseen: the Romans greeted them first of all with a shower of spears and then drew their swords and charged. The Helvetii had advanced in what is described as 'a phalanx': that is, a compact line – presumably row after row of them – with their shields overlapping. But bravery alone cannot defeat superior weaponry, and it was now that the Roman *pilum* showed itself so far in advance of the simple spear. The weight of the iron shaft behind the head, coupled with the forceful throw of men who had been exhaustively trained in just such an exercise, overwhelmed the enemy. Furthermore, 'The Helvetii were much impeded in their movement by the fact that a single *pilum* often pierced two overlapping shields, pinning them together. Then, as the iron bent, the men could not pull them out. So, with their left arms thus hampered, they could not fight properly and, despite many attempts to free themselves, they were forced to drop their shields and fight unprotected.' It was a triumph of science and discipline over unthinking courage. The Helvetii were decisively defeated, and all night long – after a battle that had lasted throughout the day – the stream of refugees fled northward. It was the end of this hardy tribe from Switzerland, whose bravery had long been famous among their fellow men. The disgrace of that Roman legion over fifty years before had been expunged, and it was as if a great voice had shouted throughout all the unconquered lands that no one was any longer safe to enjoy his freedom.

The defeated followed their old and their women and children into the area around Dijon, where the local tribe soon received warning from Caesar that they should on no account give any help to the Helvetii on pain of suffering a similar fate themselves. Contemplating the ruinous condition of the survivors, and hearing of their over-whelming defeat, the local inhabitants were not unwilling to obey and the remaining Helvetii, in danger of starvation, were compelled to send envoys to their conqueror. Caesar had given his troops three days' rest – they too had many dead to bury and more wounded to attend to, for the fighting qualities of the enemy had not been exaggerated – then the march after the Helvetii was resumed. One hundred and ten thousand of the conquered waited upon Caesar, while many others who had slipped away were later to return and surrender. (The latter, as a punishment, were either slaughtered or sold to the slave-dealers who always followed like vultures behind the Roman troops.) The main body were ordered to return to the land that they had so rashly left and rebuild their towns and villages. Meanwhile, as they were without provisions, the neighbouring tribe of the Allobroges were ordered to supply them. Caesar's decision was clear and politically wise. They had felt the might of Roman arms, they had surrendered, and now they would return to their country and serve as a buffer-state between the Germans and the Roman province.

This devastating victory over a tribe with such a high military reputation naturally had a great effect upon Gaul. Many were the tribal leaders who now came forward to secure their peace with Rome, while the Aedui – as representative of the Gauls who favoured the Roman cause (however half-heartedly in fact) – now became the dominant power in this area. At the same time, there existed a secondary option for the free peoples of Gaul. This was to ask for help from their near neighbours, the Germans – more than neighbours indeed, for there were no fixed boundaries in those days and Germany and Gaul overlapped and coexisted on both banks of the Rhine. The Germans, however, had had less contact with the Roman world than the Gauls and were feared in distant Rome even more. In the days of Marius – who had won much of his reputation by defeating them – two Germanic tribes, the Cimbri and the Teutones, had swept down as far as Italy itself. The dominant tribe at the moment was one hailing from Suebia far across the Rhine, but which already, under their king Ariovistus, had infiltrated Gaul and begun to flood across the Rhine in the vicinity of Mainz. The Gallic Sequani, to secure assistance against their neighbours (all Gaul was not just 'divided into three parts' but was a compendium of tribes constantly fighting one another) had very rashly called upon the Suebi to act as mercenaries for them. This was something that they soon bitterly regretted, for no sooner were

Ariovistus and his warriors firmly entrenched on the west bank of the Rhine than they decided that they liked the look of this rich and fertile land.

It was largely on Caesar's initiative that, during his year of consulship, Ariovistus had secured recognition as an independent king and as a friend of the Roman people. Caesar had probably been thinking of the adage 'Divide and Rule', hoping that Ariovistus might distract the Gauls from any combined nationalism. Now, a year later, he was confronted with the reality of the Gallic chieftains in assembly asking the Romans to stop the Suebian flood that threatened to engulf the tribes on the west bank of the Rhine. (Ariovistus, it must be noted, had been careful, in accordance with his concord with Rome, not to assist the Helvetii in any way during their march.) Caesar, who had supported Ariovistus the year before, now found himself faced with the necessity of curbing him and protecting the Gauls, and in particular the Aedui, against any further German incursions.

The senate had described the Aedui in glowing terms as 'blood brothers'; so when they, together with many other Celtic chiefs, now asked for help he had the excuse – if one were needed – to take arms against the Suebi and their chieftain. For the fact was that a good excuse was indeed needed, and Caesar was well aware that there were those among his officers who were constantly reporting his every move to Rome. The Roman senate did not believe in preventive war, but the cycle of events which Caesar had set in motion called for just that. He now looked to Ariovistus to provide him with the necessary excuse.

CHAPTER FOURTEEN

Ariovistus and After

Having promised the Gallic leaders the protection of Rome, Caesar sent an ambassador to Ariovistus asking him to meet him at any place midway between their two armies. Ariovistus, far away in Suebia, had no intention of crossing the Rhine into territory where most of the Gauls hated him. He sent a message back that he could not come to see Caesar without being accompanied by an army. 'If,' he added ironically, 'he had wanted to see Caesar he would have gone to see him, but since the reverse was the case, then let Caesar come to Ariovistus.'

He pointed out that the Aedui owed him money in accordance with a treaty which they had made with the Germans, but the presence of Roman troops meant that the Romans were taking what was rightfully his. The Aedui had given him hostages as guarantees for this treaty, and he had no intention of returning them until they showed that they were prepared to keep up their regular payments of tribute money. Caesar's reply was to send further ambassadors to the Suebian leader stating the conditions under which the Romans were prepared to continue their friendship with Ariovistus: these included a return of the hostages and a renunciation of the use of force against the Aedui or any of their allies. But Ariovistus had really won this contest of words: he had given his reasons for retaining the hostages, and his unwillingness to venture halfway to meet Caesar without an army to protect him was justified enough. Caesar had sought a *casus belli*, but the German, while remaining intransigent, had not provided him with one. Meanwhile, whether acting on Ariovistus' instructions or not, numerous Germans continued to cross the Rhine and pour into France.

Caesar considered that he had cause enough for action – even if many of those who were with him were to show that they disagreed. He ordered the legions to march on Vesontio (Besançon), thus forestalling Ariovistus who was already moving in the same direction. He was full of elation, seeing ahead of him a further campaign that would crown the year during which he had already defeated the Helvetii and had, to his satisfaction, solved that problem by getting them to return to their former country. He looked forward to throwing the Germans back across the Rhine and of being able to write to Rome that he had completely stabilized and secured the security not only of the Narbonese province but of their Gallic friends to the north of it.

His enthusiasm was not shared, however, by his officers – and certainly not by his troops. The latter had been hearing from the Gauls horrific stories about the fighting prowess of the Germans, their barbarism and their cruelty. The soldiers had been enjoying themselves in a rich and pleasant country after a hard campaign, and now they had been suddenly ordered by forced marches to a land unknown to Romans, to find that, having already fought well for Caesar, they were going to be ordered out once more against what appeared to be monsters. The legionaries could be calmed down if Caesar could only secure the undivided enthusiasm of their officers for the fight that lay ahead. But here – to his surprise and no doubt to his inner fury – he discovered that the latter were practically in revolt. Young Romans of good families and no doubt the products of soft living had thought it would be 'interesting' or 'amusing' to take a look at the barbarous Gauls; it would give them something to talk about when back in Rome. Instead, they had been hauled off at breakneck speed into Switzerland, confronted by a savage race migrating to the west, and then – just as this seemed to have been satisfactorily settled – told to march again and make war upon the very people whom they had happily considered pacified. There had been heavy fighting, with many dead and wounded in the last battle against the Helvetii: they themselves had survived and had congratulated themselves on a good campaigning year. Now Caesar was leading them into even more barbarous territory to fight a people whom, they heard, even the Gauls and the Helvetii considered irresistible. Caesar of course does not say as much, but it seems very probable that some of this apparent indiscipline among his officers was not due to fear at all but to pressure from Rome, where it was constantly being said by his opponents that Caesar's campaigns were unnecessary and that he was bent only on self-aggrandisement, whereas he had been sent out to administer a province: no more. Dio Cassius records that it was said everywhere that they were entering upon a war merely to satisfy Caesar's personal ambitions. It was a war that was neither just nor sanctioned by public decree.

Caesar was faced with what looked very much like mutiny, not only from his troops but also from the military tribunes and prefects. Despondency prevailed, and 'throughout the camp there was nothing but the sealing of wills'. When it became evident that even the centurions, the backbone of discipline and the legions, were infected by the malaise Caesar realized just how dangerous the situation was. He knew at once where to strike – and that was with them. Convince and win over the centurions, and the army was his. As for the senior officers, he could deal with them himself. He knew how to handle the centurions: 'To argue that we ought not to go to war is only to say that we ought not to be rich, that we ought not to rule over others, that we ought neither to be free nor to be Romans.' Yes, they were a thousand miles away from home, but the centurions were men who were in the army of their own choice and 'because of the honours and advantages that can be gained by war'. He spoke to them as a soldier to soldiers and his approach was successful. He disparaged these absurd legends that the Germans were unconquerable, reminding them that Marius had soundly trounced them some forty years ago. (He did not need to remind centurions, steeped in all the history of the army, that Marius had been his uncle.) He did remind them, however, that there had been many Germans in the army of slave-revolt led by Spartacus – and look what had happened to them!

It was true that the Germans had achieved some success over the Gauls, but the Gauls were 'barbarous and inexperienced', as they themselves had found out. He reminded them of his success against the Helvetii and said that he intended to march that very night – alone if need be, but he knew that the Tenth Legion would never let him down. The Tenth Legion under his friend Labienus was, of course, certain to obey, but Caesar had played cannily upon that rivalry between the legions which the Marian system of individual numbers and eagles had fostered. When he had finished speaking, 'his words were applauded by all' and particularly by those who had given credence to the previous rumours, and who now wished to show that their legions were every bit as reliable and stout-hearted as the Tenth. They came forward to offer their apologies and excuses and, as he puts it tersely in his account, 'Caesar accepted their explanations'. Six days later, with all doubts and hesitation quashed by his own superlative self-confidence and by the trust in him now so clearly felt by the centurions, he was some twenty miles from the camp of Ariovistus in Upper Alsace. The German leader certainly knew of the trouble there had been in Caesar's camp, for he was kept posted with intelligence from Rome and knew that the proconsul had many enemies there. He must therefore have been somewhat surprised when Caesar, having apparently overcome the opposition and any semblance of mutiny, suddenly appeared within an easy march of his own lines.

He could no longer prevaricate. He had asked Caesar to come to meet him if he wished to have a discussion, and the latter had done so. Accordingly he sent envoys to the Roman camp to inform the proconsul that Ariovistus was now prepared to meet him personally. Five days passed, with the almost inevitable haggling about how many should be present at the conference and what kind of escort each should be allowed, both men naturally being suspicious and fearing some kind of trap or ambush. It was a historic moment when the great German leader met the Roman proconsul: the representative of the powerful, unknown North and the representative of the Mediterranean world.

Gallic was the *lingua franca* used by the interpreters between German and Latin, Caesar speaking in his own tongue but Ariovistus, long familiar with Gallic, being able to speak directly through the interpreters. On and on went the long arguments: Ariovistus maintaining that the Romans were interfering in his sphere of influence, Caesar maintaining the opposite, that if the Germans kept out of Gaul then there was no reason for any quarrel. In his *Commentaries* Caesar was anxious to establish that he was doing no more than his duty in protecting the Roman province (now far away to the south). He was also pleased to be able to insert a statement by Ariovistus that there were many men in Rome who would be happy to see Caesar removed – thus showing up his political opponents as traitors who had inspired disaffection in the legions and were also guilty of trying to betray a Roman proconsul and his legions almost on the field of battle! And Caesar was determined that it should come to battle, for he realized that this powerful and wily German could never be trusted to hold to any agreement that might be hammered out between them. The long dialogue was cut short by a more or less trivial incident in which some of the German troops made a half-hearted attack upon Caesar's bodyguard. It was enough. Caesar ceased his speech, rejoined his troops, and hastened back to camp. A stupid indiscipline had given him the opportunity he sought.

It was clear that Ariovistus did not want to fight, for he sent a further delegation to the proconsul, seeking another meeting. But Caesar now had his excuse for battle and he was not relinquishing it. He sent back two comparatively insignificant envoys with orders to listen to Ariovistus and report back what he had to say. The German was justifiably angered at what seemed clearly intended as an insult, and had the two men imprisoned in chains. This was, indeed, against all the conventions and Caesar had a further (quotable) excuse for having nothing more to do with this barbarian. War was now inevitable, and both sides began to manoeuvre for position, Ariovistus attempting to cut off Caesar's supply route and the latter denying him this advantage by establishing a secondary camp south of the Germans. The battle when it came was swift, bloody and decisive.

Caesar made the first move. The autumn rains were approaching and he wanted to capitalize on the new mood which had been aroused among his troops. To delay would be to the advantage of the enemy. He attacked the camp of Ariovistus with his six legions, advancing in three lines, and the German, forced to fight, ordered his troops out in a counter-attack. Caesar himself took command of the Roman right wing, and before long the German left began to yield before the weight of his attack. But in the turmoil of battle Caesar seems to have lost command of the overall picture, and failed to notice that on the left it was the Romans who were giving way before the onslaught of the Germans. The situation was rectified by the young son of the millionaire Crassus, a youth fresh from the soft life of Rome who showed an instinctive grasp of tactical opportunities. Stationed in the rear with his cavalry he observed the position on the Roman left and, without waiting for any orders from his commander, immediately sent up the third legionary line (the reserves) to the relief. Both German wings finally fell back, and the battle turned into a rout. (Like most barbarians they were fine offensive fighters, but they lacked the discipline to maintain an ordered withdrawal.)

There followed a disorderly flight towards the Rhine, a race between pursuers and pursued that was made doubly tragic for the Germans by the fact that their camp lay in the path of the advancing legions. Their wives and children were put to the sword. The two wives of Ariovistus himself perished in this slaughter, one of his daughters was killed and another was taken prisoner. The German chief himself managed to cross the Rhine but he had probably been badly wounded: all we know is that he died soon afterwards. The great reputation of the Suebi was destroyed. Only the scattering of a few German tribes, of little importance in themselves, was left in Gaul. For many years to come it was as if a great silence hung over the grand, divisive river of the Rhine. The peace of the sword had descended.

By the end of 58 the first year's campaigning was over, the threat of the Helvetii eliminated, and the most powerful German tribe so heavily defeated that all the others in that dark land heard of it and withdrew into their forests. If he had acted in accordance with the wishes of the senate Caesar would now have led his troops back into the Roman province. Instead of this he ordered the legions under the command of Labienus to take up winter quarters in and around Vesontio (Besançon), the heartland of the Sequani tribe. The Sequani, who by soliciting German assistance against their neighbours had been so largely responsible for the recent trouble, now found firm shackles laid upon themselves. One thing was clear to all, from tribune to centurion to legionary – they would not have been quartered so far north of Narbonese Gaul if Caesar had no intention for further expansion in the year to come. He himself was off and away before the onset of winter to Cisalpine Gaul: there in the north of Italy to make his circuit administering justice, to raise new legions, to secure close contact with his friends in Rome, and to appraise the situation in the city.

This had changed greatly since his departure in March, and the change cannot have been agreeable to Caesar. Clodius, without a firm hand to rein him in, had exceeded any latitude that Caesar might have allowed. He had turned against Pompey to such an extent that the latter had inclined towards the *Optimates*. Then, on the disclosure of a plot by Clodius to have him murdered, Pompey had withdrawn into his house with the avowed determination not to leave it until the end of the tribunician year, when Clodius would no longer be protected by his position. Crassus was preoccupied by business and, apart from his aptitude for making money, seems to have been without political ability or real character. Pompey had long shown himself incompetent politically, and Caesar had recognised – as probably he had done all along – that without his presence the triumvirate ceased to function. In this desperate situation, when the city was at the mercy of thugs employed by rival political parties, it was not surprising that a move was afoot to recall Cicero. After all, it was now remembered how well he had dealt with the Catiline conspiracy, and Clodius was another Catiline, equally unstable and violent. One of the senators who supported Cicero's recall travelled north to see Caesar to try to secure his approval of such a move. Caesar might possibly have agreed if he himself had been in the city, able to keep an eye on Cicero and Clodius alike, but as things stood he gave a temporizing reply. Cicero did not receive permission to return to the city until the summer of the following year.

The situation in Gaul demanded Caesar's return and for the moment Rome must wait. The quartering of the legions among the Sequani, deep in the heart of Gaul and far removed from the Roman province, had naturally provoked considerable concern among the native peoples. They were not stupid and could read the writing on the wall: the Romans are here to stay. Labienus had not helped matters by actively concerning himself with local politics, favouring the pro-Romans and persecuting those whose nationalism was openly declared. Caesar also heard that the northern tribes of Belgic Gaul, alarmed by what had happened the previous year in the south, were mustering for a collective action against the invaders of the homeland. As evidence of his intentions (though quite unknown to the senate in Rome) Caesar raised a further two legions in Cisalpine Gaul, thus bringing his army strength up to twice that which had been authorized. Hardly had the legions been formed than he sent them across the Alps, under the command of his nephew Q. Pedius, he himself following about a month later at a time when 'it began to be possible to get fodder'. The campaigning year of 57 was about to begin.

In these and all subsequent campaigns the Roman attitude was very different from that of other imperialistic and colonizing nations in later centuries. There was not even the pretence of bringing a superior culture or religion to the conquered. It is true that over the years the civilization of the Mediterranean did spread northward throughout Gaul, finally even reaching Britain, but this was an accidental by-product of the presence of the legions in the conquered countries. First in the wake of the soldiers came the slave-dealers, always ready to conduct business as soon as a battle or a campaign was concluded. Healthy strong slaves such as Gaul was to provide were always welcome in a civilization based on slave-labour. Even so, the dealers did not like a glut on the market and, to maintain the price, would tend to regulate their quotas for release, keeping back much of their 'raw material' in slave-camps for training in talents suitable for the home, while simple brutish strength could be quickly disposed of to farm or mine. All roads did indeed lead to Rome, but precious little came back in return. The city was not, as Carthage had been, a great manufacturing centre and furthermore it lived largely on grain imports from Sicily, Egypt and North Africa. Rome, at any rate during this period of its history, ran much as did the later Ottoman Empire on a principle of 'ever-extending conquest'. The loot of conquered lands and captured cities went back to swell the city's wealth and power – as well as rewarding the conquering generals, officers, and legionaries – while the permanent possessions of a country, iron and silver for example, would be worked on the spot by the conquered inhabitants for the benefit of the ruling power.

After the soldiers and the slave-dealers came the merchants and the tax-gatherers, the former (as in later colonial Africa, for example) to trade the insubstantial for the substantial, and the latter to drain into Italy the wealth that had previously gone to tribal chieftains. No missionaries followed the eagles, for in one thing Rome was, however unwittingly, more farsighted than later conquerors – completely toler-ant or indeed indifferent to foreign religions. (Most of the Sky Gods, Mother Goddesses, Gods of War and so on were usually easy to equate with those already existing in the Greco-Roman pantheon.) The Romans did later persecute the Druids, the centre of whose Celtic cult was in Britain, but this was less because of their practice of human sacrifice than because they were at the heart of nationalism, and therefore resistance to Roman power. As for Caesar, he had no civilizing mission, nor real sense of racial superiority. From the conquered he sought money and fame, and above all fame as a world general sufficient to eclipse Pompey. The slaves, the loot from temples and chieftains' houses, the profit from metals and mines, all helped to enrich him. But the bodies, living and dead, of the conquered were the raw material which he used to further a political career. Pompey had erred in thinking that the fame he had gained by his conquests in the

East and his reorganization of ancient states for the benefit of the republic would make his position unassailable. Where he had erred, and where Caesar did not err, was in failing to understand that the real levers of power lay always in Rome.

CHAPTER FIFTEEN

Conquest of the Belgians

One thing that cannot have pleased Caesar during his months in Cisalpine Gaul was that his visitors from the capital, as well as his correspondents in the city, revealed that his first Gallic successes had made comparatively little stir. The Helvetii, after being thoroughly defeated, had gone back to their original territory, but in consequence of this and of being a migrating tribe without much in the way of possessions, had yielded few if any slaves and practically nothing worth plundering. Similarly, Ariovistus and his Germans had been soundly beaten and forced to retreat beyond the Rhine but, because they were engaged not on their own territory but in that of the Gauls, there had been no towns, temples or chieftains' houses to sack, and few slaves to take since those who were not killed on the battlefield had escaped back to their own land. Caesar's victories, then, meant little to the Romans, who were almost totally absorbed by the state of affairs in the city. The latest street fighting between Clodius and his gangsters and those who opposed them was of more moment to the citizen concerned about the safety of his house and family than some distant campaign against people no one had heard of, in unknown regions of the earth. Pompey had had one advantage, in that the kings and nations of the East as well as their cities had been well-known to Roman and Greek for centuries: their names meant something. Caesar now required a campaign that would disturb and bedazzle his countrymen. The massing of the Belgae to the north seemed as if it would provide him with the kind of campaign that, if successful, could not be overlooked.

Having rejoined the army, supervised stores and provisions – a practical point which Caesar never ignored – he listened carefully to all the information that was coming in and prepared to march. In the summer of 57 he struck camp and, at the head of some 50,000 men, moved north as far as the river Aisne to confront the enemy. But, despite their vast concentration over the winter and their declared intention of preventing their free lands from falling to the Romans, the assorted tribes, who were loosely classified as 'Belgae', had run into the usual situation so often to be found among the less-civilized. Malad-ministration meant that their supply services were totally inadequate. Used to inter-tribal wars, when each contestant operated out of his own territory, they were totally unable to foresee the necessity of organizing supply dumps and transport between their bases and the fighting men at the front. The Remi, the inhabitants of the area of Rheims, were the first to come forward with protestations of affection and submission to the Roman legions. This was good news for Caesar, for now at the very beginning of the campaign he had a powerful tribe – rather like the Aedui in the south – upon whom he could rely for help, information, and corn if necessary. Hostages, the children of the chiefs of the country, were handed over as a bond for good behaviour.

The tribes which had fallen apart through lack of provisions and organizations were now picked off piecemeal: the Bellovaci (around Beauvais), the Suessiones (Soissons) and the Ambiani (Amiens) all surrendered to Rome and handed over hostages. There were, of course, a few engagements. These were individual actions, often fierce in themselves, but with no unifying hand to direct the tribes against the controlled precision of the legions. It was not until Caesar reached the region dominated by the Nervii (Hainault and Flanders) that he encountered the kind of resistance which he had anticipated from the beginning. The most powerful tribe among all the Belgae, the Nervii were renowned for their fighting qualities and they had been careful to keep themselves well away from the demoralization and disintegration of their neighbours to the south. There was no sense of nationhood in those days – tribal loyalty was all. The spectacle of other tribes collapsing probably rejoiced the hearts of the Nervii and their neigh-bours the Atrebati (around Arras) and the Viromandui (Vermandois) much as in later centuries one Scottish clan could rejoice over the discomfiture of a neighbour, even though it was at the hands of every Scotsman's enemy, the English.

When they heard of the advance of the legions into their territory, the Nervii at once prepared for all-out war. They sent their old, and their women and children back into safety and themselves, having pro-claimed that they would never send ambassadors to Caesar (like their cowardly neighbours) nor accept any offers from him, prepared to make the Roman invasion of their land as difficult as possible. Together with their allies they took up position in thick woodlands on the right bank of the river Sambre and awaited the moment when the enemy should begin their crossing. Caesar reached the river after a three-day march – and blundered. He had clearly not foreseen that so large an army (possibly as many as 80,000 men) would be concealed in the woods opposite, nor anticipated anything like the vigour of the attack that they launched while his own troops were still in the process of 'digging in' and fortifying what was to be their base-camp.

Having waited until Caesar's scouting cavalry had crossed the river, the Nervii suddenly burst from their concealment, thousand upon thousand of them, overwhelmed the horsemen and stormed across. 'With almost unbelievable rapidity' they raced up the far bank and soon were upon the unprepared legionaries, many of whom had not even had time 'to take off their shield-covers or put on their helmets – let alone details like fixing their crests'. There was no time either for the legionaries to find their own centurions or their own officers; they just joined up with the first group that they saw, never mind what standard they were fighting under. In the chaos that prevailed there was no chance for a commander's eyeview of the action, and each separate group was fighting its own battle for, as Caesar comments, 'thick hedges obstructed the view'. In some places the Romans were successful, managing to throw back on the right wing the allies of the Nervii, the Atrebates, and even drive them in flight across the river. But on the right wing, where the attack had fallen fiercest, there were signs of collapse – the two legions at this point having become isolated owing to the advance of the Roman centre and left wing. It was here that Caesar showed that instinctive grasp of the fulcrum of power – 'Give me a place to stand, and I will move the earth', as Archimedes had said – and, seizing a shield from a soldier in the rear, made his way to the front. Here his personal knowledge of his troops served him in good stead. He was able to call to individual centurions by name, ordering them to push ahead and open out the ranks so that each man's sword arm could have full play. But it was the presence of the general himself that produced so great an effect. Individual generals, however brave, did not show themselves in the front rank – and on foot. This was the birth of the 'Caesar Legend' that would last him all his days. On many another occasion throughout the years, when things looked bad, when another general would have been seen on horseback some distance away, directing the action by messenger, Caesar would be found at the weakest point. He was no Napoleon, masterminding from a distant knoll but 'in there with the troops'. This was his great secret, and part of his magic.

The day might still have gone badly for the Romans, but the return of Labienus with the indomitable Tenth Legion from the far side of the Sambre, where he had been ransacking the enemy camp, coupled with the arrival of two reserve legions who had hastened up on hearing news of the battle, changed everything. The Tenth Legion stormed back across the river and took the Nervii in the rear, while Caesar's nephew, in command of the two reserve legions, seeing his uncle and the Twelfth Legion surrounded and almost cut off on the right flank, divided his troops and attacked the Nervii on both sides. The Belgae proved every bit as brave as reputation had it and fought to the bitter end. 'As the bodies of their men piled up, so they stood on the mound that they made and shot arrows at our soldiers and hurled back javelins which had missed their mark.' But it was the end for this warrior tribe and, although it is almost impossible to accept Caesar's account of the numbers that fell – for many must have escaped across the river – the fact remains that their chiefs and elders now sought peace. Caesar readily granted it, 'leaving it to them to enjoy their land and their towns and ordering their neighbours to respect their persons'. This was most important in this kind of warfare, for a tribe which had been thoroughly defeated by the Romans was often, in its weakened state, immediately attacked by its neighbours. In other words, Caesar more or less took them under the protection of the Roman state.

Their allies, the Atuatuci, who had arrived late for the battle and then, seeing how things were going, had immediately returned to their own lands, were the next to feel the onslaught of the conqueror. Huge men, like so many of these northerners, it is clear that they despised the shorter, smaller Romans, but science as applied to warfare was to defeat them. When they withdrew inside their principal stronghold (probably the citadel of Namur) they were terrified by the spectacle of the Romans building a gigantic tower which far out-topped their own defences. After an apparent surrender, during which they threw down many of their arms from the battlements, they attempted a treacherous attack on the Romans by night – an attack that had been foreseen – and paid the penalty for their action. At daybreak the legions burst into the city and, to punish the breach of faith, the whole population was put up for sale, along with their property. According to the account, 53,000 people were sold by auction. This was the kind of profit, the evidence of which would soon be paraded in the slave markets of Rome, that could not be ignored even by Caesar's enemies.

While this siege had been in progress Caesar had sent off one of the legions under the young son of Crassus, who had already distinguished himself, to deal with the tribes who inhabited the areas now known as Normandy and Britanny. Although these hardy seafaring people might have been expected to put up a fierce resistance, so great had been the impact of Caesar's successes that Crassus moved with triumphal ease through tribe after tribe who came out to offer their submission. The hegemony of Rome and this conquering Caesar (already equated with a god) was recognized everywhere.

The campaigning year was ending, but before he left for his other responsibility, Illyricum in the east, Caesar laid down the framework by which he hoped to hold all Gaul within the domain of the Roman republic. For each of the two main divisions of the people, the Celtic and the Belgic, was appointed one master-tribe: The Aedui for the Celts and the Remi for the Belgians. Their kings were directly responsible to Caesar, administration (on the surface at least) was left in their own hands, but all major decisions were to be taken at an annual assembly to be held under the presidency of Caesar. Those who were hostile to Rome, secretly hostile and biding their time, or waiting to see which way the dice finally fell, were thus eliminated from any positions of power. It seemed to Caesar as he left that, after two years, all Gaul was conquered and pacified. This time there could be no doubt in Rome about the astonishing successes that had been achieved in this remote part of the earth. The elaborate Celtic goldwork, the massive golden torques and gem-studded shoulder-clasps, the unfamiliar weapons, the swords and daggers with their decorated hilts (for it seemed that these 'barbaric' people could not leave any metal surface unadorned), the jewellery incorporating amber, garnets and enamels – all these made a profound impression. But no less did the steady stream of slaves, the motive power of the ancient world, daily remind the Romans of victorious Caesar. The names of unfamiliar towns and tribes, rivers and immense tracts of land hitherto unknown which featured in the carefully promulgated reports of Caesar's campaigns opened up the vista of a new world to the Roman citizen. Not until, centuries later, Europe discovered America and the Far East would there ever be such a sense of novelty, and of expansion into a realm which seemed to have no limit.

Whatever their private feelings, the senate could not resist the public mood, and Pompey, who may well have felt some jealousy over Caesar's triumphant success, was the first to propose a public thanksgiving in the conqueror's honour. To mark the unprecedented nature of Caesar's achievements, this was to last for fifteen days – five more than had been allotted to Pompey for his triumphs in the East. Moreover, no less a man than Cicero, who had been brought back from exile at Pompey's instigation, was the seconder of this proposal to do such great honour to Caius Julius Caesar. History can record few greater ironies.

CHAPTER SIXTEEN

Politics and a Revolt

When he returned to Italy Caesar had every reason for feeling that his conquests were permanent and that his arrangements for the administration of the newly conquered territories were more than adequate. Quartered among the Gauls and Belgians were the conquering legions, permanent evidence of the controlling hand of Rome: Labienus with one legion in the area of Angers, two other legions to the east near Tours and Chartres, another to guard the Great St Bernard pass, and four in the territory of the Belgae. All seemed secure. But winter, which immobilizes, also gives men time to dream, and in the cold north seated around their fires, to remember old days and deeds and plan a new future.

Even if he could not personally visit political Italy (something which was forbidden proconsuls during their term) Caesar was able to keep in constant touch from his own province of Cisalpine Gaul and to know what was happening in the city almost from day to day, and he found plenty to interest him. Clodius, whose tribunate was over in December 58, was still terrorizing the city with his gangs of thugs, dashing Caesar's hopes that he had found another Catiline, but one subservient to his will. Moreover, the fact that Clodius had displayed such open hostility towards Pompey did not make for any confidence between the two triumvirs, while the third, Crassus, was now almost as envious of Caesar's military triumphs as he had formerly been of Pompey's. The three horses of the triumvirate were all straining in different directions, and there were many who were delighted to note that the alliance between the three most powerful men in Rome seemed to be disintegrating.

Cicero, who firmly believed that he had saved the state during the Catiline affair, still dreamed of the restoration of the old *Optimate* republic, with himself as its leader and mentor. With Caesar's reluctant consent, and Pompey's hope that Cicero would apply himself to restoring order in the city, he had come back happily convinced that old triumphs would repeat themselves. Caesar, distanced from Rome by his station in northern Italy, and infinitely wiser politically than either of his colleagues, saw that it was essential – for the moment at least – that the triumvirate should forget any differences and cement their alliance against all the other forces in Rome. While Cicero continued in one bitter speech after another to offend as many as he pleased, and Clodius had become a liability rather than an asset, the strength of the triumvirate must be re-established. If it was not clear to Pompey and Crassus, it certainly was to Caesar, that their shared power must be exerted for their mutual benefit. The differences between Pompey and Crassus, which Caesar had managed to heal before, once again needed attention and the pride of Crassus soothed by providing him with the opportunity to achieve some equal measure of success in the field. Crassus might be one of the richest men in the world, but he still hankered for the medals and laurel crowns and cheering crowds that only a triumph could provide.

The all-important meeting took place at Luca (Lucca) in Cisalpine Gaul, and it was here that the three men decided on the main policies for Rome during the next few years. Crassus and Pompey were to become consuls in 55, their elections being postponed until the winter so that men on leave from Caesar's legions could be available to lend support. Once consuls, they were to secure for themselves commands commensurate with that which Caesar now held. (Caesar was well aware that even Pompey was chafing at his current eclipse.) Crassus was to take command in the East and confront the great Parthian empire beyond the Euphrates, the only power in the lands known to Rome that still challenged the might of the legions and the city, while Pompey was to have the rich provinces of Spain, which he might administer through delegates, thus leaving him free to attend to the affairs of Rome. Both men would secure an *imperium* similar to his own, brooking no interference for five years after the date of their consulships. Meanwhile, to avoid the risk of Caesar's being left as a private citizen, exposed to danger from his enemies, Crassus and Pompey as consuls would secure a further extension of Caesar's *imperium* over the two Gauls. So, in the quiet town of Luca, the rich cake of the Roman world was divided up in, as Plutarch puts it, 'a conspiracy to share the sovereignty and destroy the constitution'. Over that winter Luca knew the comings and goings of many of the most powerful men in Rome, who, although they are unlikely to have known the precise arrangements between the triumvirs, knew enough to smell out the sources of power. Of those who might have protested at the republic's fate being decided not in Rome but in Caesar's own province, Cato was far away in Cyprus, while Cicero was muzzled because his brother Quintus, who had been working for Pompey, now transferred to the service of

Caesar. His main trouble was that he was not a man of action, but of letters and rhetoric, so that for the rest of his life – while dwelling constantly on what had and what might have been – he was compelled to trim his sails to whatever strong political wind was blowing. At the moment it was clear that it blew from Caesar, and Cicero found himself defending, and even praising, the conduct of the proconsul in the far regions of Gaul.

Caesar had hoped to spare some time for Illyricum, a part of his command which had gone untouched by his ambition, but the news from Gaul soon had him hastening back to Brittany in the west. The annexation of large areas previously unaffected by the Roman sphere of influence had had unfortunate effects upon such hitherto free and independent peoples as the maritime Veneti. The advent of Roman traders, whose arrival in any newly conquered territory was always akin to the descent of vultures, threatened the whole of their economy with ruin. Their trade with their kinsfolk in Britain was endangered, and Roman officers entering their territory to requisition corn were seized as hostages. The Britons, equally anxious to secure their trading routes, offered them help, and even the inhabitants of Marseilles, for so long the most faithful allies of Rome, seeing the threat to their own trade with Britain, promised assistance to the Veneti. The importation of tin from Britain was one of the mainstays of the Marseilles trade, and the likelihood that Caesar would soon mount an expedition to the island threatened them with the loss of one of their main sources of income, since it was obvious that Roman merchants would secure this all-important metal for their own interests.

As soon as he heard of the rebellion, Caesar – even before leaving Italy – ordered the construction of a great Roman fleet on the Loire and the recruitment of crews for it in the Narbonese province. He had realized that, without control of the Channel, he would have no chance of invading the northern island, which he had every intention of doing. He himself arrived in the region of Angers early in May and saw at once that he was confronted not with a local revolt, but with one that was spreading from one area to another. The great province, which he had thought was tamed for permanent occupation, showed every sign of fragmenting into its old tribal structures, every one of them hostile to Rome. It was clear that so great an example must be made of these 'rebels' (although the term could hardly be applied to people who had done no more than willingly welcome the Romans into their territory) that the spark of insurrection would be quenched at source.

An indication of the dangers that Caesar foresaw in the changed situation in Gaul was that, contrary to the usual Roman practice of keeping the entire army concentrated in one place around the general, he now divided the legions into five groups, his intention being to hold down all the tribes from Brittany eastward to the Rhine and southward to the Pyrenees. He himself took command of the troops destined to reduce the Veneti to submission, the core being his trusted Tenth Legion. To lead the seaborne attack on the Veneti coast he picked a young commander, not yet a senator, Decimus Brutus. His brilliance, subsequently proved, was to confirm Caesar's judgement, and he would ultimately play an important part in Caesar's life.

Throughout the summer the troops under Caesar worked hard and fought desperately, but all to no avail against an enemy who always retreated to fortified places at the sea's edge, and who was always reinforced from the sea before he could be starved into submission. The Roman fleet took a long time to prepare and assemble, and Caesar, who at first had envisaged a simultaneous attack on the Veneti from both land and sea, was compelled to fight only from the land – and without success. The summer drew on and it was already August when at last the long-expected fleet arrived. Caesar was apprehensive, for he realized he was dealing with a race of seamen quite alien to any Roman conception derived from the Mediterranean.

The boats of the Veneti were built for the Atlantic and the Channel, heavily-timbered, the oak iron-fastened; even their cables were of iron chain (something unknown before), and their sails were of leather, designed to withstand storms such as the southern seamen hardly knew. Quite apart from that, the Veneti were completely familiar with their own rockbound coasts and with the high and relentless tides – a phenomenon again unfamiliar to the Romans. Their high stems and sterns, built to withstand the roaring seas, overtopped the turrets erected aboard the Roman ships, while the projectiles hurled from them could clear the Roman decks. The latter, indeed, had only one advantage over their enemy and that was the speed which their lean lines and their trained oarsmen gave them. Once again the ingenuity and superior thinking of the Romans, which in an earlier century had defeated the Carthaginian marines, gave them the mastery. They had studied the ships of the Veneti and observed that they were totally dependent upon their sails. Once without them they would be floundering in the ocean swell, while the superiority of the Roman soldiers would soon show itself in a land battle fought afloat.

They had therefore prepared sickles fastened to the end of long poles, somewhat like the grappling hooks used in sieges, and when the day came for the major action they knew what they had to do. The culminating sea battle took place in Quiberon Bay, with Caesar and the army gathered as spectators on the shore. As the galleys closed with the great ships of the Veneti, they grasped the halyards of their leather sails, and then the men at the oars pulled hard away. As the strain came on the halyards and the sickles began to cut, yards and sails came thundering down and ship after ship was disabled. To add to the distress of the Veneti a calm descended, and those who had not yet lost their sails also swayed immobilized upon the heaving sea. The Romans ran alongside with the agility of dogs attacking a bear and the soldiers swept aboard to overpower men more used to the tactics of the sea than the land. The whole engagement lasted throughout the day, from ten in the morning until sunset, and at the end of it all the proud fleet of the Veneti was either taken or sunk.

Deprived of their ships, with many of their best men killed, the Veneti surrendered. Caesar, who was usually disposed to clemency towards a brave enemy, was determined on this occasion to make an object lesson. They had laid hands upon Roman officers and citizens (the phrasing suggests peaceful ambassadors rather than avaricious merchants, requisitioning officers, and civilians calculating tax), and this 'treachery' must be denounced and paid for. Accordingly all the Gallic leaders were executed, and the rest of the tribe was sold into slavery. Like the Nervii, who were spared, they had been brave but, like the Atuatuci, the Veneti were considered to have broken a trust.

The year which had opened so threateningly ended peacefully enough. Labienus had kept everything quiet among the Belgae, young Crassus had gained a great victory in Aquitania, and the rebels in Normandy had been defeated by another of Caesar's handpicked subordinates. Caesar himself had projected a further minor campaign against two tribes living in Flanders, who had as yet refused to submit to the Romans. These tribes, however, refused to give battle in the usual fashion but, living as they did in an area thick with forests and marshland, merely withdrew before the advancing legionaries and allowed the weather of their native land and coast to work for them. Soon even Caesar had to confess himself beaten by the torrential rain and by the earth which turned into so soft a mud that not even tents would stay erect. He had been anxious to secure a base for an expedition to Britain the following year and to investigate the coastline opposite the island, but was finally forced to call a halt and withdrew. Having once again quartered his legions in the conquered lands, he made his way back to Italy.

In the electoral struggle for the new consulships Crassus and Pompey would almost certainly have failed if it had not been for Caesar. Despite all the bribery and corruption that had been used, it was neither Pompey's reputation nor Crassus' money which gained them their places but a thousand or more legionaries. Released in batches under the command of young Crassus (eager to see his father elected because of the benefits it might confer on himself), their entry into Rome produced the desired result. Pompey and Crassus, once elected, saw that the bill was pushed through which would in due course secure the province each had asked for at the Luca meeting, and shortly afterwards they fulfilled their obligation to Caesar, prolonging his powers for a further four years. None of this took place without great opposition, but the climate of violence triumphed. Four were killed and many wounded in affrays, Crassus himself even stabbing a senator.

Caesar turned back to the west earlier than usual in the year 55. He had news of a further migration of Germanic tribes across the Rhine. Immense numbers of Germans from two major tribes, the Usipetes and Tencteri, themselves squeezed out of their land by the Suebi whom Caesar had crushed, were now moving towards the lower Moselle at the invitation of Celts and Belgians planning to use them to free themselves from Roman domination. Caesar, having summoned up his Celtic cavalry, moved in the direction of Coblenz where the bulk of the invading Germans were encamped. Here events took much the same course as they had with the Suebi, the chiefs coming forward to say that they had no wish to make war against the Roman people: they just wanted somewhere to live, and asked Caesar to grant them an area where they could settle in peace. Caesar reiterated that there was no place for them anywhere in Gaul but that, if they went back across the Rhine, they could find living room among a tribe there who had already asked him for protection from the Seubi. He aimed, in fact, to make use of these migrant German tribes as a kind of buffer-state, hoping that they and the remaining Suebi would fight it out and leave Gaul alone. Unfortunately a cavalry clash ensued in which his Gallic horse were ignominiously routed. The Germans, again making it clear that they had no wish to engage the Romans in war, sent a deputation of all their chiefs and leading men to apologize for the incident and to ask for a further armistice. Caesar ordered their immediate arrest and then, having deprived the body of its head, pressed on with the legions in the direction of the German camp.

In the absence of their leaders, and taken totally by surprise, the Germans turned in confusion and flight when the disciplined legions and the Gallic cavalry – anxious to wipe out the stain on their reputation from their previous defeat – fell upon them without warning. Like the Helvetii before them the Usipetes and Tencteri were whole tribes migrating, impeded by civilians, noncombatants and baggage-carts. As Michael Grant rightly says, Caesar's account of what ensued is 'one of the most chilling passages in ancient literature':

> When they reached the confluence of the Moselle and the Rhine, they realized that they could flee no farther. A large number was killed, and the rest plunged into the water and perished, overcome by the force of the current in their terror-stricken and exhausted state. The Romans returned to camp without a single casualty, and with

only a few wounded, although a grim struggle had been anticipated against an enemy four hundred and thirty thousand strong.

This massacre, for which no excuses can be adduced since the leaders of the tribes had been taken prisoner when on a mission of peace, was quickly promoted by Caesar's propagandists in Rome as a magnificent victory. 'Four hundred and thirty thousand barbarians killed in a single battle!' was a headline that none could ignore. There was nothing comparable in history! Caesar was surpassing Alexander . . .

CHAPTER SEVENTEEN

From Germany to Britain

When the news of Caesar's successes against the feared and hated Germans reached Rome, there was of course an immediate outcry for a further public thanksgiving to be held in his honour. The enthusiasm of the masses for such festivities could be taken for granted, since they implied a holiday, feasting and entertainment – at whose expense was no concern of theirs. This demand naturally had to be brought before the senate, which in its demoralized state would probably have acceded. Cicero was now trimming his sails to the Caesarian wind, and there would have been no spokesmen of consequence to raise any objection, had Cato not been present.

Cato's indignation would have done credit to many a modern sensibility, and it seems strange to find it in the Rome that bred Caesar, Clodius and Crassus. He maintained that instead of honouring this criminal leader for his breach of faith they should hand him over to the Germans for punishment, in that way the sins of their general might not be visited upon his soldiers and his city. (Cato clearly had received reports from the front of what had really happened in the Usipetes and Tencteri affair.) In his anger he did, however, forget that there was another side to the argument: the Germans were a very real and constant threat to the Gaul which Caesar was establishing. They had indeed previously threatened Rome itself, and there was a case to be made for the surgical treatment of this infection at source. But Cato's eloquence, and a certain uneasiness among the senators themselves, meant that the proposal to accord Caesar further honours was not followed up. (After all, even to a Roman of the 1st century BC the extermination of nearly half a million people – if Caesar's own figures were to be credited – was hardly commonplace.) As soon as he heard of Cato's speech Caesar replied by letter with an attempted character-assassination of his old enemy, but the fact was that he could not, either at this time in his life or years later when he tried again, find any justification for traducing Cato. The latter's honesty and stern morality was as evident to his contemporaries as that of his great-grandfather Cato the Censor, who had long served as a model of all the best republican virtues, had been. Nothing more was heard of fresh honours for Caesar, and he was already too occupied with a new development in his German campaign to pursue the issue any further.

According to Dio Cassius, Caesar 'wanted an excuse for crossing the river Rhine for he was ambitious to do something that no other Roman general had done before him.' There can be little doubt that this was true, but the matter was not quite so simple. Caesar – as usual, one might be justified in saying – could manage to combine a private ambition with a practical policy of benefit to Rome. Being daily in contact with the moving mass of peoples in this vast extent of 'new Europe', he knew – as Cato did not – that the Germans presented a very real threat not only to the extended Romanized Gaul that he was creating, but ultimately to Rome itself. They were savage and fierce warriors, whereas the Gauls of the Narbonese province and even the others whom he had recently conquered were already softening under the impact of civilization. The Cisalpine Gauls, who had once terrorized Rome but who had now become agriculturalists and lived quietly in northern Italy, were hardly a match for their ancestors – and it was a nightmare to imagine what might happen if the Germans in their tens of thousands, hardy, prolific, and inured to warfare, were to descend on the soft citizens of the capital. Now that the blood-stained tide was so clearly running in his favour, Caesar intended to protect the new provinces of Gaul and Belgium, the old Narbonne Province, and ultimately Italy itself, with a *cordon sanitaire* that would isolate them from turbulent Germany. Gradually, no doubt, this could be extended, for the horizon of potential conquest seemed limitless.

He was soon provided with an excellent excuse. A detachment of German cavalry who had been away from the main body of the two tribes at the time of the massacre, returned, heard what had happened, and at once made their way across the Rhine to seek shelter with the Sugambri, another tribe on the right bank of the Rhine. They were only a fragment of the defeated enemy, but Caesar immediately sent orders for them to be handed over as 'men who had borne arms against him and against Gaul'. The Sugambri proudly, and rightly, replied that the sovereignty of the Roman people did not extend beyond the Rhine, and if he complained that the Germans had no right to come into Gaul, what right had he to come into Germany? Ignoring the logic of this, Caesar now had his pretext for the crossing. He intended to make a demonstration, no more, unless any Germans were so foolish as to attack his troops. He wished to show them that the power of Rome could easily be extended into Germany if need be, and he also wished to demonstrate by the Romans' superior skills, that the Germans were technically and in all other respects inferior. Although the river could have been crossed comparatively easily by boats, he elected to have a bridge built, across which the legions would march in parade-ground style. For them there was to be no floundering in the shallows, no awkward embarkation and disembarkation. Something that the Germans had never seen before was to be achieved by the Roman engineering skill – a bridge across the turbulent, wide and deep river that symbolized their untamed country. All the available workforce on the left bank were pressed into service, cutting down trees and shaping timbers at the direction of the engineers, while the legionaries – as adept with mattock and agricultural tools as with their arms – now showed they were also bridge-builders. Within no more than ten days a bridge on the trestle-system had been erected, fifteen hundred feet long and forty feet wide. Across it marched the legions with the eagles, and at their head a balding man in elaborate armour on a white charger – symbols of a power that stretched from the Atlantic to Africa, from Gaul to the Caucasus and Asia Minor.

The proconsul and the legions were only eighteen days on the far bank of the Rhine: long enough to reassure the Ubii, who were friendly to the Romans but who must often have feared what that friendship might lead to among their neighbours. The other tribes fled back into their dark, mysterious woods. They had seen what these people, who had conquered the Gauls and Belgians, could do even to their sacred father-river. But the Germans in their tens of thousands were soon gathering, and Caesar had no intention of hazarding his legions in unknown country against impossible odds. 'He returned to Gaul and cut the bridge behind him.' He had, at least, been where no Roman general had ever been before.

Nothing was known of Britain except the white cliffs that could be seen from the Calais area, while Roman and other merchants who had been there had never ventured into the interior. The island was reputed to be rich in cattle and corn, iron, gold, silver and tin, but little was known of its people except that they harboured many refugees from Gaul, and that some of them had even fought with the Veneti against the Romans the previous year. Caesar, if we are to believe the story, was also interested in this remote and strange place because of the high quality of its freshwater pearls, and his passion for pearls was well known. (Certainly there was no legend in this, and the freshwater pearls from the pearl-bearing mussel, although far less common than centuries ago, are still found in some of the country's rivers.) There were further good reasons for investigating this island at the world's rim: the availability of the fleet that had defeated the Veneti, and the fact that the trade of the Veneti was now passing into Roman hands. For this to succeed, warehouses would need to be established on the south-east coast of Britain and these in their turn would require protective strongpoints that could be garrisoned – with the ultimate view of extending roads into the country and preparing it for conquest. There was perhaps yet another good reason for this expedition to Britain. Caesar had crossed the Rhine, where no Roman general had been before, but the Rhine was only a river while the Channel was an unknown sea. Nevertheless the Romans were finding out, as have all similar conquering races subsequently, that an ever-expanding conquest poses more problems than it solves – and this was to be emphasized in Britain.

Leaving the harbour of Boulogne, the Seventh and Tenth legions, embarked in eighty ships, set off in the wake of Caesar and his staff officers. The ground had already been prepared by diplomatic negotiations with a number of British tribes. One foretaste of the difficulties inherent in a sea-crossing, however relatively small, was that the cavalry had not been ready as scheduled, so that the legionaries would be without their support in a land known to be furnished with many horsemen and charioteers. There was to be no friendly reception either, for, on reaching the coast off Dover, massed crowds were seen on the heights and their appearance was anything but welcoming.

Dover was clearly no place to land, under the threat of javelins and rocks, so the fleet moved a few miles westwards to reach a wide beach, very probably near Deal. Once again the Britons, having followed them along the coast, were waiting, and Caesar realized that his legions would have to land and charge up a sloping beach in the face of the enemy. It was not an attractive proposition and it was made more awkward because the transports, on account of their draught, were unable to get right into the shallows. The legionaries, heavily-burdened with their arms and armour, would have to jump into an indeterminate depth – and this was no pellucid Mediterranean but moving, silt-ridden, tidal waters unfamiliar to Romans. A standard bearer of the Tenth is said to have been the first to jump into the water, and the legionaries, with their usual disciplined resolution and determination not to let one division put another to shame, followed him. The Britons, although they had the commanding position and should by rights have driven the invaders back into the sea, were totally unfamiliar with troops – let alone disciplined ones like these – landing on their native shore. The legionaries, on the other hand, no doubt relieved at being back on dry land and conscious of that superiority which they had found in themselves everywhere else, followed their centurions and drove the natives back. If they had had their cavalry, now would have been the time to rout the defenders and chase them back into the woods beyond the foreshore.

The next day the Britons returned to sue for peace, bringing with them Caesar's envoy, whom they had bound as a traitor but now apologetically released. They appeared to be cowed, but this was probably no more than a gesture designed to keep the Romans inactive while they called up other tribes from inland. Some of the delegates even offered themselves as hostages, and many more were promised. The legionaries, in any case, immediately began building a camp, probably on the cliffs at Walmer, and establishing themselves in the immediate area. Caesar waited for the arrival of the cavalry, without whom any advance into this unknown land would be impossible. Then, 'on the fourth day after his arrival in Britain' as the *Commentaries* record, 'the eagerly expected convoy arrived in the vicinity'. While it was closing the shore a gale from the west sprang up and the transports were forced to run off before it. Many of them were driven back towards the Continent, while others tried to anchor but had to give up the attempt and stand out to sea. That night, 'it happened to be full moon, a time at which the Atlantic tides are more than usually high – something unknown to the Romans'.

Not only had the long-awaited transports disappeared into the night and the storm, but their own ships, which were beached or riding at anchor (thoughtlessly as if in the Mediterranean) were cast up by the tide. Some of the vessels, with insufficient lengths of cable out, were either constrained by the tide until they began to dip their bows and fill, or broke from their cables and headed out to sea. 'This state of affairs,' writes Caesar with some understatement, 'moved the whole army very deeply.' They had no cavalry, they had come with only limited provisions, baggage and shelter, and it now seemed as if they were marooned on a hostile shore. The natives who had watched the events began discreetly to disappear; no promised hostages arrived, and it soon became clear that the earlier protestations of friendship might be forgotten.

In the days that followed, the Tenth legion, turning to boatbuilding from work on the camp, began to resurrect the ships that were left, while the Seventh scattered over the nearby countryside in search of grain and other food. It was not surprising that the natives took advantage of these men foraging more or less independently through the land to launch a surprise attack upon them – an attack that would have succeeded if Caesar had not realized by dust-clouds rising over the fields what was happening and gone to their rescue. In their usual fashion, the Britons on encountering organized opposition took to their heels and faded away into their omnipresent forests. While the boats were being completed, some that were seaworthy being sent to Boulogne for further materials, more attacks were made on the embattled beachhead and camp.

It became clear enough to Caesar that this island, whose size and geography remained unknown, would not yield except to a carefully-planned invasion with all the logistical preparations that this entailed. At the first sign of fair weather, he, his staff, and the legions set off across the Channel, leaving the Britons with the comfort of seeing them go, but also with the uneasy awareness that their isolation at the end of the world was drawing to a close.

Caesar's interest in this potential new conquest, coupled with his concern about affairs in Gaul, led him for the first time since he had become proconsul to forego his annual visit to northern Italy during the winter of 55–4. There had been trouble among some of the Gauls in his absence, the Morini in their marshy districts refusing to accept the dominance of Rome, while there were signs elsewhere that at the slightest slackening of the rein things could get out of hand. In Britain the expeditionary force had suffered some casualties, but he had been lucky to get away without more, or without being forced to attempt to winter in that inhospitable land. Furthermore, the promised hostages had failed to appear before his departure. Preparations for the invasion of Britain were carried on over the winter and every port from Spain to Belgic Gaul was put to work on the assembly of an invasion fleet, while conquered towns on navigable rivers were also given their quota to fulfil.

It was a difficult year to justify in despatches, and the senate, quite apart from Cato, was becoming concerned about the way in which Caesar seemed to be constantly involving the state in new wars – entirely on his own account and without reference to Rome. First Gaul, then Belgium, then Germany, and now this island, Britain, somewhere at the end of the earth. The old *Optimates* must have snarled disapprovingly. Cato took the moral stance of the Stoic that he was, and indicted Caesar for treachery and unwarranted massacre. Then there were those who sneered; even Pompey was later to maintain that the Channel was no more than a mudflat.

That was on one side, but on the other the populace was excited by these reports of new countries and peoples, rivers, mountains and forests, and – now – of a great unconquered island in the Ocean. Petitions pursued Caesar from men with suitable – and unsuitable – recommendations, all looking for a job and hoping for plunder in these newfound lands. Even Cicero, who was now inclined in his favour by the way in which Caesar included him in his correspondence, was moved to seek posts for people whom he knew. Caesar's voluminous correspondence with his friends and agents in Rome was balanced by their reports to him on every aspect of life in the capital. From the writings of poets such as Catullus who traduced him (but whom he later forgave because he recognized his talent), and from men like Oppius and his friend Balbus, who more or less ran a news-service for him, he knew the climate of the distant city. Above all, unlike the *Optimates*, he knew the feelings of the people, and he knew that to them these foreign conquests and discoveries were exciting, a promise of an ever-expanding Rome with more and more wealth for distribution.

The report that was sent off to Rome detailing that year's campaigns has long been lost, but it is probable that the gist of it can be discerned in Caesar's *Commentaries*. Caesar was adept at propaganda and he knew that almost anything can be so arranged to create a favourable impression. The massacre of a German tribe, following the arrest of their ambassadors and leaders? It was in return for a treacherous attack on his own troops, and it had led to a glorious victory which had saved Gaul from invaders. The crossing of the Rhine? An important advance into hitherto unknown territory and a valuable display of strength – 'Showing the Eagles'. The crossing to Britain and the landing on this remote island? It was but an earnest of things to come. Another conquest lay ahead.

CHAPTER EIGHTEEN

Invasion

The second expedition to Britain was a well-prepared invasion, backed by all the weight and resources of the Roman Empire. Caesar was well aware that he had started too late the previous year and that the island was clearly a very large one. He knew too that the natives showed every sign of being as belligerent as the worst of the Belgae or Gauls. Then, just as everything was being readied for an invasion to take place in late spring or early summer 54, his whole timetable was disrupted.

Having seen that all the preparations were in hand, he had travelled to Cisalpine Gaul, hoping to make his legal circuit quickly, deal with anything outstanding in the quiet province, and then return to the scene of operations. He was frustrated in this by an urgent report from his neglected province of Illyricum that wild tribesmen from the hinterland were laying waste the borders. At the garrison-fortress of Aquileia he immediately summoned out the militia (paid for by the local communities) to deal with the invaders. This in itself was enough to bring them to heel, and they meekly handed over hostages and accepted an arbitrator appointed to assess what damage they had done and ensure that reparations were paid. It was all over neatly and quickly – a typical example of the work that had to be constantly carried out around the frontiers of the empire – and Caesar returned to Gaul.

The construction programme was almost complete, some eight hundred ships in all. Although there were a few armed galleys, they were mainly transports, and two hundred of them had been built by private enterprise. The merchants concerned were willing to invest in ships and lend them to the fleet in return for profits (human and otherwise) at the end of the campaign. While all these preparations were being made and the fleet was beginning to assemble at Boulogne the powerful tribe of the Treveri (whose base was probably near Trèves) openly repudiated its ties with Rome. In the two previous years, 55 and 56, it had taken no part in the Gallic assemblies called by Caesar, and news now reached him from his agents that its chieftain

Indutiomarus was only waiting for the Romans to cross the Channel to call on his neighbours to revolt. As was often the case in tribal communities there was rivalry for leadership among the Treveri, the anti-Roman faction being led by Indutiomarus, while his son-in-law Cingetorix, looking towards an inevitable future, was the head of the Romanophiles and planned to supplant his father-in-law. (The news of the planned revolt may well have come from him.)

Clearly Gaul could not be left under so dangerous a threat, and Caesar summoned four legions to deal with the situation. The Treveri were among the finest horsemen in Gaul (had indeed fought in company with the legions during the Belgic campaign) and if, as it appeared, they were in communication with their German neighbours the only solution was sharp action. But the younger party who followed the chieftain's son-in-law came over to Caesar *en masse* and Indutiomarus found himself increasingly isolated. He realized in time that against the legions and so many of his own tribe he had no chance of succeeding, so he sent envoys to the proconsul and finally – having received a list of two hundred hostages whom he was to hand over – was allowed to give formal assurances of unquestionable loyalty.

Indutiomarus was left as official chief of the Treveri, but his son-in-law was promoted to the position of 'friend of Caesar' – which meant that the chieftain knew that every move he made while the latter was away would be watched and reported. It was a neat solution from Caesar's point of view for, by maintaining Indutiomarus as the formal head, he had satisfied the old 'conservatives' of the tribe, while at the same time he had given them warning that they were under observation by the younger man who opposed them. Caesar's troubles, however, were not over, for next he had to deal with problems among the Aedui, upon whose pro-Roman stance he had based much of his policy. Here the nationalist leader Dumnorix, who clearly had the idea of taking over the kingdom during Caesar's absence, refused to supply the cavalry that had been agreed upon for the invasion and made to ride off home taking them with him. Caesar's reply was to send all the Roman cavalry after him and cut him down. As so often happened with the Gauls, once his men were deprived of their leader they accepted Caesar's command and dutifully joined the embarking forces. These two episodes alone, however, should have been enough to tell Caesar that the newly-conquered territories were a simmering cauldron. It only required the right man at the right time to rise up and shout 'Liberty!' and everything would boil over.

A combination of these political difficulties, together with unsuitable weather, meant that the second expedition to Britain, well-planned though it had been, started several weeks earlier than the previous one but still nearly a month later than it should. There would be too little time to achieve any major conquest or advance before the onset of autumn would badly upset both ships and plans. Pompey might joke about mudflats, but Caesar was finding out that the sea to the north of France was more formidable than any fast-running river or battlement built by men.

After being subjected to the vagaries of the tides (alarming enough for the Mediterranean men) the fleet, which for a time had run out into the North Sea clear of the land with a south-westerly behind it, finally fetched up somewhere near Sandwich. The landing was unopposed; no natives at all were to be seen and Caesar comments, rather naïvely perhaps, that they had been frightened by so many ships and had gone inland to hide. It was true that 800 ships – of whatever size – was something that the Channel would not see again in a combined fleet for some 2,000 years But all that had happened was that the threatened British in the south-east of the island had sensibly withdrawn, while making up their minds whether to place themselves under the command of a supreme chief. This was Cassivellaunus, whose kingdom was in the area of St Albans in Hertfordshire. Also, well aware from the reports circulating about the arms, equipment, and fighting abilities of the Romans that they were no match for them in an open battle, the Britons hoped to lure the Romans into unfamiliar territory, much of it still untamed forest land.

Caesar was eager to make contact with the enemy, for he knew that he dare not hazard his troops in the interior. Only an open engagement in which the weight of the legions could make itself felt (he had five with him) would sufficiently overawe the Britons to compel mass surrender and the default of one tribe from another. (He knew that all barbarians – Gauls, Belgians, Germans and now Britons – were consumed by inter-tribal warfare and that, given one hard blow, their uneasy alliances crumbled in a flash.) Unfortunately for him, his eagerness to get the troops ashore and into action as quickly as possible, coupled with his ignorance of this northern sea, led him into an error that almost proved fatal. He left the invasion fleet well-guarded by some cavalry and one legion, but he left it at anchor. The weather seemed fair, there were men to watch over the ships, and they looked secure enough off a sandy shore. Then, as had happened before, the unpredictable wind and weather of this northern climate took its toll. When Caesar had marched inland with the legions as far as the Great Stour and was in rapid pursuit of the enemy, who had fallen back before him, the news came up from the coast – there had been a violent gale which had totally destroyed a number of the ships and severely damaged almost all the others.

This would have daunted many a man and would have broken the spirit of some, but Caesar – while he had to abandon his lightning offensive – turned back to the first task in hand. He had taken a great interest in the construction of this invasion fleet, and it was to some extent due to his own negligence (for a commander is ultimately responsible for everything) that for the second time the Romans had been unprepared for the vagaries and violent shifts of wind and weather in this sea. Why had the boats not been beached (they were later)? And why had the cables which had proved too light in the blow of the year before not been doubled up or more?

He acted with his usual practical efficiency and had every man with boatbuilding or carpentry experience drafted from the legions to work on the ships. Other vessels which were still capable of getting to sea were sent back to Gaul to bring over more experienced workmen, as well as to order the construction of replacements. Labienus, who had been left in charge of Gaul during Caesar's absence, was ordered to put all his troops on to this new project. Meanwhile, only three days after landing in Britain, all military operations were suspended and the entire force was set to hauling the ships ashore and building a fortification to contain not only the remains of the fleet but also serve as a garrison for the army. Again, it is important to give his full due to the Roman legionary, the man who made the empire possible and who made the reputations of generals and the wealth of senators. From roadbuilder to boatbuilder, from bridges to battlements, from fortified camps to siege-engines, the legionary and his centurion *were* Rome. For ten days now they laboured to erect this camp-cum-boat-pound in an unknown land. On the eleventh day Caesar conducted a final inspection of the work; and then the legionaries, after polishing their arms and armour, fell in again to march to war.

During this respite the British tribes had temporarily sunk their differences and had nearly all elected to come under the leadership of Cassivellaunus. An exception were the Trinobantes in Essex, who had been conquered by Cassivellaunus and the young son of whose defeated king had already come over to Caesar. But the amalgamation of the other tribes under the coordinating intelligence of this British leader was to provide Caesar and his legionaries with a very tough opposition, as well as a style of warfare which the Romans had never encountered before.

Cassivellaunus was well aware that the Romans sought a straight-forward pitched battle and was determined to deny it to them. Battles of this type, proposed by the Romans and accepted by Gauls, Belgae and Germans, had invariably led to the latter's defeat. In any case, the Britons did not rely on infantrymen in warfare but on horsemen and chariots – the latter being something with which the Roman infantry-man was unfamiliar. Chariots had been used from Homeric days in Europe and in the East by most of the early civilizations, but they had been found unsuitable in later warfare and had survived only for races in the public games or for processions where (like the State Coaches in modern Britain) their function was decorative and symbolic of power. Those which the British now brought out in their hundreds against the Romans were purely functional, designed for war and nothing else.

Caesar says that at one moment about 4,000 charioteers were brought up against the legions, but this does not necessarily mean that number of chariots. There were enough in any case to cause grave disruption in the Roman lines, when Cassivellaunus launched his first attack just as the legionaries were digging in. The soldiers on guard at the perimeter were hurled aside by the weight and number of the galloping horses and chariots, while the fighting men aboard them leapt down and attacked the legionaries within. When Caesar sent reinforcements to back up the threatened positions the Britons immediately jumped back aboard the chariots and disappeared into their forests.

This was, as Caesar put it, 'a new kind of warfare'. Similarly the British cavalry did not operate like the Roman or the horsemen encountered in Europe – where the sheer weight of the charge was used to overwhelm the enemy – but fought in open order, with groups of reservists posted at various points to the rear who, when the advance horsemen tired or weakened, swept up to take their place. No more than the charioteers or the men on foot would they fight a standing battle, but would constantly withdraw, seeking to extend the Roman horsemen and draw them away from their compact groups. Seeing that his heavily armed legionaries were at a disadvantage in this warfare where mobility played so large a part, Caesar tried to entice the Britons to attack the fortifications behind which the legionaries took up their positions, and out of which raiding parties were sent to ransack the countryside for food and cattle. But Cassivellaunus steadily withdrew before him, retreating to his own land on the north side of the Thames, so that, still seeking an open battle or at least the siege and conquest of a town, Caesar followed him north to the river. At a place where the Thames was fordable, Cassivellaunus had driven stakes into the riverbed and banks in an attempt to deny the crossing to the enemy, while he and his army waited for them on the northern side.

Caesar, who had thought of so much in his preparations for this campaign had not neglected one master-card, something which he had kept in reserve, either for a pitched battle or for just such a case as this. He had brought across from Boulogne an Indian elephant (and we know that it was Indian because the large African bush elephants are untamable while the African forest elephants – which Hannibal had used in his famous campaign – were too small to support a large howdah such as is described). Elephants had been used in warfare in the East for many centuries but they were principally useful in war when organized in massed lines, especially upon the wings of an army, to break up the cavalry of the opposing forces (horses unfamiliar with them being afraid of their smell and size), and also to act like tanks upon the infantry. It is easy to see why in the deserts and flat plains of the East they had long been a formidable weapon and why they had been abandoned in Europe's less suitable terrain. The elephant had, however, one other use, which for a time had proved an advantage to the Carthaginians in Spain and, until they had discovered its weaknesses, even against the Romans in Europe. This was a purely psychological one: the sight of the immense and hitherto unknown animal lumbering towards a footsoldier was almost certain to induce panic. Caesar had rightly calculated that the barbarous Britons in their remote island would never have heard of an elephant, let alone seen one. He had brought it along for just such an occasion as now presented itself.

Polyaenus, a Macedonian writing in the second century AD, describes in his *Stratagems of War* how Caesar made use of this strange beast against the Britons at the crossing of the Thames:

> Caesar had with him a very large elephant, an animal which the Britons had never encountered before, and he had armoured it with iron scales. Upon its back he had put a large tower containing archers and slingers, and he had it sent ahead into the river. The Britons were terrified at the sight of this huge and unknown beast, from the tower on whose back came a volley of arrows and stones, and one and all – men, horses and chariots – they turned tail and fled. Through the terror inspired by this single animal, the Romans were able to cross the river in safety.

(We know no more about this Indian elephant, whether it died in Britain or whether it was transported safely back to Gaul.)

Caesar was nevertheless forced to admit that, unable to bring the enemy to battle, his troops were being increasingly demoralized by their guerrilla tactics. (The only success was the capture of a fortified town belonging to Cassivellaunus – somewhere in the area of modern St Albans.) As he advanced, his troops ravaging the country as they went, he was haunted by the approach of autumn and winter. He had seen what summer storms could do in the seas between the island and Gaul. The only alternative to returning with his purpose unachieved was to winter in Britain, unthinkable without a really adequate base and good supply of corn and other provisions. Besides, Gaul itself needed his almost constant supervision. But political dissension among the Trinobantes and a number of smaller tribes succeeded where the military option had failed and, as more and more Britons came over to him, support for Cassivellaunus steadily dwindled.

In some desperation the British leader sent a message to the four chieftains of Kent asking them to attack Caesar's base camp: a wise enough move which, if successful, would have left the Romans cut off in a hostile land with winter approaching. But the cohorts on guard at the base had further strengthened their defences, were alive to such a potential move, and when it came hurled back the attackers. Cassivellaunus through an intermediary now asked for terms and Caesar was happy to seize upon the occasion. Although he must have been deeply concerned at the position in which he found himself he nevertheless needed to impose conditions that would look good in Rome. Accordingly, it was arranged for hostages to be handed over, for an annual tribute to be paid, and a guarantee to the new king of the Trinobantes that he and his tribe would remain unmolested. They would, in theory, be under the protection of Rome and would fulfil the same position in Britain as the Aedui in Gaul and the Remi in Belgium.

The equinox was approaching and Caesar remembered the previous year's weather. Since there were not sufficient boats ready as yet for the whole army to sail together to France, he sent it back in two waves. Even this very nearly ended in disaster, for the convoy returning for the second load ran into a violent gale and many of the boats had to seek refuge in Gaul. Eventually the last of the troops were pulled out and made their way without incident to Boulogne. The historian Florus wrote that 'Caesar returned with much richer spoil than the first time.' It could hardly have been less, since the first visit had ended in a hurried evacuation – and this was little more. One suspects that the businessmen who had invested in the expedition got a poor return – some loot maybe from the captured fortress, and some illiterate slaves. Cicero even cautioned his friend Atticus, who speculated in such commodities, against buying British slaves since they were likely to be deficient in any civilized attainments. Before the invasion there had been much talk in Rome of the riches that the island would yield but, although the land had some mineral wealth, Caesar's costly year of 54 produced practically nothing. Even the *Commentaries* can hardly disguise the fact that the expedition was a failure. Suetonius cites it as one of only three in Caesar's whole career. It was to be a century before the Romans returned and conquered part of southern Britain. They never at any time conquered it all, and this latecomer to the Roman Empire was to be one of the first to leave when the legions were ultimately summoned back to Rome.

CHAPTER NINETEEN

Disturbances in West and East

Even before he left Britain, Caesar knew that the situation in Gaul was daily becoming more serious. Indeed, he himself reveals that his principal reason for agreeing on terms so comparatively generous to Cassivellanus was that his presence was needed in Gaul. The Gauls were becoming restless and – now that they felt the impact of the merchants, the slave-dealers, and the tax-collectors who followed in the wake of the legions – they began to value their freedom more than ever before. Caesar's mood can only have been grim as he landed at Boulogne in the autumn of 54, with an unsatisfactory campaign behind him and a certainty of trouble ahead. It will have been intensified by the news that waited for him in a letter from Rome. Julia, his only child and daughter – Julia whose name evoked the aunt who had first inspired his career and recalled his first wife Cornelia for whose sake he had suffered so much at the hand of Sulla – had died in childbirth. The child she was carrying was Pompey's son, but the child had also died.

Plutarch writes: 'Caesar and Pompey were much afflicted with her death, nor were their friends less disturbed, believing that the alliance was now broken, which had hitherto kept the sickly commonwealth in peace . . . The people took the body of Julia, in spite of the opposition of the tribunes, and carried in into the field of Mars, and there her funeral rites were performed, and her remains are laid.' Suetonius says of these years that, during them, 'Caesar lost one after the other, his mother, his daughter and his grandson.' Of his stoicism under these blows of fate Quintus Cicero, who was serving with him, wrote to his brother the orator praising Caesar's 'strength of spirit'. But he had plenty to keep him occupied and, even if his had been a quite different kind of temperament, would have been forced immediately into the world of action.

In that year the harvest had been poor and Caesar, instead of concentrating his troops into one place, felt constrained to scatter the legions so that the burden of supplying them should be spread over as wide an area as possible. Such was his account of things, but it must be noticed that he did not send the troops to the south where the harvest had been better, but concentrated them in the north, the worst affected area but the home of the tribes who had shown the greatest resistance to the Roman occupation. The disposition of the troops for the winter must have been the main talking point at the annual meeting of the representatives of the Gallic nations at which Caesar presided soon after his return to Boulogne. Hardly were these matters settled than the news reached him that the King of the Carnutes, a tribe inhabiting the Orleans territory – dark, wild country where the Druids exerted a formidable influence – had been murdered. This was a blow clearly aimed at Rome, for the young King had been appointed by Caesar himself on his usual principle of having a leader who would be personally indebted to him. In the heart of Belgic territory, and in the heartland of their religion, which must be assumed to have had a nationalist bias, such an appointment was vital. The legion which Caesar had designated to be based at Soissons was hastily summoned to winter among the Carnutes, with the task of finding the murderers – as well, of course, as keeping an eye on a disturbed area.

All the legions had now been placed and all arrangements made for the winter and Caesar was on the point of leaving for Italy, where urgent domestic politics required his attention, when the real blow fell. Revolt had broken out among the Belgic tribes. Fifteen cohorts (one and a half legions) had been massacred by the Eburones at Aduatuca in the Ardennes and their two legates killed. Quintus Cicero at Amiens was soon under attack by an army of 60,000 who were using siege engines that they had learned to make after the Roman fashion. The Treveri had risen in a body and Caesar's chief deputy Labienus was hard put to it to hold his own against this tribe, who were once more under the leadership of the same Indutiomarus whom Caesar had earlier spared. (In due course Labienus solved the problem, as perhaps Caesar should have done earlier, and had him killed.) The whole of the New Order for Gaul and Belgium, which Caesar had thought securely constructed, was collapsing. There could be no question of his proceeding to Italy that year. Suetonius tells us that so deeply did Caesar feel the blow that he vowed neither to shave nor have his hair cut until the disaster was avenged.

Quintus Cicero, after withstanding a protracted siege, was finally relieved by the arrival of Caesar, who managed to deceive the chief of the forces surrounding Cicero's legion into lifting the siege. He then marched against Caesar, attacked him without due care, and was soundly beaten for his pains. But although for the moment the Romans seemed to have quenched the main sources of the revolt, the damage to their reputation remained. The knowledge that fifteen cohorts could be wiped out and – even more disturbing to Caesar – that barbarians who only a year or so before had run at the sight of siege engines had now learned how to construct them served as grim reminders to the occupying forces that the Gauls and the Belgae were far from finished.

As the news of the uprising spread so, the *Commentaries* inform us, 'nearly all the cities of Gaul were talking of war. Everywhere messengers and envoys were passing between the tribes talking of the uprising which was to begin. It was known that secret meetings were being held, and Caesar never had a moment's peace from news about the dealings that were going on and the revolt that was being prepared.' From his headquarters at Samarobriva (Amiens) Caesar ordered the recruitment of two more legions in Cisalpine Gaul, more than making good his losses, while Pompey, still true to their agreements of mutual aid, prepared to lend another to the embattled proconsul in Gaul. Caesar would now have ten legions at his disposal. He would need them.

Early in 53, as the harsh northern winter drew to a close and before spring could bring the renewal of hope (synonymous with rebellion), Caesar summoned all the Gallic chieftains to a meeting at Amiens. Prior to this, he had set the tone for the year and used four legions to crush the Nervii. The Nervii were compelled to yield up hostages and formally submit to the Roman *imperium*, while the men and cattle captured in the expedition were all handed over as prizes to the legionaries. It was noticeable, however, that at this meeting in Amiens no representatives of the Treveri, the Senones or the Carnutes appeared: this was, in effect, a declaration of open rebellion. Caesar at once ordered the meeting to move to Lutetia (Paris) – nearer the rebel centre – and had his headquarters transferred there. He acted swiftly against the rebels, and the tribes which did not surrender were taught a harsh lesson. The Rhine was crossed yet again, to dissuade any Germanic tribes from joining the Gauls, who were once more seeking their help. The Eburones were so savaged, and their countryside so plundered and laid waste, that the name of this tribe to all intents and purposes disappears from history. Ambiorix, the Belgic king who had been responsible for the massacre of the fifteen cohorts at Aduatuca, managed to escape but Acco, leader of the Senones, was tried, condemned to death, and stripped and bound to a stake before the leaders of all the Gauls. He was beaten to death and his corpse was then beheaded. *Vae Victis.* It is safe to say that, after a year in which the iron hand had been so clearly shown, never had the Romans been so hated. A stunned peace fell over Gaul, and Caesar was able to spare the time to winter once again in Italy.

There was much to engage him. The death of his daughter Julia, and of the grandson who would have strengthened the ties between himself and Pompey was a grievous blow. Pompey himself, exercising his right to govern Spain *in absentia*, had stayed in the capital while Crassus, taking up his command in the East, had begun by ravaging Mesopotamia and had then wintered in Syria. After plundering the temple at Jerusalem, he had crossed the Euphrates once more, and in the summer of 53 he had been defeated in the dry plains near Carrhae (the Biblical Haran) and killed shortly afterwards. The triumvirate was thus ended, and things looked insecure for Rome and greatly to Caesar's disadvantage, for 'the richest of all the Romans' had generally tended to favour Caesar's arguments when it came to any conflict of interests among the triumvirate. There could be no gainsaying the fact that Caesar's political position had weakened since 55. That year had begun with great promise – which had not been fulfilled – and the invasion of Britain in 54 had done nothing to redeem his reputation, while 53 had seen the beginning of chaos in what had been previously considered in Rome Caesar's new world in the west. Despite his careful cultivation of correspondents in the city he had lost the ear of many of those who counted, while his public image of golden success upon the battlefield had become somewhat tarnished.

Pompey, on the other hand, had slowly learned how to improve his image with the masses and, above all, how to manipulate political power. With Crassus dead, and Caesar away, he had become the dominant figure in the state and indeed it looked as if he could easily secure the dictatorship if he so wanted. So much had public and political life declined into anarchy since Caesar's consulship that the Roman world was at the mercy of street gangs and thugs. Money dominated all. In so sordid an arena even Pompey, whose personal reputation was far from stainless, seemed to many a source of strength round which some elements of the republic could still maintain their function. There was indeed a considerable movement afoot to make Pompey dictator and, in the absence of his fellow triumvirs, the proconsul for Spain was, because of his continued presence in Italy, granted authority to maintain law and order in the city. The dictatorship, however, was resolutely opposed by Cato; and indeed only Cato throughout all this period managed to continue to fight for the virtues that had once been equated with the word 'republican'. Cicero for his part had trimmed and, as he wrote revealingly to his friend Lentulus:

We must assent, as a matter of course, to what a few men say, or we must differ from them to no purpose. – The relations of the Senate, of the courts of justice, nay, of the whole Commonwealth, are changed. – The consular dignity of a firm and courageous statesman can no longer be thought of . . . We must go with the times. Those who have played a great part in public life have never been able to adhere to the same views on all occasions. The art of navigation lies in trimming to the storms. When you can reach your harbour by altering your course, it is a folly to persevere in struggling against the wind.

Over the winter of 53–52 Caesar contemplated the situation in Rome from across the border in Cisalpine Gaul. He had made his headquarters at Ravenna, and it was here that he heard shortly after his arrival that his erratic agent Clodius had finally been killed. In an affray between his own gang and that of another unscrupulous aristocrat, Titus Annius Milo, he was cut down by armed followers of his rival. (It is indicative of the state of things in Rome that both these scoundrels were candidates for the consulate in 52.) Immediately following upon the murder serious rioting broke out in the city, the meeting house of the senate and other buildings near the Forum were set on fire and it was clear that public order was collapsing. It was essential for the senate to find a strong man whom they could (to some extent) trust, and Pompey was elected to the consulship – his third – but with the curious provision that he was to be sole consul, although with the right to choose himself an associate. Cato had won his way, but so desperate was the situation that Pompey had more or less achieved the power of dictator without the title. Pompey, wrote Dio Cassius, was less anxious to curry favour with the people than Caesar, and the senate considered that they could more easily detach him from the people and win him over to their way of thinking. In this they were right. Pompey had already shown that he had more sympathy with the outlook of the *Optimates* than with Caesar. After all, as a young man he had been in favour of Sulla and against Marius, so it was not very surprising that the conservative in him should once more emerge.

Caesar recognised the facts, and with almost brutal cynicism proposed to Pompey that he should marry Caesar's grand-niece Octavia while he Caesar put aside Calpurnia (who was childless) and married Pompey's daughter. The fact that Octavia was already married and that Pompey's daughter was engaged mattered not at all – marriages could be annulled and engagements broken. But Pompey had no desire to bind himself to Caesar quite so closely and openly. He surprised everybody by electing to marry the daughter of Metellus Scipio, one of the most revered men in Roman society and one of the most outspoken in the anti-Caesar camp. Then, as if he had not made his views clear enough, Pompey now nominated his new father-in-law as his fellow consul. On the other hand, he did not wish to alienate Caesar entirely and he supported a popular decree that would allow Caesar to stand for the consulship of 48 *in absentia*, thus permitting him to keep his office of proconsul and escape the prosecution that would otherwise have been brought against him. For although Caesar's consulship had led to his present position of power and would lead on farther, the rank smell of his year of office would never be forgiven or forgotten by some.

Curiously enough, although Pompey now appeared to be dominant upon the board he had made an error of the kind that, although not immediately clear at the time, would ultimately lose him the game. He was in a strong position and Caesar was in a weak one. If he had pressed harder he could almost certainly have secured the dictatorship, whereas to be consul – even with his new father-in-law as fellow consul – was still to be subject to the senate and constrained within a one-year term. Caesar's power-base in Gaul was very far from secure, whereas in the desperate state of the republic and the confusion of the empire Pompey could probably have held office as dictator for almost as long as he wanted. Pompey had temporized, seeking for favour with the *Optimates* without overtly offending Caesar. He had miscalculated Caesar's weight in the scales of power and had not acted decisively enough to bring them down on his own side: he would never be given a similar opportunity.

Caesar did not need to have his former partner's actions spelled out for him. He was aware that Pompey's new relations and friends would do all that they could to weaken the link between the two surviving triumvirs, and would indeed try to make an open break between them. It was also clear to Caesar, even if it was not yet to Pompey, that the death of Julia, the death of Crassus, and Pompey's remarriage into the heart of *Optimate* country, all tended towards a direct confrontation between the two men.

CHAPTER TWENTY

The Great Gallic Uprising

Throughout that winter the eyes of the world were upon Rome and the contest for power that was taking place. Those who are on the sidelines can often see more clearly than those who are engaged, and the leaders of the Gauls and their informants were far from ignorant barbarians in a distant country. They knew, to some extent at any rate, the relative positions of Caesar and Pompey in their struggle. They knew also that it was Caesar whom they had to fear, and their experience of Roman occupation had not endeared their new masters to them. Even the favoured tribes knew that they would never enjoy real freedom again and, in Caesar's absence, the mood began to harden throughout Gaul. It was clear that individual uprisings were of no avail and that only a massive insurrection on a *national* scale (something never previously envisaged) could secure them their liberty.

Caesar's reaction to Pompey's elevation to the consulship, and to his move towards an alliance with the *Optimates*, was to counterbalance the consul's power with the aristocracy by seeking the affection of the people – an area in which Pompey had never had much success. Suetonius details the means that Caesar employed to win a popularity that would benefit him privately and also stand him in good stead when he became a candidate for his second consulship. Almost for the first time, he had money to spare – not borrowed as before from Crassus and others, but money of his own. It stemmed of course from Gaul, partly the loot of captured towns and villages, but also from deals with tribal chiefs, Roman merchants, tax-collectors and slave-dealers. A large section of the continent that had hitherto known only the economic requirements of its leaders and their immediate supporters, was now open to methods of extracting money from the conquered that Rome had perfected in its dealings throughout the East and the Mediterranean world. From the spoils taken in Gaul Caesar began building Rome a new Forum, paying (as Suetonius tells us) more than a million gold pieces for the site alone. A gladiatorial show (always a way to the people's heart) and an immense public banquet in memory of his daughter Julia were followed by arrangements for the training and provision of gladiators of a high standard for shows in the future. He was careful not to forget the real source of his strength, doubling the rate of pay of the private soldier, while at the same time he increased his ration from the state granaries and, whenever the market was glutted, would allocate a Gallic slave to every soldier. He became 'a certain and reliable source of help to all in legal difficulties, or in debt, or living beyond their means . . .'

For those with serious criminal records or whose affairs were in such a state that even he could not help them, he had only one thing to say: 'What you need is a civil war.' (If it should come to that, he knew well on whose side they would be.) Nor did he look only to Rome and Italy, for he knew – especially if there should be a civil war – that it was in the vast provinces of the empire that allies would be needed. Not only Rome benefitted from his architectural munificence, but also the other major cities of Italy, for he knew better than anyone that an imposing work of architecture makes its donor's name reverberate a thousand times a day. Magnificent public works were presented to the main cities of Asia and Greece, as well as to Spain and Narbonese Gaul. 'Everyone,' writes Suetonius, 'was amazed by this liberality and wondered what it might signify.' Thinking men knew of course, and saw that everything was leading up to a conflict between Caesar and Pompey for the rulership of the world.

But everything – money, power, legions and his continued freedom from prosecution in Rome – hinged upon Gaul. Caesar had staked all on his possession of that great new power base, and he needed it solid behind him or he was ruined. The first signs that Gaul was again stirring uneasily came early in 52. The Carnutes were once more among the first to raise the banner of independence, putting a number of Romans to death in their town of Cenabum (Orleans). Then his faithful ally and friend, Commius of the Atrebates, after surviving an assassination plotted by Labienus, proved to be at the heart of the rebellion, organizing a rising designed to take advantage of Caesar's absence and to cut him off from his legions in Gaul. But the centre of the revolt was finally to be a tribe which, although one of the most powerful in Gaul, had hitherto not been conspicuous in opposition to the Romans. Indeed, the man who led them had fought in Caesar's Gallic cavalry and had been dignified by the proconsul with the title of *Friend*. This tribe, the Arverni, came from the region of the Auvergne, and had probably failed to take part in previous uprisings only because its people were bedevilled by the usual struggle for power between two rival chieftains. They and almost all Gaul were ultimately led in the great revolt against Rome by the son of the man who lost this power struggle, the man who had distinguished himself fighting with the Roman cavalry, the man who was to remain a Gallic hero throughout all the ages – Vercingetorix. (This is the name that Caesar gives him, while Plutarch calls him Vergentorix – in either case, probably a title rather than a name.)

Despite opposition from the other Arvernian leaders, who were not anxious to provoke the Romans, Vercingetorix managed to arouse the ordinary peasants in the country to take up arms against Rome. This was new in itself, since all previous revolts had started with the Gallic chieftains and nobles. He even enrolled slaves in his ranks, promising them their liberty, and – a fact that Caesar comments upon – 'he welcomed robbers'. Vercingetorix, proclaimed King by his followers, managed to rouse the neighbouring tribes and persuaded them to accept his overall leadership. Inspired very probably by the way in which Caesar had begun to weld the various Celtic tribes into a single province, he conceived the dream of the Celts as a nation – united against Rome and in their shared language, customs and religious beliefs. It was something completely new in their history and for this reason acted as a leaven among people previously divided by clan loyalties. At the same time another leader declared himself, one Lucterius, from the Cadurci, a tribe neighbouring upon the Arverni, a man whom even Caesar was to call 'of unusual courage'. He was unusual too in that he was prepared to accept Vercingetorix as his leader, and he rapidly began to draw into the revolt a number of tribes which had hitherto kept out of entanglements against the foreign power. Vercingetorix was meanwhile rousing the tribes from the Parisii to Armorica; the whole territory was bursting into flame and the rising even threatened the Roman province of Narbonne. Once the Gauls began to work together like this there was real danger for the Romans, and Caesar acted immediately. After crossing the Alps he made straight for the provincial capital, rapidly organized its defence and saw to it that the frontiers were well garrisoned. Lucterius, who had been moving southward threatening the province, found himself forestalled by that immense speed with which Caesar was always able to move his troops, impressing everyone around him with the necessity for immediate action. Time and again his enemies would discover to their discomfort this quicksilver quality, whether in the civil war, in Alexandria or later in Spain. It was something quite matchless. Plutarch catches its quality:

But Caesar, who above all men was gifted with the faculty of making the right use of everything in war, and most especially of seizing the right moment, as soon as he heard of the revolt, returned immediately the same way he went, and showed the barbarians, by the quickness of his march in such a severe season, that an army was advancing against them which was invincible.

Coming up from the south Caesar was confronted by the Cevennes mountains, where the pass was deep under snow and Vercingetorix to the north of it had reckoned himself secure for the time being. He little understood as yet the capabilities of the Roman legionary. The snow was six foot deep, yet the pass was cleared in a night and a day and the Romans suddenly appeared upon the borders of the Arverni. So confident had Vercingetorix felt, that he had been away urging upon another tribe the necessity of breaking with the Romans, and by the time the news reached him, the legions were moving deep into his own country. Plutarch again takes up the tale:

> For in the time that one would have thought it scarcely credible that a courier or express should have come with a message from him, he himself appeared with all his army, ravaging the country, reducing their posts, subduing their towns, receiving into his protection those who declared for him . . .

Vercingetorix was now forced to concentrate on the defence of his own lands, while Caesar, leaving Decimus Brutus with enough troops to keep the enemy occupied, moved on rapidly towards Vienne where he was met by a detachment of cavalry, in whose company, travelling overnight, he made for Langres where two legions were stationed. Two other legions stationed in the country of the Remi were ordered to Agedincum (Sens), and the main body of his troops was already forming. Vercingetorix, having observed from Caesar the value of rapid movement in war, now marched north and began to besiege a town called Gorgobina, the centre of the Boii tribe whom Caesar had placed under the sovereignty of the Aedui. He knew that the Aedui were wavering in their attachment to Rome, and that if they could be made to join the revolt the whole of the Roman scheme for the new Gallic colony would collapse. But Caesar realized this as well, and realized too that all the waverers would abandon their neutral or their pro-Roman position if it were seen that Caesar could not protect a small and relatively unimportant tribe.

Despite the great difficulties over provisions at this time of the year (the legionaries even had to be put on a meat diet, which they disliked intensely) Caesar started off with eight legions. After a two-day siege of one town (the inhabitants capitulating on the third) he moved into the country of the rebellious Carnutes and prepared to make them pay bitterly for the murders which had been the spark for Vercingetorix's revolt. At Cenabum (Orleans) the inhabitants fled before the advance of the legions but, trying to escape by a bridge over the Loire, were caught in a bottleneck and killed or captured. The deserted town was looted and set on fire, and Caesar made a present of everything within it and of all its inhabitants to the legionaries. He now crossed the Loire and headed into the land of the Bituriges, whose particular assistance Vercingetorix was now soliciting, for he had been caught by the speed and the success of Caesar's moves and forced to abandon his threat to the Boii (thus proving to the undecided that Caesar's protection was of more value than joining the revolt) and had moved to protect the Bituriges.

This tribe, which had wholeheartedly responded to Vercingetorix's call, had shown their willingness even to the extent of adopting a scorched-earth policy in the path of the Romans. They balked, though, at destroying their capital Avaricum (Bourges) and, despite Vercingetorix's pleas that they should abandon the city, forced him to yield to their arguments that the place was so strong by nature that not even the legions could capture it. Vercingetorix and his troops remained outside Avaricum, their mission being to harass Caesar's lines of supply and prevent food getting through to the legions (in which they nearly succeeded). But the legionaries, remembering the spoil from Cenabum and seeing this far richer city in front of them with its supposed wealth of treasures, remained steadfast at the siege in spite of the winter weather and their starvation rations, for neither the Aedui nor the recently rescued Boii came to Caesar's aid despite constant requests for supplies. With the erection of towers by both sides, the digging of sap-works and the display by the besieged of a bravery and ingenuity that Caesar remarked upon, the siege dragged on for three-and-a-half weeks. On a day of torrential rain, when both sides had more or less decided that nothing further could be done, he ordered the legionaries to attack. Surprise was all. The defenders' walls and towers were thrown down, an entrance was forced, and the citizens were put to the sword.

Gone were the days when Caesar had spared gallant adversaries. Gaul had given him too much trouble in recent years, and this revolt had been more dangerous than anything before. Everything hinged for him on Gaul's being safely secured for the Romans by a Roman whom they would accordingly honour – himself. He noted that out of forty thousand men, women and children within the walls, not one survived the subsequent massacre. (In fact the only survivors were about eight hundred who had fled at the first sign of the attack.) The city was immensely rich and, almost as important to the legionaries after their days of semi-starvation, it was also found to be well stocked with grain and every kind of supplies. It may seem curious but, despite this defeat, Vercingetorix did not lose his hold over the Gauls and indeed even derived some political benefit from it. He was able to point out that he had always advised abandoning the city – and that his policy of leaving nothing anywhere for the Romans to capture, nor grain to eat, was right.

Caesar was now deeply concerned that the Aedui were becoming less and less reliable. They had failed to supply him with provisions during the recent siege, and he decided to make his headquarters at Noviodunum (Nevers) in their territory. He had learned that a civil war was imminent in this tribe, due to the usual disagreement between two rivals, and all his political skills were needed to sort this out. Meanwhile, as the revolt still threatened the whole of Gaul, he took the decision to divide his forces into two, sending the much-trusted Labienus north to Lutetia (Paris) while he himself moved to attack the very heart of the Arverni – their main stronghold, Gergovia. Vercingetorix, he may have reasoned, while willing enough to urge others to abandon their cities, could hardly let Gergovia fall. He would therefore be forced to abandon his policy of laying waste the land and conducting a guerrilla strategy out of the forests, and have to stand and fight. Vercingetorix did withdraw into the fortress-capital, but Caesar had underestimated the strength of the place. Gergovia, standing on a natural hill, furnished with water, well-garrisoned and full of provisions, could only be forced to yield by a frontal assault. The strength of Gergovia, as of so many great fortresses, lay not in its walls, towers and ditches, but in its natural site – a plateau standing over 2,000 feet above the surrounding land. He 'despaired of taking it by force', thus leaving himself with no option but a prolonged siege – carried out in a hostile land and with no certainty that his so-called friends such as the Aedui would keep him supplied.

The Aedui under their new leader (whom Caesar had himself appointed) had, in fact, already decided to withdraw their support from the Romans. The news that Caesar's troops had attempted to storm Gergovia and had met with a serious reverse – several hundred legionaries and, even worse, forty-six centurions killed – must have encouraged them in their decision. Caesar was compelled to raise the siege and turn back to deal with this new danger. No general, whatever his skills, could have carried on with a siege when his principal allies had risen against him. The Aedui had indeed thrown their hand in with the insurgents with a vengeance, massacring all the Romans at Noviodunum and seizing their stores and provisions. At the same time, evidence enough of how well-coordinated was the rebellion, the Parisii burned Lutetia (Paris) to the ground in defiance of Labienus. At this juncture Caesar realized that his only sensible recourse was to retreat with his six legions and join up with Labienus and his four since the latter, being only second-grade troops, would be unable to cope on their own with the weight of enemy forces massing against them. With his ten united legions he felt confident that he would be able to crush the Gallic uprising and impose a peace upon the territory that would last.

Finally, after a march of amazing rapidity towards the Loire through a country in which tribe after tribe seemed to be defecting, Caesar met up with Labienus who had withdrawn from Lutetia on hearing rumours that Caesar had been defeated by Vercingetorix and was retreating towards the Roman province. The reunion of the two halves of the army resulted in an upsurge in morale that from then on never seemed to leave the soldiers. This was as well, for a conference at Bibracte (Autun) of the Aedui, the Arverni and the league led by Vercingetorix, confirmed the latter as commander-in-chief.

This was the high point of his career. Caesar had been forced to retreat from Gergovia and all Gaul, so it seemed, was united under a single Celt. The Aedui, however, were far from happy at submitting to the leadership of this Arvernian chief, who, despite the formidable preponderance of manpower available, seemed to keep as his overall strategy the idea of starving the Romans out by the scorched-earth policy that he had consistently urged upon his allies. Vercingetorix had ridden with the Romans; he knew their formidable discipline and capacity for war, and he did not want to engage Caesar and his legions in any set-piece battle. To the south he had the Roman province apparently at his mercy (Caesar's cousin who was in command had little more than two legions with which to defend it), and he had Caesar and his army cut off to the north, unable even to communicate with Italy. He also trusted in his immense cavalry superiority and thought that he would be able to throw the weight of his horsemen against the Romans at some favourable opportunity, without risking a stand-up battle involving great numbers of infantry.

His opportunity came as Caesar, Labienus and the ten legions, made their way in the direction of the Sequani, who it was hoped were still faithful to Rome and willing to allow them to pass so as to effect a junction with his cousin's two legions. Vercingetorix misinterpreted Caesar's move as an indication that he was in flight and, in the area of Dijon, unleashed a massive cavalry attack upon the marching legions. His own infantry were held back – to give a show of force, no more – while a three-pronged charge was launched against the Roman columns, from ahead and on both flanks simultaneously. Despite the weight of the attack the legionaries fought back fiercely, assisting their own cavalry and – unlike the Gallic footsoldiers held in reserve – took part in every moment of the battle. Caesar, furthermore, had an unpleasant surprise in store for the Gauls. He had noticed from his very first encounter with the Germans how admirably-mounted, well-equipped, and stern-spirited were their horsemen, and he had hired a considerable number of them from across the Rhine to put some additional weight into his own cavalry. At the height of the battle they were unleashed from a position on high ground, and drove in the right wing of the Gauls, putting Vercingetorix's cavalry to flight. The Gallic infantry who had been kept back in their thousands as passive spectators of the battle – the aim being to throw them in when their cavalry had completed the demoralization of the Romans – now found themselves facing the victorious German cavalry. The legionaries, heartened by their successful containment of the enemy horsemen, were eager for revenge. Vercingetorix, witnessing the flight of his cavalry, could think of nothing but withdrawing his fighting men from the field – even abandoning his camp. Caesar was already in full pursuit and, leaving two legions to guard the Roman camp, stormed after the retreating Gauls. Now, as was so often the case with brave but undisciplined troops, these had turned into a demoralized mob and were making for shelter in the great fortress city of Alesia, standing proud and isolated on the high plateau of Mount Auxois. Whether either of the leaders realized it or not – the end of the great Gallic revolt was in sight.

CHAPTER TWENTY-ONE

Alesia and an Example in the Dordogne

Alesia was so situated that it would have been almost impossible to storm. Caesar remembered his defeat at Gergovia, and Alesia was built on a similar high plateau and was even more formidable. On all sides the ground fell away steeply, in some places precipitously, while two small rivers, the Ose and the Oserain, enclosed the area, forming natural defences as well as ensuring a supply of water. Inside Alesia were Vercingetorix and some 80,000 men, as well as the permanent inhabitants. But herein lay his weakness for, although there was adequate water, there would hardly be enough provisions for so many people. Vercingetorix had counted on defeating Caesar by a scorched-earth policy combined with guerrilla tactics and then, when he thought that the Romans were retreating, by a major cavalry attack while they were on the march. He had not counted on his cavalry being defeated, nor on a siege, and there was no reason to imagine that the storerooms of Alesia contained enough provisions for such an army as well as the inhabitants. Caesar knew this and, while he had not been prepared to sit out a lengthy siege at Gergovia, he now counted on the legions being able to supply themselves from the country around Alesia and to reduce the citadel before reinforcements could come up to relieve Vercingetorix.

He settled down confidently for a lengthy siege as, on their very first day before the walls, the legionaries began digging. The tenacity and endurance of the Roman soldier was never shown to greater advantage than during the conduct of a siege, and their engineering skills as well as their perseverance became so well known throughout the world that those familiar with Roman techniques usually abandoned hope when they saw siege-works rising around their town or fortress. One Roman commander was said to have replied to a delegation from a town he was about to besiege, who told him that they had enough food for ten years, that in that case he would take it in the eleventh year. The delegation went back within the walls and the town at once capitulated. The process by which Caesar intended to reduce Alesia (described in detail in the *Commentaries*) was bicircumvallation – surrounding the town with two double lines of fortified trenches; the circumference of the outer being some fourteen miles and of the inner ten. Between these two great lines of entrenchments there was ample space for Caesar's troops and cavalry as well as all the baggage and provision carts. Within this area, protected also by tall watch-towers, the troops could face both inwards towards Alesia and outwards, if and when Gallic reinforcements came to relieve the city.

Before the noose could close around the threatened fortress Vercingetorix decided to send all his horsemen out secretly by night to take word to their tribes that Caesar was besieging Alesia, and that their only hope for a free Gaul was to come in their thousands and break the siege. Once Caesar and his army had been in their turn surrounded and defeated, the Roman threat to the people of Gaul would be over. It has often been debated why Vercingetorix decided to send all his horsemen away from the threatened city – surely a hundred at the most would have been enough to take the word to the other tribes? Lack of forage seems an obvious answer, but the horses could have been methodically slaughtered for rations (and there is no evidence that the Gauls had the Roman aversion to horsemeat), while the horsemen themselves would have proved useful in the garrison force. In any case, they rode out through gaps in the unfinished entrenchments – with the knowledge that Vercingetorix had supplies for thirty days – and made their way throughout Gaul to summon help.

Then the noose closed, the days passed, and after a month starvation began to grip the besieged. The difficulty of summoning so many men from so many tribes (many of them at variance with one another) and the slowness of communications, all contributed to Vercingetorix's next action. After an assembly of the Gallic leaders within Alesia, capitulation having been rejected, as well as a suggestion that the old and those unable to bear arms should be killed, the decision was taken for all the noncombatant civilians to leave the city. Vercingetorix may have hoped that the Romans would let them pass through their lines to the outside world; in which case he knew little about the real purpose of a siege. This was to ensure that the excessive numbers of those within a city or a fortress would lead to mass starvation and, in its turn, to capitulation. The strength of the besieging army lay in the numbers and weakness of the besieged. The inhabitants of Alesia were rebuffed when they came up to the Roman lines and when in desperation they turned back towards their own city, they found that the gates had been closed against them. So they wandered about between the encircling Roman cordon and the doomed garrison until they died.

The corn in Alesia had run out and the Romans were also reduced to minimal rations when the relief force finally arrived – a swirl of dust in the distance beyond the river Brenne into which the two tributaries that encircle Alesia emptied. Caesar estimated the relieving army at a quarter of a million infantry and eight thousand cavalry, but these figures – like others in the *Commentaries* – must be regarded with some suspicion. There could be no doubt, however, that the relief force by far outnumbered the besieging Romans, who were outnumbered in any case by Vercingetorix's besieged army. Certainly, they represented a large part of that Gaul which the Romans had thought was willingly accepting the New Order, and they were led by senior chieftains: Commius of the Atrebates, Vercassivellaunus, an Arvernian cousin of Vercingetorix, and the two Aedui, Eporedorix and Viridomarus, who had been responsible for taking their tribe into the great revolt against Rome. Vercingetorix is reputed to have said that the Romans won their victories, not by superior courage, but by superior science. Certainly it was the scientific ingenuity of the bicircumvallation with all its outer defences of staked pit-falls, calthrops and barbed spikes (the minefields of the day) which, combined with the courage of the legionaries, were to defeat the Gauls.

For four days, lashed by spears and arrows within their double lines, the Romans fought off wave after wave of attacks from both sides. Cavalry charges (in which the Germans again proved their superiority) were followed by massed infantry assaults in which both Caesar and Labienus showed not only their tactical abilities but their personal courage. At one moment, when the fighting had grown desperate around a weak point, Caesar 'left his own station: he called up the reserves which had not yet been engaged, and he rode across the field, conspicuous in his scarlet dress and with his bare head, cheering on the men as he passed each point where they were engaged, and hastening to the scene where the chief danger lay'. The final attack came about noon on the fourth day. Caesar in person took charge of a legion plus an extra cohort, to fall upon the Gauls at their thickest point. The loyal German cavalry came to his assistance, taking the great mass of Gallic infantry from the rear, and the last major assault was over.

The relieving army, their morale shattered, turned in flight as the legionaries swarmed from their positions and took the offensive. By the end of that day – while thousands of Gauls dispersed throughout the countryside around – it was clear that Alesia would never be relieved. Seventy-four captured standards were piled at Caesar's feet, while the broken Vercingetorix, seeing that the great relief force had failed in its purpose, turned back into Alesia, a man without hope. So many thousands had come to his assistance and yet they had been unable to break that cordon of steel which surrounded him ... Too many thousands was perhaps the answer, for it seems as if many of them had never been able to get even near the Roman perimeter, while the problems of food and weaponry supply for so vast a number were beyond their simple logistics. The horsemen and foot soldiers, who now spread back into Gaul like a great ripple on a pond, carried with them a very different message from that which Vercingetorix had originally sent out. The message was that the Romans had triumphed at Alesia and that the dream of a free Gaul was over. The dream of a united Gaul was something that few had ever been able to understand.

On the following day, seated formally on a curule chair on the Alesia side of the encircling Roman defences, Caesar accepted the submission of the defeated Gallic leaders. His own cool prose tells it all: '. . . the commanders were brought before him, Vercingetorix was given up to him, their arms were cast at his feet.' His verdict on the rebellion and on those who had taken part in it was pronounced. Vercingetorix was to be kept a captive in chains until the time came for his death. The other leaders were pardoned. The prisoners of war were to be divided among the Roman soldiers as slaves. (This meant that, if not personally wanted, they could be sold to the contractors.) The Aedui and Arverni, however, were separated from the other prisoners and, after a short detention, were restored to their states. The Arverni had to produce a large number of hostages, but the Aedui were even restored to their former position of free allies. Caesar's magnanimity was to yield dividends, for his preferential treatment of the two major tribes secured them to his interest permanently. Nationalism was over for them, they had 'swallowed the toad' and would remain faithful to Rome. And Caesar had every reason for requiring all the assistance he could find in the current tumultuous state of Gaul.

Although the dream of a single Gallic state had dissolved, it would be some time before he could be confident that the land was quiet. As for the defeated Vercingetorix, he had to wait for six years in Roman jails until his death after Caesar's Gallic Triumph in 46. And the Roman soldiers on the vast perimeter around Alesia?

. . . they knew nothing of the victory till they heard the cries of the men and the lamentations of the women who were in the town, and had from thence seen the Romans at a distance carrying into their camp a great quantity of bucklers, adorned with gold and silver, many breastplates stained with blood, besides cups and tents made in the Gallic fashion. So soon did so vast an army dissolve and vanish like a ghost or dream . . .

(Plutarch)

The heart of the great revolt had collapsed with the defeat of Vercingetorix and the fall of Alesia, but the embers still smouldered in various part of Gaul – most noticeably among the Belgae who had contributed little. Caesar, who had gone into winter camp at Bibracte, was soon compelled to take action against the Bituriges and, even though it was the depths of winter, to move in person at the head of two legions and occupy their country. He did it with that rapidity which had the customary effect of taking the enemy completely by surprise. After six weeks of what seems to have been more a man-hunt than a campaign, the Bituriges 'were brought to accept peace' and the legions could go back to winter quarters. They were rewarded, however, for this disturbance of their routine by what amounted to about half a year's pay a man.

Early in 51 some of the Belgic states, including the tough Bellovaci, began – too late – to prepare for war, and Caesar was finally compelled to bring six legions against them (he had initially considered four to be enough). So bad at one moment was the situation that the news even got back to Rome that he had suffered a major disaster. But his enemies rejoiced too soon, and in the end Correus, the leader of the Bellovaci, who had been conducting a very intelligent guerrilla campaign, was killed in the fighting. Even with this defeat the resistance to the Romans did not end, other leaders and other tribes continued the struggle – proof enough that the Roman Peace was never desired but only forced upon the inhabitants of the land.

The final act in the great drama occurred in 51. The rebellious Belgae had all surrendered, handed over hostages and paid an immense tribute calculated on the proportion of their previous engagements against Caesar. From the land of the Eburones (devastated yet again) to the area of the Loire and the Treveri in the east, the people were brought back into the Roman allegiance and reminded by the marching legions of Caesar and Labienus, and his other lieutenants, of the consequences of 'folly'. In only one place, and that far away in the Dordogne, was there any survival of the spirit of resistance that only a year before had swept through the land like a great fire. In the hill-fortress of Uxellodunum (Puy d'Issolu) a number of Gauls under two distinguished leaders were holding out, waiting for Caesar's departure and hoping, once he had gone, to raise the revolt again. He determined to make an example of them 'so that other cities, following their lead, should not try to regain their liberty . . .'

The siege and fall of Uxellodunum, told by Hirtius, Caesar's friend and fellow-author (he completed the *Commentaries* of the Gallic War), is one of the most moving episodes in all the history of great sieges. The fortress-town built on almost solid rock held out throughout a hot summer against all the skill and ingenuity of the Romans, until their engineers finally managed to divert the underground stream that provided Uxellodunum's interior water supply. Caesar had shown clemency after the fall of Alesia, but now he decided that an example must be made: he would show the other side of the Roman *imperium*. The lives of the inhabitants were spared, but all those who had borne arms against him had their hands cut off. The survivors would wander for the rest of their lives throughout Gaul, living witnesses of the fate of rebels.

One thing that is noticeable about the *Commentaries*, more even than their laconic style, is the shortage of reference to the many other men who made the conquest of this great country possible, although, of course, Labienus, young Crassus, a centurion, and one or two others are mentioned. These were the official accounts of the proconsul (Caesar always refers to himself in the third person), but they must also be seen as the report of a general of immense political ambition who wished to appear in the most favourable light to people in Rome. It was natural enough that Caesar, with his literacy and rhetorical ability (witness the accounts of his speeches), should inevitably show himself in a favourable light and, since he was the commentator, that the actions in which he himself was engaged should have a vivid quality that could hardly be extended to others. But there were a number of commanders – Labienus was an outstanding example – who clearly were extremely fine professionals and who, although their actions are necessarily recorded, fail to command the attention that they should. This may well be the reason why Labienus chose the other side when it came to the civil war.

There can be no doubt at all as to Caesar's ability, and his place among the great commanders in world history is safe for all time, but the reader of the *Commentaries* should never forget the unknown legionaries and, above all, the centurions who made the victories possible. Caesar found in the legionary system (created by Marius) the ideal instrument for his purpose and honed it to perfection. The skill of the Roman engineers, whether at mining operations, bridge-building, or the construction of assault towers, battering rams and other weapons of war such as the missile-throwing *ballista*, was outstanding. It is evidence of that 'superior science' which, as Vercingetorix said, played so large a part in the Roman victories. Something else that must always be borne in mind – when Gauls were starving or short of weapons, the Romans remained supplied. The commissariat, the supply side of the Roman army, was brilliantly organized – from helmets, breastplates, swords and boots, to grain and all other provisions. Even when the conquerors were living off the country, the food available still had to be obtained and distributed.

Able men like Labienus and Balbus, who was Caesar's personal adjutant for a time, made fortunes out of Gaul, and so too did Mamurra, who replaced him. Mamurra was a knight from Formiae who aroused the envy and hatred of the poet Catullus because he was *nouveau riche* and had at one time stolen the poet's mistress. He was also reputed to be bisexual, and Catullus in one of his most savage poems accused him and Caesar of having sexual relations, calling them

> . . . the pervert Mamurra and Caesar
> . . . sharing the same vice, this pair of twins
> Clever lads at love, sharing the same bed . . .

There must have been many others like Mamurra who

> . . . squandered the wealth that once
> To long-haired Gauls and farthest Britons belonged.

Every war produces its crop of profiteers – invariably able men, and usually hand in glove with politicians.

CHAPTER TWENTY-TWO

Tension and Dissension

In the year 58 Caesar had justified moving his troops beyond the province of Narbonese Gaul on the grounds of protecting those old friends of Rome, the Aedui. He had been forced by the mass-migration of a Swiss tribe, the Helvetii, to invade areas which had never before been claimed by Rome nor had any ties with the Roman republic. Successive years had steadily increased the territory to which it was now clear that Caesar (in the name of Rome) was laying claim, and by the end of 51 a Roman province had been carved out of Europe that stretched from the Pyrenees in the south to the Alps in the east, to the Rhine in the north and to the Atlantic Ocean in the west. This new province, which he gave to the Roman people, but out of which he sought political power, comprised an area of 200,000 square miles, many different tribes, numerous dialects of the Celtic language, and one basic religion (on the decline) Druidism. The land now lay exhausted after the conquest, a conquest in which Caesar claimed to have conducted thirty formal battles, captured more than eight hundred towns and fought against over three million men. Quite apart from those killed in the conquest, the numbers of those captured and sold as slaves was so great that the markets of Rome and Italy were glutted. The immensity of his achievement could not be ignored by any Roman, or indeed anyone living in the Mediterranean world. He was the first of all the kings, conquerors and generals, who for millenia had campaigned around the Inland Sea, to bring Mediterranean civilization and northern Europe into close contact. In doing so he transformed the Roman empire as well as the Gallic world, and ensured that the empire of the future would be a very different thing from that of the past. Pompey's conquests had been among the old and known: Greece, Asia Minor and the Near East, whose cultures long predated that of Rome. Caesar by bringing in this fresh blood from the north changed the whole of Roman (as well as European) history, and at the same time secured from the conquered territories a fresh infusion of manpower which would enable him to challenge for the leadership of the Roman world. He had well assessed the fighting capabilities of the Gauls and saw that, with the addition of Roman discipline and technology, they would make magnificent soldiers. The Gaul grew up believing that the right and proper life for a man was warfare: agriculture was for the conquered, for slaves, and women. Caesar would give him all the warfare he wanted, only instead of fighting against rival Gallic tribes he would now fight Caesar's battles – against other Romans if need be.

At the close of 51, after sending the legions into winter quarters, Caesar made a tour of the old province, Narbonese Gaul, rewarding all those in positions of authority for their steadfastness throughout the tumultuous years that had passed. Once again he was unable to visit Rome because of his proconsular status, but in any case, so much needed to be done in setting up the administration and organization of the new Gaul. He remained in the position of being able to reward his supporters in Rome and buy his way into the good graces of a great many senators and men of influence, including such unlikely diehards of the right as Cicero. As part of his propaganda campaign, 51 saw the publication of his seven volumes on the Gallic war. As well as slaves, gold from the captured temples and towns of Gaul flooded Rome, to such an extent that even the money market was upset. In his summing up of Caesar's character, and after giving earlier instances of his financial malpractices in Spain, Suetonius makes the classic understatement: 'he was not very honest in money matters'. The financial aftermath of the Gallic campaigns is stated as follows:

He plundered large and small temples in Gaul of their votive offerings, and very often allowed his troops to plunder towns not because they had offended him but just because they were rich. In the end he collected a great deal more gold than he could possibly handle and even began selling it in Italy for silver at 750 denarii to the pound – about two-thirds the official rate.

At the same time, absent in Gaul though he was, he knew from his correspondents that Pompey was making every possible use of his consulship to strengthen his position in Rome, Italy and the empire. Caesar well understood that the military gains in Gaul must now be consolidated by political and administrative foundations.

Without reference to Rome and the senate, entirely on his own authority, he proceeded to give Gaul its constitution. In doing this he could justifiably say that he was doing no more than Pompey had done in the East (something which Caesar when consul had hastened to ratify). From his headquarters at Nemetocenna (Arras), convenient for Belgic territory, he spelled out the relationship between Rome and the various states of the new Gaul, in which each individual nation or tribe was to keep its own name, laws and boundaries. Some, like the Aedui, Lingones and Remi, were recognized as equal allies of Rome, the others had their tribute assessed at 10 million denarii. This in itself was a comparatively small sum, and can only be explained by the fact that the country had been so devastated by the long years of war, and deprived at the same time of its means of production, that this was the highest figure at which the tribute could be fixed. The almost incalculable loot in men, money, specie, minerals and *matériel* which had flowed through the conquerors' hands in recent years had in themselves comprised several years of advance tribute. The manpower of Gaul, trained to fight alongside his legionaries and owing their allegiance not to some abstract state, city or senate, but to Caesar, would – for him – make up the balance. In his dispensations he was courteous and clement and at the same time careful to see that the reins of government in the various states were in hands that had been well paid to hold them in the way he wanted. That they kept their own identities, boundaries and laws was to his advantage, since he had no wish to see any kind of unified Gaul grow up which some future Vercingetorix could turn against the Romans. As for their religion, let them keep that too. In many ways it seemed that their gods more or less equated with those familiar in the Mediterranean world, and the High Priest of Rome had never been particularly dogmatic on religious matters.

The day was fast approaching when Caesar's proconsulship would come to an end. It was convincingly argued in the senate that, now that the Gallic War was over, Caesar was no longer needed as general and proconsul, but must take his place as a private citizen if he wished to campaign for the consulship of 49. Pompey was fully aware that, while Caesar remained in Gaul and he was in power in Rome, he must do all he could (as evasively as possible, for he had no wish at this moment for an open break with his former ally) to see that his colleague was undermined politically. A bill was brought in, for instance, which authorized any Roman citizen to institute proceedings against any holder of public office since the year 70 who had been guilty of illegal intrigue or public corruption. Both the date and the wording of this bill held Caesar within its net, for it was open knowledge that bribery and corruption had been synonymous with his consulship. (But what candidate for high office in Rome did not use money to secure his object?) Caesar knew that the bill was aimed at him, and that Pompey without openly declaring his enmity had made his peace with Caesar's enemies. At just about this time he was able to send word back to Rome that Alesia had fallen and that the Gallic revolt was over – a triumph, in fact. An uneasy senate could do no more than decree twenty days of thanksgiving celebrations, pleasing to the people but odious to his enemies.

Caesar well knew that in his absence he needed good friends, with power to exert on his behalf – so he bought them. One of the consuls for 51, a certain Paullus, Caesar obligated by paying off his massive debts; while he for his part agreed not to obstruct Caesar in any way during his year as consul. Since the other consul Marcellus was an *Optimate* and an enemy of Caesar this meant, in effect, that whatever Marcellus proposed was nullified by Caesar's man. One of the tribunes of the people for the following year 50 was also bought, and C. Scribonius Curio proved to be one of Caesar's wisest investments, for a tribune had the power of veto and Curio used this well in his interests. All Caesar's enemies were endeavouring to get him back to Rome without the power of his army behind him, and with a successor appointed to take over his commands in Cisalpine Gaul, Illyricum and, above all, in this great new Gallic province to the west. Every time a proposal was made that a successor to Caesar should be appointed Curio vetoed it, thus prolonging a stalemate with Pompey that maintained the peace but kept the Romans in a tremor of fear. Curio also made a proposal of his own which seemed at the time a reasonable solution to the whole problem: Caesar would resign his governorship on condition that Pompey would equally resign from the governorship of Spain, exercised *in absentia*. Curio's argument was lucid: 'In view of the state of mutual suspicion between these two citizens, there are few chances of an enduring peace in Rome unless both men at the same time return to the condition of private individuals.'

Pompey, who had improved over the years in his capacity at political in-fighting, surprised most people by agreeing to the proposition. He promised to renounce his powers on condition that Caesar did the same. His thinking behind this was clear enough: he, Pompey, was secure enough in Rome and furthermore he had the backing of the *Optimates*, whereas Caesar, if he returned as a private citizen, would immediately have legal proceedings taken against him for events that had occurred during his previous consulship. Pompey, moreover, still had the veterans from his previous campaigns on call in Italy, whereas Caesar would be without any military support to hand.

Throughout this period Cicero, who was in Asia Minor, was in constant touch with one of his correspondents, Caelius, who wrote to him in August 50:

I have written to you often that I can see no chance of peace lasting as long as a year, and the nearer the inevitable clash, the clearer looms the danger. The issue over which the powers that be are going to come to blows is, that whereas Pompey is determined not to allow

Caesar to become consul unless he gives up his army and provinces, Caesar is convinced that he cannot be safe once he has parted with his army. Caesar does, however, propose this compromise, that both should give up their armies. So all that show of affection and their detested alliance is not merely degenerating into bickering behind the scenes, but breaking out into open war.

Using his authority as a tribune, Curio managed to get the debate in the senate on the question of both Caesar and Pompey renouncing their proconsulships adjourned, and the matter was left as much in the air as before – but without the threat to Caesar of being left defenceless while Pompey held the reins of power in Italy. The ideal solution for the senators, of course, would have been to get rid of both Pompey and Caesar but, 'who holds the armies, holds power', as Caesar had remarked. The senators trusted neither man, but they feared Caesar the more.

It was probably on this account that they did achieve one significant action. Since the disaster and death of Crassus against the Parthians, the state of Syria had become of some concern, and the senate accordingly asked that one legion from both Caesar's and Pompey's forces should be detached and sent to reinforce this important province in the East. If their idea was to weaken each of the opponents equally they failed, for Pompey, while readily agreeing to their request, asked his associate Caesar to detach the legion that Pompey had lent him during the previous Gallic troubles and send it to Italy *en route* for Syria. This meant in effect that Caesar had to deprive himself of two legions, and Pompey of none. Caesar, although of course well aware of the ploy, agreed – on the surface readily enough. But he was determined to make this gift of the two legions something of a Trojan Horse within Italy. He knew that he could rely upon his own soldiers for their attachment to his cause. He had always known how to handle the legionaries, and his bravery in battle and military brilliance made him their favourite, while his successes naturally brought them money. As a parting gift, however, he saw to it that each soldier received a handsome gratuity and he then left with them and their officers the words with which he intended to fool his opponent. All the soldiers, they were to say, were worn out with Caesar's incessant campaigns, they suspected him of seeking the monarchy, they would all desert him if it came to a conflict between him and Pompey, and all they wanted was to leave Caesar's command, come home to Italy and serve under Pompey. The latter was, in due course, as deceived as Caesar had hoped:

Upon this Pompey grew presumptuous, and neglected all war-like preparations, as fearing no danger, and used no other means against him than mere speeches and votes, for which Caesar cared nothing.

(Plutarch)

These two legions, when they reached Italy, were not embarked and sent on to Syria but were posted to Capua north of Naples – on the grounds that the situation in the East no longer warranted their despatch. Pompey relaxed and, when danger threatened and there were rumours of Caesar massing troops in Gaul, he smiled and said: 'Wherever I strike the ground in Italy with my foot, legions will spring forth.'

The consul Marcellus, who had shown himself violently anti-Caesar (and nearly all of whose moves had been blocked by Curio's veto), believing or pretending to believe the rumours that Caesar was massing troops in Gaul for an advance on Rome, asked the senate to declare Caesar an enemy of the republic. He further asked that the troops now stationed in Capua should be moved north to block any advance that Caesar might make. Curio once again opposed him, and brought evidence that the news was false. (Caesar had, in fact, stationed three legions in the south of Narbonese Gaul in case of any threat arising from Pompey's legions in Spain.) Marcellus, acting on his own behalf and accompanied by the two consuls designate for the next year, now called on Pompey who was by arrangement waiting for them outside the city boundaries – where the authority of a tribune such as Curio was not valid. There Marcellus, backed by his colleagues, gave Pompey the authority to march against Caesar 'in defence of the country'. He was entrusted with the command of the troops at Capua as well as others throughout Italy, and authorized to raise further troops as he saw fit. This arbitrary action by Marcellus, without the approval of the senate, had the result of precipitating the conflict which, in theory at least, it was intended to avoid. Pompey accepted the charge laid upon him and began at once to prepare orders for mobilization. Cicero, who had somehow or other managed to remain on good terms with both Pompey and Caesar, still hoped that some compromise could be effected between them. But, meeting Pompey on his way down to Capua in early December, he was told that war was now inevitable.

CHAPTER TWENTY-THREE

Across the River

Caesar had spent part of the summer of 50 in a tour of his province of Cisalpine Gaul, where he had been received with such enthusiasm that one cannot help suspecting his election agents had been busy among the people well in advance. Certainly he had wanted the Romans to hear how popular he was among those whose lives he administered, and possibly hoped too that his enemies in that quarter would note how these hardy provincials (who had proved their worth in the legions) reacted to his presence. Now, in December, having made his dispositions for the troops in Gaul, he came back again to hear it confirmed that the two legions he had sent for the senate's use in Syria were held in Capua, and that Pompey was in command of them and was preparing to mobilize others. Curio joined Caesar in Ravenna, straight from the capital, where, according to Appian, he feared for his life and 'could no longer hope to serve Caesar's interests' – being no longer tribune since December. Other supporters would follow him to Ravenna as the unlikelihood of any reconciliation between Caesar and Pompey became more and more obvious. Meanwhile in Rome another of Caesar's protégés, Mark Antony, who had been elected as tribune in Curio's place, was already busy doing his best to protect his interests.

In Cisalpine Gaul Caesar was busy seeing to the concentration of the single legion in Cisalpine Gaul, and arranging with great secrecy for other legions from Transalpine Gaul to start for Italy. With only one legion to hand, he was far outnumbered by the forces at Pompey's disposal, and for this reason he temporized as far as possible and continued negotiations with the senate. It was far from certain, if it came to civil war between himself and Pompey, that his followers would be in the majority – and almost certain that they would be among the most disreputable. Ever since the days of Catiline, indeed ever since Caesar had begun to practise the political arts, he had made himself the champion of the bankrupt, the dispossessed, the unscrupulous and the ill-famed. If 'the people' also followed him it was largely because they too, wittingly or unwittingly, had been bought. It was true that many members of the equestrian order were among his followers, as well as senior officers, the centurions and the soldiers, but most of the old ruling class looked on him askance.

Pompey, for his part, could lay claim to the support of a better and more well-established class of followers – differently, but not better-intentioned. When he had first come to Rome he had seen himself as Princeps, first above all, but he had gradually reconciled himself to being first among equals. Since his new marriage and his reconciliation with the *Optimates*, he had inclined towards their position. He had, after all, been a follower of Sulla and he never significantly changed. Earlier that year Cicero's correspondent Caelius had analyzed the situation in Rome as he saw it:

> I am sure of course that you realize that, in the case of a domestic dissension, men should support the side that is right so long as it is a matter of politics, but that when it comes to weapons and warfare then they must support the stronger side, taking the view that might is right. [Caelius finally chose Caesar's.] Now in this quarrel I perceive that Pompey will have with him the senate and the judiciary, but that Caesar will have the support of all those who have anything to fear and nothing to lose. In any case, the latter's army is infinitely better than Pompey's.

Caesar knew this as well as anybody, but it is clear that right up to the last he hoped that he could maintain his official dignity, acting in accordance with the rule of law and the requirements of the senate.

Early in December he informed the senate privately that he would be willing to give up his command of Transalpine Gaul and content himself with Cisalpine Gaul, Illyricum and only two legions until such time as he was consul. Although on the surface this meant that he was relinquishing the fruits of all his endeavours of recent years, it still meant in effect that he would not be standing for consul as a private citizen. Marcellus and those of Cato's persuasion remained adamant against making any concessions. Meanwhile Antony in his position as tribune continued to harass Pompey and his followers, carrying an edict through the popular Assembly requiring the immediate departure of the two legions for Syria and forbidding Pompey to mobilize any troops. While Cicero, who was now back in Italy, attempted to persuade Caesar to reduce his demands to Illyricum and one legion alone, and Cato spoke out against having any truck with him at all, one obscure senator proposed that Pompey should leave for his own province of Spain and thus armed conflict could be avoided. Naturally those who were dependent on the protection of Pompey indignantly rejected the suggestion. Prior to this, Curio had brought an official despatch from Caesar in Ravenna that, if he was not allowed to keep his provinces pending the elections, then he and all other holders of military commands (by which he meant Pompey) should resign their authority simultaneously. This met with such antagonism from the senate that it was clear to the tribunes, Antony and Cassius, that no further dialogue was possible.

The senate now hastened towards the fatal decree: Caesar, by a date which should be fixed at once, must disband his army on pain of being considered an enemy of the State. Antony attempted to use his veto but was ruled out of court on a legal nicety, debate about which then kept the members busy for many hours. But the real decision had been taken, although it was not until three days later that the senate finally gave the charge to the consuls and others in authority in the vicinity of the city (this included Pompey) to 'protect the interests of the state'. The two tribunes, Antony and Cassius, fled Rome disguised as slaves and made their way north to Caesar, and no doubt a good many others followed them. They knew that this was the real declaration of war against Caesar. Short of handing over his proconsular commands and coming to Rome as a private citizen (to deliver himself to his enemies) Caesar had no option but to act as he did. Arms were already being requisitioned throughout Italy, mobilization had been ordered, and the man appointed to relieve him of his command was L. Domitius, a sworn enemy ever since his consulship.

It was probably on the morning of 10 January 49 that Caesar heard of the senate's decision (it took three days to cover the 140 miles between Rome and Ravenna). He had at the moment only his one legion, whereas Pompey had the two at Capua and was mobilizing the resources of Italy and the Empire. Caesar had to move fast and – fortunately for him – this ability, which had proved itself so valuable in Gaul, remained one of his greatest assets. Pompey, a slightly older man, had never felt the necessity in his eastern campaigns for the mercurial flexibility that Caesar had required against untried enemies in unknown countries. Any doubts Caesar may have had in the preceding weeks were resolved by now. The news from the senate that he had been declared an enemy of the state was unknown as yet to his men; so too the fact that the two tribunes (whose persons were supposed to be sacrosanct) had fled the city. His dispositions were all made. Two experienced legions were on their way from Gaul, as well as twenty-two new cohorts, while the three legions in the south of the province guarded his western flank against any attack by Pompey's supporters in Spain. Many legends were later to surround all the circumstances of that fateful day, and both Plutarch and Suetonius have their own accounts, which, though they vary in details, present the same overall picture. Suetonius writes as follows:

> When the news came that the veto of the tribunes had been disallowed and that they themselves had fled the city, he immediately sent a few cohorts ahead with all secrecy, and disarmed suspicion by appearing at a public show, inspecting the plans of a gladiatorial school which he proposed building, and dining as usual with a number of guests. After sunset he set out very secretly with some members of his staff, having borrowed the mules from a nearby baker's shop and harnessed them to a small carriage. When the lights went out, he lost his way and they wandered aimlessly for some time, until at last at dawn they found a guide who led them back on foot by narrow lanes until they reached the road. Caesar overtook his advance guard at the boundary of his province, the river Rubicon, which formed the frontier between Italy and Gaul. Well aware of what a step he was taking he paused a while and then turned to his staff, saying: 'We may still draw back, but once across that little bridge and the issue rests with the sword.'

Appian, on unknown authority, has him hesitate at this moment, while Plutarch, basing his account on Asinius Pollio, an intimate of Caesar's who was present at the time, also has him debate what calamities his crossing the river might bring upon the human race. But such hesitation as there may have been was clearly momentary. With the gambler's cry 'The die is cast!' or, in another account, with the words from Menander, his favourite Greek poet, 'Let the dice fly high!' he gestured forward across the river.

The Rubicon (now called the Fiumicino, little river or stream) was nothing in itself; it was what it represented. By taking his army across the boundary between his province and the Italian homeland, Caesar was breaking a Sullan law which forbade governors to do just this, for the great dictator had foreseen the dangers to the state from ambitious commanders. Caesar was now guilty of the very treason of which he had already been accused.

CHAPTER TWENTY-FOUR

Civil War

One legion was little enough with which to invade a country and attack an empire. There must have been those in Rome who, knowing the situation, felt confident that Caesar would never dare to move – at least until he had been reinforced from Gaul, by which time Pompey would have more than adequate forces to deal with him. But Pompey had seen no active service since 62; he was now in his fifties; his life since 60 had been lived in Rome, and he had recently been seriously ill. Most important of all, although he boasted that he could call on ten legions, except for the two Caesar had sent him from Gaul, the only troops available in Italy were unseasoned recruits, and his own veterans from the Eastern wars retired to their farms and small holdings.

After crossing into Italy Caesar's legion, divided into two columns of five cohorts each, struck south-east towards Ariminum (Rimini) on the Adriatic coast and due south at Arretium (Arezzo) the heart of Etruria, the first column under Caesar and the second under Antony. There was no opposition to Caesar when he arrived at Ariminum, where he addressed the troops and explained the circumstances under which he had been compelled to invade the homeland. His rhetorical skill was not wasted upon soldiers who were in any case attached to him, and who knew of Pompey only as some general who years ago had been victorious against decadent kings and leaders in the East. Caesar successfully played upon the fact that Pompey represented the men who were most remote from ordinary soldiers – the kind of senators they had heard of but never seen near a battlefield – and that Pompey himself was 'a leader enervated by a long peace'. Their indignation at the treatment that had been accorded to the tribunes by the senate in Rome (although no one had ever laid a hand upon them) and the fact that they had sought shelter with Caesar was enough to allay any qualms they may have had about invading Italy. Their general, and the sacrosanct officials, had been wronged by those insolent senators in Rome – that was quite enough for any simple soldier who probably, like most servicemen throughout history, had little time for politicians and civilians.

As soon as it was known that Caesar's forces had occupied Ariminum, the gates of other cities, as Plutarch records, were opened wide. There was no opposition, and by mid-January Arretium had been occupied as well as Ancona, south from Ariminum on the Adriatic. Caesar's purpose in sending a flying column down the coast was to cut off Pompey from the sea, for he knew well enough that Pompey, if he did not stand and fight, would try and escape to the east by sea. There was instant panic when the news of the fall of these two cities reached Rome within a day or two. Not since Hannibal had come storming over the Alps over a century and a half before had Rome been in such a state, the inhabitants from outlying cities fleeing in to add to the confusion while the adherents of Pompey were either blaming him for not foreseeing this eventuality or taking to their heels for their country estates. Two envoys from the senate had meanwhile been sent to Caesar at Ariminum, where he maintained his headquarters, conveying to him the instructions which had become invalid from the moment he moved into Italy. Privately they brought him a message from Pompey in which he maintained that the present situation was not of his making and asked Caesar to place the interests of the republic above his own. Caesar replied with a statement of his grievances and the conditions for his retiring within the boundary of his province. These were unacceptable, including, as they did, the demand that after both had disbanded their troops Pompey should retire to his province of Spain. In any case, by the time that the envoys had made their way back to Rome they found that Pompey had already left, as had the consuls, the senators and many of the people. Before this exodus Pompey had been roundly abused for his lack of foresight and energy, and mocked by a supporter of Cato who had called upon him to 'strike the ground with his foot now' and call up his legions.

As town after town opened its gates to Caesar, and as there was no opposition, his invasion with only a few thousand men was an astonishing success. Among the rich and powerful there was an overwhelming feeling that they should have accepted Caesar's conditions – that they should still accept them – and even Cato seems to have believed that submission was better than civil war. But, although his lightning advance had so far succeeded, Caesar cannot have been entirely happy about the situation. He knew that Pompey, even if he continued to retreat in Italy, would probably follow the example of Sulla and attempt to recover Italy from the east, where all the legions were at his command, as were those of Spain. He would thus be in the position of being able to attack Italy from both quarters. Furthermore, it cannot have pleased Caesar that he had been forced into committing a treasonable act and that now, with the senate having fled from Rome, he could not deal with the legitimate government but must appear in the eyes of all respectable citizens as no more than a revolutionary.

As this moment he was disturbed by the news that Labienus had gone over to the other camp and had placed himself at Pompey's disposal. This was not entirely a surprise, for Caesar had suspected for some time that his lieutenant had become jealous of him and wanted to be his equal, if no more. But Labienus could certainly give Pompey and his supporters a lot of invaluable information about the state of Caesar's troops: how many were available in Gaul and details of his supply position. Meanwhile the advance rolled on effortlessly, towns and hamlets declaring themselves open to Caesar's forces. In the few places where enemies of Caesar attempted to rally people against him the consensus of public opinion was that he deserved well of his country and that they should show no resistance. The absurdity of the military position was that Caesar, with only ten cohorts divided up into flying columns, was rolling up Italy before him, and that behind those advancing spearheads he had nothing whatsoever . . .

Meanwhile Pompey had withdrawn to the region of Capua in Campania. It seems clear that he had already decided to withdraw from Italy altogether and to fight from the East, for wherever troops of his had been left behind in garrisons they were always ordered to retire at the approach of any of Caesar's forces. Rumours were rampant that a large fleet was being prepared for Pompey at Brundisium (Brindisi) to take his army to Greece or some unknown destination in the East. This was something that did not appeal to most of the soldiers, and the steady influx of deserters to Caesar's camp suggests that Pompey's overall strategy was entirely wrong. The continued retreat in front of the invading forces, without giving battle at any time, was very bad for morale, as was the rumoured evacuation. Pompey's great weakness was that he had been out of command for too long, and that all his successes had been in the East. He was somewhat like a nineteenth-century 'old India Hand' in the British Army, dreaming always of other campaigns in another country.

Caesar had by now been reinforced by the first of the fresh troops from Transalpine Gaul, the Twelfth legion, and could continue with renewed confidence, having twenty cohorts to deal with a force that seemed to be dissolving before him. Early in February he had gained control of Picenum, a narrow strip of Adriatic coastline where his feeling of success must have been heightened by the fact that it was an area which came under the patronage of Pompey himself – although that did not prevent the citizens from inviting Caesar into their towns and many of the legionaries coming over to his side. Only in one place did it look as if he might face resistance and this was the fortified town of Corfinium in the Abruzzi, where some nineteen cohorts were assembled under the command of his bitter enemy, L. Domitius Ahenobarbus. Despite Pompey's orders for him to withdraw and join him at Brundisium, the rich and powerful Domitius, prompted by his hatred of Caesar and confident in the fact that he was the greatest landowner in the area and should be able to count on the loyalty of the local people, decided to resist. Feeling that he had sufficient troops to meet Caesar's and that the defences of Corfinium would defeat him, he was strengthened in his decision not to yield by the fact that he was the appointed successor to Caesar as the new governor of Gaul. A number of other politicians, senators and members of the equestrian order shared his views and decided to stay. Domitius sent a message to Pompey appealing to him to come to the aid of Corfinium, but the general was intent only on getting his forces out of Italy to Greece and by the time that his reply to Domitius arrived – urging him to do as he was told and not risk a siege – Caesar's troops had surrounded the town. Reinforced from Gaul, he had Corfinium completely cut off, and it was only a week before the troops inside the walls decided to abandon Domitius and hand him over to Caesar. Fifty prisoners in all were brought before him, not only Domitius but Publius Lentulus Spinther, the consul of 57 and one-time ally of Caesar, as well as Optimate senators who had consistently opposed him and who, knowing his record from Gaul, cannot have been hopeful that they would be shown any mercy. Caesar, to their complete astonishment, set them all at liberty. They were free to go as they pleased, to join Pompey if they wished, and even a large sum of money which had been deposited in the city treasury for the payment of Pompey's troops was handed over. The legionaries in the town who had revolted against these leaders all now offered Caesar their oath of fidelity and were accepted into his army. Domitius and the others, all with profuse expressions of thanks, accepted their freedom – and went off to continue to fight against him.

The clemency of Corfinium had its desired effect and even Cicero, who was nervously hesitating about coming to a decision, could not fail to realize what Caesar had achieved by this totally unexpected act. In a letter which he probably expected to be widely copied and read Caesar wrote: 'History proves that nothing is earned by cruelty but hatred ... Why should we not arm ourselves with generosity and compassion as our weapons?' The sophisticated and the cynical might still distrust him, but it soon became clear that soldiers felt differently. Nine cohorts which were being withdrawn from various places to join Pompey at Brundisium deserted their officers and made their way to Caesar's camp. Cicero, still inclined towards Pompey because of his distrust of Caesar, commented in a letter to his friend Atticus:

Do you see what a man the Republic is up against, his foresight, his alertness, his readiness? If he kills no one and takes nothing away from anyone, I guess he will be most loved by those who formerly were most afraid of him.

While the assembly of Pompey's fleet at Brundisium and the mustering of his forces continued, Caesar was still trying to renew negotiations. In *The Civil War* he reiterates how much he wanted peace, and to spare the country the horrors that must inevitably follow if no agreement could be reached. When one considers the necessity for self-justificatory propaganda and remembers (as one must always remember in Caesar's writings) that he is not the dispassionate historian but the totally involved participant, then other reasons must present themselves as to why he wanted to keep negotiations going on as long as possible. First of all, he knew the fighting capabilities and the morale of his own soldiers, and he knew by the desertions the state of things on the other side. This must have suggested to him that in Italy he could win. On the other hand, he knew that Pompey had seven legions under trusted legates in Spain and that a determined push into Gaul could overwhelm the legions he himself had left there. The Gauls would then rise, and a triumphant army, reinforced by Gauls, could sweep into Italy behind his back if he were to follow Pompey east. He would in any case have found it very difficult to follow Pompey into Greece or even farther east, for Pompey had the ships (and would leave few or none behind), and his troops had also stripped Italy of stores and weapons as they retreated. If he could not come to an agreement with Pompey – or defeat him before he left – then his first concern would have to be the elimination of the threat from Spain.

CHAPTER TWENTY-FIVE

Rome, Marseilles, Spain

Caesar's attempts to negotiate with Pompey and, in the process, detach him from his *Optimate* friends, had all failed. His triumphant march through Italy had not brought him the one thing he wanted. This was the acceptance by all those officially in authority – the senate, ex-consuls and jurists such as Cicero – that he was not acting outside the law but had right on his side. This was more important to him than bringing Pompey to battle (something which he seems genuinely to have wanted to avoid), but his enemies were equally determined that he should be made to appear in the wrong at all cost. Pompey's withdrawal from Italy, along with most of the senate, was one way of ensuring this, and Pompey managed it very successfully. In mid-March he skilfully extricated himself from Caesar's investment of the port of Brundisium, having deceived Caesar into thinking that most of his forces were inside the walls when, in fact, they had nearly all left. Both the consuls had already sailed for Dyrrachium (Durazzo), while the bulk of the senate and many of the young patricians accompanied him. As far as he was concerned this whole move (which he had long planned in the event of an attack by Caesar) was not a retreat but a tactical example of *reculer pour mieux sauter*. Following the example of Sulla, he would make for the East where so much of his strength lay and reorganize his forces before invading Italy. Not only the East was his, but Africa and Spain, leaving Caesar with only Italy itself and Gaul (a dubious asset perhaps).

Caesar was now master of all the homeland, but the war itself had not yet begun. He was faced with a further problem. Not only Africa, but Sicily and Sardinia remained loyal to Pompey, and these were important grain-producing areas upon which Rome depended. With his control of the sea Pompey was in a position to strangle the lifelines to Rome; and Caesar knew well enough that, though the bulk of the people might now be in his favour, they would very quickly change their minds when their food supplies were threatened. In the sphere of action Spain must come first, but before moving westward he hoped to negotiate with such senators as were still in Rome, using as his credentials the two tribunes, Antony and Cassius. But he needed other respected senior figures to give him support, and he clearly thought that Cicero was worth a great deal for his oratory and his moral authority. A meeting was finally arranged and took place at Formiae (Formia) which in the event proved satisfactory to neither party: Caesar wanted authentication of his actions and Cicero was unwilling to provide it. His letter to Atticus of 29 March 49 BC gives the picture:

I spoke so as to earn Caesar's respect rather than his gratitude, and I persisted in my resolve – not to go to Rome. Where I was mistaken was in supposing he would be easy to handle – I never saw anyone less so! He said that my decisions amounted to condemning him, and that if I did not come others would be reluctant to do so . . . The upshot was that, by way of ending the interview, he asked me to think it over. To this I could not say no, and so we parted. The result is that I don't think he is very pleased with me.

The meeting of the rump of the senate, legally summoned though it was by the tribunes Antony and Cassius, was a sorry affair and poorly attended. It was clear that Caesar would not be able to run the country with such senators as remained and that, against his wish, he would have to do it on his own – illegally or not. Having come to this conclusion he committed himself to the use of force against the sacred treasury held in the temple of Saturn, which the Pompeian consuls in their undignified flight from the city had omitted to take with them. Thousands of bars of gold and silver as well as millions of coins were transferred into Caesar's keeping, his argument being that he needed the money to prosecute the war. 'And so,' as the poet Lucan wrote, 'Rome was for the first time poorer than Caesar.' But he left the city in a very bad humour, for the senate had contributed nothing towards any feeling of legality to his cause, while even his popularity with the common people had taken an abrupt fall after his looting of the treasury.

Before leaving for his Spanish campaign he secured the grain so urgently needed in Italy by having Sicily occupied and Sardinia taken under protection. Mark Antony was left in command of the troops in the peninsula, and the Adriatic and Tyrrhenian seas were held by fleets under reliable friends. After the initial impetus of his invasion everything had turned into frustration and inaction, but Caesar now felt cheerful again and joked that he was about to take the field against an army without a leader, and that when he returned he would deal with a leader without an army. However first he was to meet an unexpected and unwelcome event on his route to Spain. Rome's ancient ally Massilia (Marseilles), that famous Greek city-state, had declared for neutrality in the civil war between Caesar and Pompey. No fault could have been found with this decision, but it was reached by senior citizens who, while maintaining that their state was equally indebted to Pompey and Caesar, now clearly demonstrated that they preferred Pompey's cause. Furthermore, they even admitted Domitius, Caesar's defeated enemy from Corfinium, into their harbour with a squadron of ships and put him in charge of defence measures. The importance of Massilia, lying on the flank of his route to Spain, was obvious enough, and Caesar immediately began to besiege it with three legions, as well as ordering the construction of a number of ships to enforce a blockade. Although he began supervising all the details himself, eager to see Massilia reduced before he left, so tough were the walls and the resistance that things dragged on and he could no longer delay.

In Spain six of his legions from Gaul were awaiting his orders. With his legate, Gaius Fabius, in command they were stationed near the fortified town of Ilerda, facing the five legions of Afranius and Petreius, the two most experienced of the Pompeian generals. Caesar had superiority over them in his excellent Gallic cavalry, 3,000 of them, all Celtic noblemen selected by Caesar himself (a method which served to distribute honour and at the same time keep their country quiet). For a time, however, his plans were upset by a flood disaster; bridges upon which he was dependent for supplies were swept away, and his enemies, experienced in the local terrain, were having some success. At Massilia, too, things were not going well for the besiegers, and all the signs – as they were read at Rome – seemed to indicate that in these first stages of the war fortune was favouring Pompey. There were a number of surprising political desertions and the rumour, which had no substance in truth, that Pompey was moving round by North Africa to march through Spain amid the cheers of the Spanish people caused a heavy fall in Caesar's stock. Then Caesar managed to get his forces in Spain out of their predicament -- largely by building a number of small leather boats (of the coracle type such as he had seen in Britain) by which means he secured his supply position. At the same time affairs took a turn for the better in Massilia, where Decimus Brutus, in command of Caesar's new blockading fleet, successfully held the ring around the city against a desperate attempt by the besieged to break out.

This improvement in events led to a number of the Spanish communities, particularly those north of the Ebro, declaring for Caesar, which in its turn led to the two Pompeian leaders deciding to shift their basis of operations into territory where they felt the magic of

Pompey's name still held sway. Finally, after a long and gruelling chase, Caesar came up with them near Ilerda, and it soon became evident that many of the officers and soldiers in the Pompeian army were only too eager to fraternize with the Caesarians. The heart of many of them was not in Pompey's cause and when, Caesar having cut off their water supplies, they were forced to sue for peace in the hot Spanish summer, there could be no doubt that the policy of clemency which he had initiated at Corfinium would again yield dividends. For although men such as Domitius had gone straight to Massilia to fight against Caesar again, and other senators had gone on to join Pompey, the bulk of the centurions and the legionaries had come over to his side – and it was they who won battles. At Ilerda Pompey's two legates, Afranius and Petreius, were allowed to go free while their troops were dismissed from service. Caesar's one wish was to see these armies which Pompey had kept for so many years in Spain, solely with the aim of threatening his position, disbanded so that they could no longer be used against him. He had proved his ability to his own soldiers and to the rest of the Roman world in this second round of the civil war. In just forty days, he had defeated Pompey's Spanish legions under his two best generals and at almost the same time the people of Massilia were forced to capitulate. It was the end of the long and fine history of an independent city-state and from now on Massilia would pay the penalty, losing much of its trade to Narbonne. In Farther Spain, where Caesar from his earlier activities had preserved a faithful following of clients, the whole province went over to him without demur. In so short a time had Pompey's Spain – and Pompey's legions in the west – fallen from his grasp. Those who, like Cicero, had at long last decided to commit themselves to Pompey's cause must have felt a distinct shiver down the spine . . .

At the same time, not everything upon the great canvas of the war showed in Caesar's favour. Curio, who had successfully secured Sicily for him, had gone on from there to North Africa where he had been defeated and killed by Juba, the pro-Pompey King of Numidia. At sea, the old master of the naval arm had triumphed over one of Caesar's lieutenants, the brother of Mark Antony, in the Adriatic. The worst news of all, however, came from northern Italy itself, an area where Caesar normally felt secure in the affection of its people and its legions. A mutiny had broken out among the troops at Placentia (Piacenza). It is worth observing that there is no evidence of this important and unusual event in Caesar's *Civil War*: the whole incident is passed over as if it never happened. Appian and Dio Cassius tell the story which Caesar clearly preferred not to record. The mutiny began in the Ninth Legion, which had suffered badly in Spain and was dissatisfied with the very limited spoils which had come out of that campaign. The legionaries who had served in Gaul had been able to amass considerable private fortunes (and slaves to carry them) but in the Spanish campaign, fighting against fellow Romans and conforming to Caesar's new policy of generosity towards the Pompeian enemy, the ordinary soldier found that a hard-fought campaign had yielded very little profit. Furthermore, Pompey's defeated troops had gone off happily to return to their homes, while they, the victors, only saw a never-ending road of war stretching ahead of them – with very uncertain returns.

Caesar's relationship with his legionaries was a very personal one. It stood or fell by the fact that there was mutual trust and that, in return for their allegiance, he would see that they enjoyed the spoils of war and, ultimately, the gift of suitable farmland on which to retire. At the same time his command as *imperator* had to be respected and obeyed implicitly. Arrived at the scene of the mutiny, Caesar addressed the mutineers and pointed out that long-established military usage held that there was only one answer to their crime: decimation. One man in every ten accordingly should be taken from the Ninth Legion and executed. At this the whole legion begged to be allowed to remain in his service, and the officers fell at his feet in supplication. Caesar, who could ill spare a single man, granted them stay of execution but insisted that 120 ringleaders should be handed over, twelve of whom were chosen by lot to be put to death. When one of these twelve was able to prove that he was absent at the time of the conspiracy, Caesar had the centurion who had accused him put to death in his place. Discipline and respect were maintained: the mutiny was over.

Just before the trouble at Placentia Caesar had received the agreeable news that he had been nominated dictator by order of the people, on the grounds that – both consuls being away from Italy – the affairs of the republic required a dictator to provide a legally constituted authority. This nomination earned the praetor Marcus Aemilius Lepidus, who had proposed him on the people's behalf, the governorship of Spain. Caesar could now, for the first time since crossing the Rubicon, feel that he had constitutional authority on his side and, as dictator, he had the right to hold consular elections. He was now lawfully elected to the consulship for the following year together with one of his close supporters. For the moment, however, the significance of the dictatorship was that it gave him the power to deal with the greatest national emergency of all – the state of the economy. The chaotic conditions of the past half century had meant that more and more citizens had fallen into debt and, since the outbreak of the civil war, all financial transactions had come to a standstill. The wealthy, alarmed that their money might be seized, had simply ceased to put any into circulation. Nothing could be borrowed, debtors refused to pay, and creditors were driven to every possible means to attempt to recover their loans. In such a situation it was hardly surprising that there were those who, remembering Caesar's own financially unstable past, hoped that he would make a clean sweep by the general cancellation of all debts.

He moved with great circumspection through this minefield. He fully realized that, if he listened to the demagogues who were calling for the abolition of all debts, he would automatically antagonize those with money and power. At the same time he could not ignore altogether those many debtors whose votes were one of his sources of political strength. By a dictatorial edict, with the force of law, he came down against abolition but declared that the real estate offered by debtors, which creditors were obliged to accept in settlement, was to be assessed by specially appointed commissioners at its pre-war values. This was the best that he could do but it made no one happy, for the debtors had hoped to escape without payment and the creditors were bitter at receiving less than they felt was their due. In order to promote the liquidity of money he now limited the amount that anyone might hold in cash to 15,000 denarii. Naturally, this was difficult to enforce, but Caesar totally rejected the suggestion made in plebeian circles that slaves should be rewarded for denouncing masters whom they knew to be hoarding money. Rich men were uneasy enough as it was, and Caesar's measures, though they could hardly be popular, were felt to be far less severe than many of the wealthy had expected. Gradually confidence began to be restored on both sides and the movement of money began once again throughout the land.

Caesar now turned to the vexed questions of legislation which had been left in abeyance, first of all seeing to it that many friends who had been condemned to exile were allowed to return to Rome. Juba, the King of Numidia, who had defeated and killed Curio in his North African campaign and who staunchly supported Pompey, was declared an enemy of the Roman people. The people of Gades, in Spain, who had been promised their citizenship for their support of Caesar, were rewarded and the long-promised citizenship rights were awarded in Cisalpine Gaul. The descendants of all the victims of Sulla's rule were also recalled from exile.

These measures, to restore the economic stability of the state and to secure the support of many who now owed their return to his favour, were carried out, with his usual capacity for hard work and high speed, in ten days. He was named consul on the eleventh and, laying down the dictatorship, immediately left Rome for Brundisium. It is recorded that the people everywhere indicated that they wanted peace rather than a victory, but Caesar knew that he had done all that was possible to come to terms with Pompey. Peace would only be attained by his defeat.

CHAPTER TWENTY-SIX

War in Greece

Although it was the depth of winter Caesar determined to cross the Adriatic as soon as possible. Undoubtedly he knew that Pompey was still in eastern Greece, and Pompey will equally have heard of Caesar's arrival at Brundisium from his agents in the port. But Pompey was unlikely to believe that his enemy would dream of crossing the stormy Adriatic – harassed by the dreaded northerly (the modern *Bora*) and guarded also by his fleet under Caesar's long-term enemy and one-time fellow consul, Bibulus.

However Caesar was disappointed to find that there were not enough ships available to transport all the men he needed, and dismayed to find the low morale and poor health of the troops. The epic marches down the length of Italy, short rations, and ill health had reduced his army by many thousands (there had been desertions as well). They were also daunted by the thought of a dangerous sea-crossing, followed by further campaigning – once more against their fellow Romans, so with little chance of profit. Arms and equipment were short and the commissariat was a far call from that which had operated in Gaul. Caesar's instinct (almost invariably right in such matters) was to act, to move at once before poor morale should weaken into indiscipline and shortage of food turn into actual privation. The answer, it seemed to him, was to sail as soon as possible, seize the ports and towns in Epirus, the eastern coast of Greece, and re-arm and re-victual at Pompey's expense before the latter could move back across Greece to check him. A week in Brundisium was enough to tell him that Pompey's fleet was not keeping a tight blockade of the coast, being confident that no invading army would try to cross at that time of the year. But although the weather was often bad, Caesar knew that even in December/January calms intervened long enough to make the seventy-mile crossing feasible. He had hoped for more ships and more men, but all that he could muster was some 15,000 legionaries and 600 cavalry. As he was fond of saying, 'Luck is the greatest power in all things and especially in war,' adding, 'Luck can be given a helping hand.' It was here that in character he scored over Pompey, for the latter, a master planner and organizer, was accustomed to the deliberate, almost 'set-piece' battles of the East and not to the rough-and-tumble impromptus with which Caesar had grown familiar in Gaul. An enforced delay due to bad weather held up the first invasion fleet and, while the troops were waiting aboard in harbour, two more depleted legions arrived, so that it was with about 20,000 men that he finally set sail early in January 48.

Landing unopposed on the coast of Epirus, and undetected by any ships of Pompey's fleet, he moved rapidly towards Apollonia, a number of almost undefended small towns automatically coming over to what was, for the moment at least, the strongest side. Bibulus, waiting with the bulk of the Pompeian fleet at Corfu to guard the coast of Greece, flew into a rage when he learned of the landing and put to sea at once, determined to catch the invaders on the beachhead. He failed in this, but managed to fall in with the empty ships as they headed back to Italy to collect further troops. For the first time in his life he had some small revenge on Caesar – capturing thirty of the ships and killing all their crews. Ashamed at having failed in his main duty of preventing the invasion, he determined to see that no more ships got through and that the coast was tightly blockaded. In this he was successful, isolating Caesar from Mark Antony and his other lieutenants in Italy, preventing the much-needed reinforcements from arriving, and sowing some doubt in Caesar's mind as to whether he had been abandoned by his supporters in the homeland. It was three months before Antony was able to join him, bringing a further three legions and 800 cavalry.

Being master of Apollonia and another major town, Oricum, Caesar now turned to the politics of peace. He had been enjoined by both senate and popular assembly, and indeed all the people of Italy, to bring the matter to a conclusion without any further bloodshed. Civil war, they had clearly indicated, was not wanted and peace was desired by all. As bearer of his proposals to Pompey he sent the latter's former adjutant, Vibullius Rufus, who had been taken prisoner first of all at Corfinium, released and then captured once again in Spain. Caesar's proposals were that both sides should disarm, their respective generals taking an oath to do so in front of their assembled troops, and that the operation should be concluded within three days. Since neither he nor Pompey had been able to reach an agreement, the whole matter should next be referred to the senate and the popular assembly. In this way the public interest would be served and both leaders must accept their decision.

There can be no doubt that Caesar was accurately expressing the wishes of the people in these simple proposals, which also conformed exactly to his own wishes. Having eliminated Pompey's power in Spain, having all Italy behind him (including the city of Rome and its magistrates), and himself holding the rank of consul, Caesar was politically in so superior a position that he could hardly be challenged. Pompey, on the other hand, was faced with the fact that his army and his supporters were seriously disturbed by Caesar's unexpected arrival in Greece, and that if he refused the proposals it would be tantamount to accepting the blame for the continuation of the war. Nevertheless, on receiving the message as he was making for Dyrrachium (Durazzo), he was compelled to turn them down. For the first time since Caesar had crossed the Rubicon, Pompey was now technically and morally in the wrong.

Dyrrachium, the main seaport on the Greek mainland looking towards Corfu, and almost impregnable by reason of the broad marsh-lands that surrounded it, was the favourite debarkation port for Roman armies and the starting point of the Via Egnatia, the road that ran across Greece to Thessalonica. Caesar well knew that this was Pompey's main base and commissariat centre, and he was eager to reach it before his opponent. The conflict now turned into what amounted to a race to get to Dyrrachium first, both armies travelling by forced marches night and day, the men hardly pausing to eat, stragglers falling behind to die in the harsh wintry weather, and both sides destroying the country through which they passed in order to deny it to the other. 'If he or Caesar,' wrote Appian, 'saw dust or smoke in the distance each reckoned that this marked the passage of their foe, and urged on their troops even faster.'

It was Pompey who just managed to reach Dyrrachium first, thus fending Caesar away from his main store and supply base and preserving for himself the port from which he hoped ultimately to launch his attack on Italy. Caesar was forced to take up his stance on the north bank of the Apsus near Apollonia, while Pompey advanced against him as far as the river; and thus the two sides lay for several weeks facing each other without any major move being made. Caesar for his part was still waiting for his reinforcements from Italy, and Pompey was training his recruits up to a condition where he hoped they would match Caesar's battle-hardened veterans. By March Caesar was deeply worried by the lack of word from Italy, let alone the long-expected reinforcements, and began to wonder if he had been betrayed. He decided, as so often, that no one but himself could deal with an unknown and somewhat intangible situation. He remembered his earlier crossing of the Adriatic in a small boat and decided to repeat it. Plutarch tells the story:

At last he resolved upon a most hazardous experiment, and embarked, without anyone's knowledge, in a boat of twelve oars to cross over to Brundisium, though the sea was at that time covered with a vast fleet of the enemies. He got on board in the night time, in the dress of a slave, and throwing himself down like a person of no consequence, lay along the bottom of the vessel. The river Anius was to carry them down to sea, and there used to blow a gentle gale every morning from the land, which made it calm at the mouth of the river by driving the waves forward: but this night there had blown a strong wind from the sea, which overpowered that from the land, so that where the river met the influx of the seawater and the opposition of the waves, it was extremely rough and angry; and the current was beaten back with such a violent swell that the master of the boat could not make good his passage, but ordered his sailors to tack about and return. Caesar, upon this, discovers himself, and taking the man by the hand, who was surprised to see him there, said 'Go on, my friend, and fear nothing: you carry Caesar and his fortune in your boat.' The mariners, when they heard that, forgot the storm, and laying all their strength to their oars, did what they could to force their way down the river. But when it was to no purpose, and the vessel now took in much water, Caesar finding himself in such danger in the very mouth of the river, much against his will permitted the master to turn back. When he was come to land, his soldiers ran to him in a multitude, reproaching him for what he had done, and indignant that he should think himself not strong enough to get a victory by their sole assistance, but must disturb himself, and expose his life for those who were absent, as if he could not trust those who were with him.

Approaches were made to Caesar by members of Pompey's party suggesting to him that they might be prepared to lift the blockade of the coastline, although they could still hold out no prospects of a positive response by Pompey to his peace proposals. But Caesar realized that, although the blockade was preventing his reinforcements from crossing the Adriatic, it was causing great hardship and difficulty to the blockading fleet. Pompey's men could not get ashore either for stores or water so long as he maintained his grasp on the coast, and he decided to make no concession, since they themselves had little to offer him. (He had already managed to get a staff officer across with a message to Antony stressing the urgent need for reinforcements, and the latter was preparing to leave with a convoy while his legate Gabinius, mistrusting the sea crossing, was marching his troops round from Italy through Illyria.)

Remembering the mood of the Pompeian soldiers in Spain, Caesar used the long period of inaction to try and undermine the morale of his enemy. Before Ilerda there had been informal talks between individual soldiers and centurions, and here in Greece these were soon followed by discussions between members of Caesar's staff and their opposite numbers in Pompey's army. The latter's staff, however, finally realized the danger and decided to prevent any further fraternization; a rain of missiles was directed at some of Caesar's officers as they were attempting to address some Pompeian troops. Labienus, Caesar's former right-hand man, finally broke up this informal meeting by shouting out: 'Stop talking about any agreement! There can be no peace as far as we're concerned until the head of Caesar has been brought to us!'

Bibulus, worn out by his exertions on the wintry Adriatic, died of illness – but the blockade still continued. And then there came a day when the fleet of Antony was seen off the Illyrian coast, driven by the wind past Dyrrachium to fetch up some thirty miles to the north of Caesar, safe from the enemy. A few days later their forces were united and Caesar now had at his disposal some 34,000 soldiers and 1,400 cavalry – sufficient to enable him to initiate some action, even though still considerably outnumbered by Pompey's forces. Pompey however, true to his nature, had no intention of moving out to give battle, but was content to stay within his long fortifications, hoping that sickness and shortage of food would gradually wear down Caesar's troops until they could be despatched with ease or forced to surrender. He saw the treacherous marshlands around Apollonia as his greatest ally.

Caesar was well aware that time was on the side of his enemy, and that Pompey could wait as long as he pleased, with his supplies to hand and his fleet in command of the sea, while his own troops, already short of provisions and without the comfort of a garrison town behind them would gradually disintegrate. Action suited his nature, but it was clear in any case that it was up to him to make a move. Pompey had advanced a little north of the Apsus and Caesar followed suit, offering battle – which was refused. He now decided on a bold stroke and took his army round behind Pompey's lines, suddenly interposing himself between Pompey and his base of Dyrrachium. The latter, out-generalled, realized Caesar's intentions too late. He was forced to move his army onto a rocky plateau south of Caesar, whence he maintained his connection with Dyrrachium by sea. Despite the magnitude of the task, Caesar called on his veterans to surround the enemy with encircling fortifications (such as veterans from Gaul will have well remembered), while Pompey, in order to extend his already over-extended enemy, built a semi-circle of fourteen miles of fortification around his own troops. Throughout the spring and well into the summer the long chess game between the two masters carried on with move and countermove, Caesar seeking to complete the encirclement of his enemy while the latter blocked him wherever possible. The old master showed that he had lost none of his cunning in this positional warfare and, as events were to show, could even turn the tables on his younger opponent.

In the middle of July, when Caesar's investing forces were stretched to their utmost capacity, and when he was planning to arrange a break into Dyrrachium with the aid of traitors in the city, Pompey suddenly struck at the southernmost point of Caesar's line where it hinged upon the sea. He burst through, driving the Caesarians in flight, and set about consolidating his position and establishing a new camp on the spot. At a single blow the months of work that had gone into investing the Pompeian army were nullified. In a desperate attempt to conceal the gravity of this defeat from his troops Caesar attacked a legion that had become isolated in the enemy's camp. He was on the point of taking possession of it when the sudden appearance of Pompey, coming up in support with some five legions, caused a panic among Caesar's forces. They turned and fled, at least one thousand men were lost and – that gauge of morale – thirty-two standards. Coming at such a moment, when Caesar's main strategy had been smashed, this flight and these losses suggested that the end might be in sight.

From within his interior lines of communication Pompey looked set to lash out and destroy the whole Caesarian army. It may be that he did not realize the full gravity of what had happened, or it may be that his nature was always to 'Hasten slowly', but Pompey failed to take immediate advantage of the day's events. Caesar regrouped and the success was not followed up. After a desolate night, in which Caesar felt that he had entirely mishandled the campaign and that he should have marched deep into Greece rather than linger by the sea where Pompey had all the advantages, he roused himself next morning. He then gave his troops one of those speeches which, although we have his quoted words, can only be imagined in terms of its effect upon his hearers. The previous night he had privately said to his staff, 'The war would have been won today if the enemy had a man who knew how to conquer.' Now he reminded his troops of their successes throughout the long campaign, with Italy rid of the enemy and Pompey's forces in Spain completely worsted; the hostile sea was safely crossed, and all that they had now suffered was but one reversal of fortune. 'If things do not always fall right, Luck can be given a helping hand.' Discipline was quickly restored when the runaway standard bearers were simply demoted (rather than executed) and no one else was blamed. Appian tells us that 'his army was so moved by his moderation that they asked to march immediately against the enemy'.

Caesar had other plans for them. He had thought things out in the night, and was not going to waste any further time on trying to patch up an operation that had gone wrong. He was not a believer in that

'Consistency which,' as Bernard Berenson observed, 'requires you to be as ignorant today as you were a year ago' and had changed his whole plan of campaign. He urged his men to restrain their eagerness for battle until such time as he should call on them to show it. During the night he had the whole of his army move out quietly by various routes deep into Greece. At dawn next day Pompey was left to contemplate the ravaged entrenchments surrounding him and the empty land where his enemy had previously been.

CHAPTER TWENTY-SEVEN

Pharsalus

After a brief visit to Apollonia in order to hospitalize the more seriously wounded, as well as raise money for the future pay of his troops, Caesar took the route for Thessaly where he hoped to find the people well disposed towards him. But bad news travels fast and, particularly in a country like Greece that had suffered so much from the Romans, the word was that in this civil war Pompey was winning. Caesar's defeat at Dyrrachium, even though he had managed to turn it into a planned withdrawal, had been magnified by messengers from the Pompeian forces into a major defeat followed by the flight of Caesar and his army. (Indeed, several friends of Pompey, eager to curry favour, had already left for the island of Lesbos, where his wife was living, to tell her that her husband had won and the war was over.) The Greeks, therefore, whom Caesar had hoped to find friendly because of his previous favours to their country, adopted a hostile attitude and at Gomphi, the first town they came to in Thessaly, he found the gates of the city closed against him. Caesar knew that an example must at once be made in order to restore his prestige with the Greeks, and it was not difficult to induce his half-starved soldiers to attack the city once he promised to give it over to them to plunder – something they had seen nothing of for many months. Gomphi fell before the assault of these veterans and the rest of Thessaly trembled – and changed its mind about the attitude to be adopted towards Caesar. Revived by food, laden with loot, and flown with wine (particularly the Germans, Plutarch remarks) the 'defeated' army passed on, 'revelling on their march in Bacchanalian fashion' and their morale completely restored. After seven days of forced marches they reached the plain of Pharsalus where they pitched camp. It was high midsummer and the crops everywhere were ripening – one reason for Caesar's decision to call a halt. The Pompeians meanwhile, most of them convinced that Caesar's army was disheartened and disintegrating, had marched to Larissa north of Pharsalus, where they had joined up with his father-in-law, Metellus Scipio and the troops he had been raising in the East. Pompey's army now numbered in the region of 50,000 as well as 7,000 cavalry, an arm upon which he greatly relied for he knew that Caesar was short of horsemen. Meanwhile, encamped in the plain not far from the town of Pharsalus on the north bank of the river Enipeus, Caesar awaited him with his veterans – not more than 22,000 of them and only 1,000 cavalry.

Pompey's army, as it marched down from the north, was outwardly full of confidence but inwardly riven by dissension. Pompey himself seems to have mistrusted the feeling prevalent among his staff and the senators and young nobles who surrounded him that Caesar was a spent force. He had had months to take stock of his enemy's troops and he may well have suspected that his own men, and particularly the allies from the East who had just joined, were not of the same calibre. Having at least twice as many men as Caesar, he seems to have favoured a war of attrition, just as at Dyrrachium where it had finally paid off. His followers, on the other hand, were eager for battle, eager to conclude this war that they felt was already nearly over, and to proceed to the distribution of the spoils. So confident were they that they were already arguing as to who should have which office in the immediate future, who should be consul and when, who should take over which particular property of which Caesarian, and who should administer the various rich lands of the empire. Pompey's wise plan to wear Caesar down, and to use the weight of his numbers to cut Caesar's communications and gradually starve him out, was interpreted by them as the delaying tactics of an ageing man. Pompey, they reckoned, was enjoying his moment of power and was procrastinating because he did not want to become once more only a senior senator and citizen among his fellows. Labienus, eager for whatever motives to see his former chief defeated, was among those who pressed most eagerly for action.

On 9 August 48 BC the encounter at long last took place between the two men, the two factions and the two armies who were disputing the leadership of the Roman world. Pharsalus was obscure, even the exact location of the battlefield is still disputed, but the result was to influence the history of the Western world and – like a great stone dropped into a lake – the ripples from it spread out almost endlessly.

Caesar had been trying to provoke a battle ever since Pompey's forces arrived at Pharsalus and set up camp on slightly higher ground. Everything seemed in their favour: more men, younger men, a superior position, and some seven times the number of cavalry, and at last Pompey was provoked, more by his own supporters one suspects than by Caesar's openly displayed readiness to put the matter to the test. When Pompey finally deployed his troops for battle, everything was organized according to the kind of carefully-prepared plan that had always suited him well, whereas there was initially some confusion on

Caesar's side. Despairing that Pompey would ever attack, and ever conscious that his troops had almost exhausted their supplies, he was on the point of withdrawing to some other area where the land was still untouched and fresh food was available. But the moment that news was brought to him of activity in the enemy camp, soldiers drawing up in formation, cavalry massing, eagles and standards moving into position, Caesar gave the order to run up the signal for battle. The men who had begged to be allowed to engage the enemy again after the failure at Dyrrachium 'all wanted to get to grips with the enemy,' writes Dio Cassius, 'for they felt that after their ten-year-long experience of war they were more than a match for green troops'. They felt also that they did not have the stamina to continue the long business of fetching and carrying, preparing encampments and digging fortifications. Let them get it over and done with now – once and for all.

Caesar quickly appraised Pompey's carefully thought out dispositions. His right wing was anchored on the Enipeus river and held by some of the cohorts who had been brought back from Spain before the general capitulation in that province; the centre by two legions of recruits from Italy; and the left wing, under Domitius whom Caesar had defeated at Corfinium, by the two seasoned legions which Caesar had sent back to Italy on orders from the senate in the year 50. Here also was Labienus in command of all the cavalry, as well as the archers and slingers. It was noticeable that Pompey's command post was also established at this point: clearly Pompey had packed all his punch on the left. He intended to roll up Caesar's right wing, while holding in the centre and his own right, then cut the Caesarians to pieces as his cavalry outflanked and surrounded them.

Caesar accordingly put Antony on his own left wing, with the other ex-tribune Cassius Longinus in the centre, while he himself took the right wing facing Pompey with his favourite Tenth Legion. Caesar's troops were drawn up in the usual Roman formation of battle, a triple line, but with one notable exception. As soon as he had observed Pompey's dispositions, he had taken one cohort from the third line of each of the legions to make a reserve force of six cohorts. This he stationed on the right flank, immediately behind his own cavalry, and inclined at an angle to the right. Since it was to be anticipated that his 1,000 horsemen would soon be driven back by Pompey's 7,000, this reserve was designed to attack the enemy cavalry if they burst through. They were given special orders to 'strike the enemy in the face' whereas normally a soldier would go for a mounted man's legs and thighs. 'These young dandies,' he said, knowing that the cavalrymen would be nobles and knights, 'unused to battles and wounds, bedecked with flowers and wearing their hair long, will be anxious to protect their handsome faces, and will not like the glint of steel shining in their eyes.'

His other instructions were for the third line of legionaries not to engage until he himself gave the order, for he wished them to be a fresh reserve. As for Pompey's allies in the centre, he said, they were easterners and slaves and could almost be ignored since they would run. He also gave his officers a list of those among the enemy who were to be spared if encountered during the battle, among whom was Marcus Brutus, Servilia's son and possibly his own.

The attack was begun by Caesar's troops, one veteran centurion Gaius Crastinus (to whom a monument was later dedicated) leading the way, while Pompey's men stood their ground under orders to let the enemy make the running. Caesar's experienced legionaries, javelins levelled, having run half the distance between the armies and seeing they were not being met, halted to catch their breath, carefully discharged their javelins, and then took up the charge again. The behaviour of Pompey's allied troops was as Caesar had anticipated, and it was only where Roman met Roman (sometimes tragically calling one to another by name) that the battle was bitterly contested. As expected Pompey's cavalry attack was too much for Caesar's horsemen to withstand and they gave ground. Now was the decisive moment, and the reserve cohorts 'made such a vigorous charge,' as Caesar writes, 'that not one of them resisted.' Pompey's cavalry was overwhelmed by the unexpected attack. Plutarch confirms that the tactics which Caesar had commended to these legionaries proved irresistible:

Unwilling to endure the blows aimed at their faces – a danger for the present, a blemish for the future – they [Pompey's cavalrymen] could not bear the sight of the javelins, but turned their heads and covered their faces to protect themselves.

The flight of his cavalry spelled the ruin of Pompey. The archers and slingers behind them fell before the advancing Caesarians and the legion on Pompey's left wing, which had been protected by his cavalry, was completely exposed and began to be thrown back too. The allies, crying 'We are lost!' fled in a panic, and Pompey's whole centre began to collapse. Always sensitive to gains available from political warfare, Caesar had the heralds proclaim that the battle against Romans was now over and that only the allies should be pursued. The word passed through the entangled lines and the main action stopped. Pompey who, along with many others of the leaders, was already seeking refuge in the camp, found himself forced to flee yet again.

The battle of Pharsalus was over – or would have been had Caesar been Pompey. But, unlike his enemy, he 'knew how to conquer'. He urged on his exhausted troops – the whole battle took place on a plain in the height of Grecian summer – to pursue the Pompeians, who were fleeing to the surrounding hills. It was not until nightfall that the pursuit was abandoned, and at dawn next day those who had managed to escape, being cut off from water, came down from the hills and surrendered in their thousands. Pompey and all the leaders had got clean away, only Caesar's old foe Domitius lay dead on the field. Casualties among the Pompeians were heavy (Caesar says 15,000 but Appian 6,000), while according to Caesar only 200 of his own men were killed (Appian says 1,200), among whom were 30 centurions.

Caesar found Pompey's tent empty when he and his officers went through the camp, and he ate the meal prepared for his rival. The tents of the other Pompeian leaders are said to have been crowned with myrtles, shiny green with their white and scented flowers – something that must have pleased Caesar since the myrtle was sacred to his ancestress Venus and it was in her name 'Venus Victrix' that his troops had advanced to battle. A contrast is deliberately made between the austerity of the Caesarian camp and that of these aristocratic *Optimates*, where precious fabrics hung and goblets and pitchers of wine stood ready for the victory feast. Caesar made a point of burning unread the correspondence between Pompey and his father-in-law Metellus when it was brought to him. Later, walking among the bodies on the battlefield, he said: 'It was all their own doing. Despite all my achievements I, Gaius Caesar, would have been condemned if I had not appealed to my army for help.' Pompey and his followers meanwhile were riding hard for the Aegean coast, headed for the East where his star had risen.

CHAPTER TWENTY-EIGHT

In the East

Unlike the Pompeians, Caesar and his followers did not arrogantly anticipate an ultimate victory. For the moment it was enough to have won at Pharsalus, and Caesar's troops still had not much more than their pay to show for this long and hard war against their fellow Romans. Furthermore, all the resources of Asia and the eastern provinces remained at Pompey's disposal – as well as Africa and a fleet which ruled the Mediterranean. Unfortunately for him, he was to find out that the apparent affection and respect which he had enjoyed in the past from the countries of the East was as evanescent as a courtesan's smile.

Caesar's determination to make sure that a victory was carried through to its conclusion, which had been shown by his pursuit of Pompey's troops after Pharsalus and which had resulted in the surrender of nearly all his army, was equally matched by his determination to continue his policy of clemency towards the defeated. The only exception he made to this was that those whom he had spared once were usually, though not always, excluded from any further quarter. He was well aware that he would need many of Pompey's leading supporters in the reorganization of the Roman world that must follow the Civil War. It was not only their names but their brains that would be essential in dealing with the multitude of problems that the war had created, and the even greater multitude that had led to it. Among those who surrendered to him after Pharsalus was Servilia's son Marcus Brutus who had not been in the action but who came to see him while he was at Larissa on his way towards the Aegean coast in pursuit of Pompey. Whether Brutus was indeed his son or not, he was the kind of young man that Caesar wanted among his supporters. In any case, his permanent affection for Servilia will have inclined him towards Brutus, and the fact that he was Cato's nephew and emulated the latter's conservative views made him a valuable acquisition.

Meanwhile Pompey was reported to have made for Amphipolis, an important town near the Macedonian coast, where it was expected that he would take ship for Asia Minor. Caesar followed at the head of his cavalry but, finding him already flown and having no transports for his troops, made his way up to the Hellespont, where he could feel sure of finding some vessels available and where a short and easy crossing awaited them. Pompey was already finding out the fickleness of fame and the friendship that is so rapidly withdrawn when conquerors became losers. Reaching Lesbos where his wife awaited him (falsely cheered by the news that his friends had brought her after Dyrrachium) he found the Greek inhabitants already asking them to leave, for they naturally had no wish to be the scene of any further battles, nor to provoke the anger of Caesar (who had helped to besiege them all those years ago in his first military posting). Many options seemed open to Pompey – Armenia, Cilicia, scene of his triumph over the pirates, Syria and even Parthia (where Crassus had perished). But on all sides he learned that his presence would be unwelcome, and even Rhodes, his next port of call, while remaining polite was clearly cool towards him. Next he heard that Antioch in Cilicia had come out in favour of Caesar, so he went on to Cyprus *en route* for Egypt, having decided that would be the best place in which to raise money and to secure grain for his troops and further military support. Ptolemy Auletes, the Flute-Player, had partly owed his throne to Pompey and, although he was dead, it was his son Ptolemy XIII who now occupied the throne. In Alexandria Pompey hoped to claim some practical return for his previous help and patronage.

Caesar meanwhile was in Asia with two legions, after an astonishing crossing of the Hellespont in which he was only saved from disaster by that audacity, or supreme self-confidence, which never deserted him. While Caesar's troops were being ferried across in such lightweight transports and skiffs as were available, a Pompeian squadron of ten galleys, northward bound to join up with some states in the Black Sea who were favourable to Pompey, came upon them. Caesar himself was in one of these makeshift transports but, far from taking to flight, boldly approached the commander's galley and demanded his surrender. A squadron of ten warships could easily have sunk Caesar's straggling armada in the Hellespont, but their commander must have decided that Caesar was going to win the war, for he promptly, as a suppliant, begged him for pardon. Happily reinforced by this useful escort of warships, Caesar proceeded on his way.

Caesar was well aware that for the past years Pompey's had been the name which represented Roman power and authority throughout Asia and that it was the princes and provinces of Asia which had given him soldiers and ships for the current struggle. He knew also from his youthful experiences in Cilicia and Bithynia something of the temperament of the East and the way in which rulers were regarded in that part of the world. It was not just as a tourist, then, that he now visited the sights of that great land, but as one who was eager to establish his connection with the history not only of Rome but of the East itself. The poet Lucan in his epic *Pharsalia*, written in the reign of the Emperor Nero, points out the many connections between Caesar and the great Homeric past exemplified by the ruins of Troy which he now visited. Troy, after all, was the city of his ancestor Aeneas, son of the goddess Aphrodite, and it was as a son returned to the ancient home of his family that he now stood among its ruins. The pursuit of Pompey could wait while he established his links with the past and with his divine origins. In various temples of Asia, notably Antioch and Pergamum, miracles were said to have occurred at the time of the battle of Pharsalus, and not surprisingly Caesar does not hesitate to report them in his account of the war. The Greeks of Asia Minor, accustomed to paying divine honours to monarchs, were quick to see in Caesar, by reason of his accomplishments and his origins, a new ruler of Rome who could be equated with Alexander the Great. What more natural than that this new Alexander should look towards the city that bore his name – and towards which the defeated Pompey was making his way?

Embarked aboard a large galley in company with his wife Cornelia, Pompey was looking to Alexandria as the place in which to rest and restore his fortunes. What he could not know was the extent of the civil war now raging in Egypt between brother and sister. Civil war, fratricide, patricide and all the variants of murder within a family were not uncommon in the relationships between the incestuous, scorpion-like Ptolemies. On the death of Ptolemy Auletes in 51 the throne had been occupied by his daughter Cleopatra VII and her brother Ptolemy XIII: she was then eighteen and he ten. Despite the discrepancy of age there can be little doubt that they were formally married. To maintain their hold over their Egyptian subjects and the powerful priesthood, the Ptolemies had to practise the traditional royal incest of ancient Egypt, for as gods on earth, it was essential that they like the Pharaohs, should mate only with one another (or, at any rate, for it to appear so). But by the law of female succession the monarch's eldest daughter had inherited the Kingdom and Cleopatra VII had shown from an early age that she had a strong character and was politically intelligent, something which did not please the guardians appointed to look after the interests of her brother while he was still a minor. They wanted an amenable monarch whom they had trained, through whom they would wield power and whom they would marry off to an even younger sister, Arsinoë, in due course. In the year 48 Cleopatra, realizing that there was a plot afoot to have her murdered, fled the country and made her way to Syria where she proceeded to rally an army to relieve her brother and his guardians of the Egyptian throne.

It was into this Ptolemaic spider's web that Pompey inadvertently blundered when his ship put in at Pelusium, the port to the east of Alexandria at the mouth of the easternmost branch of the Nile. At this very moment the young King Ptolemy with his general Achillas and his army was encamped there, ready to repel the threat of Cleopatra and her army from Syria. When Pompey sent ashore to acquaint the Egyptians with his presence and to ask permission to land in their country there was a furious debate among Ptolemy's advisers. Should they accord Pompey asylum since he had been Egypt's patron and had preserved the Ptolemaic dynasty, or send him on his way so as not to provoke the victorious Caesar? But if they told him to go elsewhere, might he not choose Syria, where Cleopatra would certainly make use of Pompey's formidable military abilities? Best, they decided, to lure him ashore and make away with him, thus also ingratiating themselves with Caesar. 'And besides,' they concluded, 'dead men don't bite.'

The three councillors and guardians of the young king were Achillas, commander of the army, Theodotus, a Greek rhetorician in charge of the boy's education, and Pothinus, a eunuch, who was minister of finance and a typically Alexandrian palace intriguer. Having decided to kill Pompey, Achillas, as army commander, was elected to go out to meet him in a small boat, accompanied by a Roman officer who had once held command under Pompey and a Roman centurion. Designed to reassure him, they intended to murder him. They urged Pompey to come back with them to meet the King, saying that the port was too shallow for his galley to enter. As he stepped ashore, first one and then the other two drew their swords and stabbed him in the back. Drawing his robe over his head (as his enemy Caesar was one day to do) he fell dying. So ended Pompey the Great, the man who had cleared the Mediterranean of pirates, one of the outstanding generals of his time, but who had allowed men more cunning than himself to play upon his vanity. As J. A. Froude puts it: 'Unfortunately he had acquired a position by his negative virtues which was above his natural level, and misled him into overrating his capabilities.'

Caesar sailed for Alexandria from Rhodes, not waiting for the bulk of his troops to arrive and taking with him only a few cohorts. He was confident that the knowledge of his victory would be sufficient to put the Egyptians on his side and that Pompey had few enough men with him to present any real resistance. The aim of the three guardians of the young Ptolemy was, above all, to keep the Romans out of Egypt and to try to preserve such independence as was possible in a Mediterranean that was by now almost completely in the hands of Rome. Caesar, therefore, was little more welcome than Pompey, and their hope was that when they showed him evidence of Pompey's death they would persuade him to proceed happily on his way to Rome.

The production of Pompey's severed head and his signet ring was conclusive enough, but Caesar, after seeming to be moved to tears by the sight of his dead adversary (and his former son-in-law), sent the ring on to Rome as evidence and showed no sign of wishing to leave. He was in something of a quandary, for the followers of Pompey had dispersed in all directions, Africa was still held by his partisans, and he himself had incurred immense debts – largely to his troops. The Greek campaign had yielded nothing, except for the sack of Gomphi, for he had given strict instructions that the Greek cities should be left alone, and while in Asia, in order to secure the support of people who had been bled white by Roman tax gatherers, he had even been compelled to reduce the taxes. Not only his troops, but even his officers were owed money and if, as seemed likely, further campaigning lay ahead, Caesar needed to see that those who followed him found it worth their while. Egypt now presented him with a justifiable excuse for improving his financial position, for there could be no doubt that Caesar was owed an enormous sum by the heirs of the late Ptolemy. He had backed the Flute-Player's restoration as king and had secured him his title of 'Friend and Ally of the Roman People' to the tune of millions of denarii – still unpaid. Furthermore, the Egyptian government had provided fifty warships for the Pompeian cause (these had just returned) and some indemnity could certainly be exacted for this unfriendly action. Accordingly, Caesar decided to go ashore in Egypt not as a Roman general but in his capacity as consul representing the Republic on a business matter.

The sight of a Roman consul, preceded by men bearing the fasces signifying Roman power, and followed by Roman soldiers, was immediately and openly resented by one of the most volatile crowds in the world. The people of Alexandria were notorious for their inflammable nature, comprising, as Edward Gibbon wrote 'a various mixture of nations, [they] united the vanity and inconsistency of the Greeks with the superstition of the Egyptians.' They saw in this display of formal Roman power an intention on the part of Caesar to take over the sovereignty of their country. In the turmoil that arose, the victor of Pharsalus nonchalantly moved into the royal palace. Ptolemy XIII and his sister Cleopatra VII were still encamped against each other at Pelusium and the only royal occupants of the palace were two children, their brother and sister. It is unlikely that Caesar intended to stay long in Egypt, but he certainly did not mean to leave until the country had paid its debts and, now that he saw its confused state, until some order had been restored in its government.

The eunuch Pothinus, possibly the cleverest of Ptolemy's three guardians, was the only one at that time in Alexandria. He was also the minister of finance, so it was natural that he was the first with whom Caesar had any dealings. Their dissension over money matters was inevitable, and Pothinus was quick to send a message for Ptolemy to return to Alexandria, while Caesar, at the same time, was sending separate messages to both Ptolemy and his sister Cleopatra requesting them to come and see him so that he could sort out the affairs of their kingdom. As consul in 59 he had had their father restored as King, and as current consul it was his duty to see that the Flute-Player's descendants ruled Egypt in amity. This is Caesar's own version of things in his account of the civil war. What he does not say, of course, is that he hoped to complete the long-postponed dream of seizing Egypt for Rome, at the same time laying his hands on all the money that he needed.

Pothinus meanwhile was doing everything that he could to make the stay of Caesar and his troops as uncomfortable as possible and, according to Plutarch,

he openly was intolerable in his affronts to Caesar, both by his words and actions. For when Caesar's soldiers had musty and unwhole-some corn measured out to them, Pothinus told them that they must be content with it, since they were fed at another's cost. He ordered that his table should be served with wooden and earthen dishes, and said that Caesar had carried off all the gold and silver plate, under pretence of arrears of debt. For the present King's father owed Caesar one thousand seven hundred and fifty myriads of money; Caesar had formerly remitted to his children the rest, but thought fit to demand the thousand myriads at that time, to maintain his army. Pothinus told him that he had better go now and attend to his other affairs of greater consequence . . .

Young Ptolemy XIII returned to Alexandria, but there was as yet no sign of Cleopatra. She could not make her way down to the city through the Egyptian army which was facing her own, for Achillas the general would certainly have had her killed. Caesar told Ptolemy (which in effect meant Pothinus) that his army must be disbanded and withdrawn from the frontier. There was a formal refusal to obey the Roman's wishes, and Pothinus secretly sent to Achillas and told him to bring his army down to the city. Caesar had only a few thousand troops and Pothinus calculated that he could easily overcome them; Caesar could be killed like Pompey, and the war could then be carried on against Cleopatra. His plans were completely upset by the courage and quick wits of Cleopatra herself who, raised in the Byzantine intricacies and stony cruelties of the Ptolemaic court, realized that only her presence in

Alexandria could block Pothinus and her brother. Conversant with all the gossip of the Mediterranean world, she knew too that Caesar was susceptible to women.

Secretly embarking in a ship at Pelusium, she set sail for Alexandria and arrived off the city at nightfall. She then had herself taken ashore in a small boat by a Sicilian friend, Apollodorus, who rowed to the royal quay just below the walls of the palace. The Queen, wrapped in a roll of bedding or carpet which Apollodorus tied together with cord, was carried on his shoulder into the palace, Apollodorus replying to any questions from Caesar's soldiers that he was one of the palace servants. A man carrying a bundle over his shoulder would not have surprised them, for in the East it is not uncommon for a man to carry all his worldly possessions in his bedroll or a carpet. The famous meeting of Caesar and Cleopatra has been described and portrayed so often that the full point of it has been lost – Cleopatra's incredible courage in venturing right into the heartland of her enemies. Pothinus, her brother, and all his court were determined on her death, while the Romans and even Caesar himself might, for all she knew, have been brought over to their side. 'This ruse of hers,' says Plutarch, 'is said to have opened the way to Caesar's heart', while Dio Cassius writes that 'he was spellbound the moment he set eyes on her and she opened her mouth to speak'. What Caesar will have appreciated above all was that here – like himself – was another real gambler.

CHAPTER TWENTY-NINE
Alexandrian Affairs

The war that was to follow in Alexandria, a war almost as complex, dangerous and strange as the city in which it was fought, was sparked off by the love affair between Caesar and Cleopatra. It is probable (indeed, knowing Caesar, it is more than probable) that the two became lovers on that first night. Caesar was 52 and Cleopatra 21, but the discrepancy in ages was easily outweighed by the similarity of their temperaments. Whatever else, Cleopatra was certainly no political virgin, for her whole life had been passed in the murderous intricacies of the Ptolemaic court, and she was typical of her family in her desire for power. Caesar might be old enough to be her father, but she knew that it was only through this Roman that she could maintain her kingdom and her place as its ruler. Caesar was the most powerful man in the world, and for that she must love him. She was determined to be Queen of Egypt and she had only one weapon that her brother, backed by his advisers, did not have – her sex. Caesar for his part could have had all the lovers he wanted, but an agreeable young woman who was also the Queen of Egypt and whose restoration to the throne could clearly help him financially was indeed a present from his ancestress Aphrodite. She was also a witty and amusing companion, inheriting the intellectual capacities of some of the early Ptolemies. Plutarch remarked that 'she easily turned her tongue to any language that she wished'. She was a fluent and expressive Latin speaker, spoke Athenian Attic (the best Greek) and also knew the language of her people as well as those of the Ethiopians, Jews, Arabs and Syrians, Medes and Parthians, while 'her royal predecessors had not even bothered to learn the Egyptian language . . .' Dio Cassius said of her that 'her delightful manner of speaking was such that she captured all who listened to her', while Plutarch commented:

To know her was to be touched with an irresistible charm. Her form, coupled with the persuasiveness of her conversation, and her delightful style of behaviour – all these produced a blend of magic. Her delightful way of speaking was such as to win the heart. Her voice was like a lyre . . .

Cleopatra's presence in the palace was revealed to Ptolemy XIII and his minister Pothinus the following morning, when Caesar summoned the young King to his apartments. Devastated at the sight of his sister lounging comfortably at ease in the presence of the Roman general and consul, their immediate thought was that Caesar must have heard Cleopatra's side of the case and decided in her favour. He merely said that he was determined to stop this war between brother and sister and see that the will of their father was carried out, that his son and daughter should conjointly rule the kingdom. On hearing this the young King flew into a violent rage and rushed from the room. He ran to his friends and then, dashing the crown from his head in full view of the crowd, cried out that he was betrayed. The Roman guards, seeing a mob gathering at the gates of the palace, dragged the young King back inside, an act which aroused the indignation of the Alexandrians even further. The word swiftly went round that the exiled Cleopatra had returned and was in the company of Caesar – and that the Roman would use her to take over the kingdom from their rightful ruler Ptolemy XIII. But for the presence of the Roman legionaries on guard, the palace would have been invaded by the Alexandria mob.

Caesar realized that something must be done to calm the situation and called a meeting of all the people in which, speaking in his fluent Greek – the international language of that cosmopolitan capital – he read out to them the will of Ptolemy the Flute-Player. This specifically stated that Ptolemy XIII and Cleopatra VII should jointly rule Egypt. As he pointed out to the assembled throng, he was only doing what was incumbent upon him as representative of the Roman people to see that their late King's wishes were respected. The young Ptolemy, still trembling with rage, and Cleopatra, smiling with satisfaction, were officially reconciled in the presence of their subjects.

Nevertheless Caesar was in a very awkward position, in a hostile city with, he had no doubt, the Egyptian army marching down from Pelusium against him, while he had only a few thousand legionaries to hand. He must temporize, and he did so now by declaring that the island of Cyprus was restored to Egypt, and would be jointly ruled by the two other children, Ptolemy XIV and his sister Arsinoë. This did a great deal to allay the fears and suspicions of the people – although not, of course, among those who saw themselves deprived of their power and position. Naturally Caesar had no intention of fulfilling this promise to give back to Ptolemaic control the important and rich island which Rome had acquired only ten years before. It would have been immensely resented in Rome and would, even with the senate as demoralized as it was, have caused more trouble than he could have handled. But he had already sent a message to Calvinus in Asia to send two legions to Egypt, and he counted on their arrival before the situation worsened drastically.

His enemies will have been well aware that Caesar only had troops enough to man the palace and its surrounds and that he must have sent for reinforcements, but Achillas and his army were expected down from Pelusium before any help for Caesar could arrive. In the meantime Pothinus continued with his opposition to the Roman presence and, in that palace of murder and intrigue, was undoubtedly plotting the Roman's death, either by poison or the sword. Although outwardly nonchalant Caesar was careful about his security, but his relationship with Cleopatra undoubtedly delayed him in a situation from which he could, at that moment, have easily escaped. As sovereign master of the Roman world he could enjoy all the flattery he wished but, at the age of fifty-two, he cannot have been insensible to the charms of a physically attractive and highly intelligent young woman whose political aims so far as Egypt was concerned roughly coincided with his own.

Achillas with the army now arrived in Alexandria, and shortly afterwards the investment of the palace quarters began. At that time the Egyptian army consisted of about 20,000 men and some 2,000 cavalry. It was a heterogeneous collection: legionaries left behind from the time when a Roman army of occupation had been imposed on the country to maintain Ptolemy the Flute-Player on his throne, slaves and criminals from all parts of the eastern Mediterranean, as well as Greek mercenaries. Although no match for Caesar's battle-hardened legionaries, they outnumbered his troops by five to one and, backed as they were by a whole city which now rose to drive him out, constituted a formidable force if properly handled. Shortly after their arrival, determined to rid the palace of at least one source of disaffection, Caesar had the eunuch Pothinus executed for treachery.

Throughout 'The Alexandrian War', as it came to be called, Caesar and his legionaries held the palace and its complex of buildings together with its valuable hostages, the Flute-Player's four children, between whom no love was lost. The first major worry arose when the freshwater canals that fed the palace complex were either dammed or fouled with seawater. Adept at sieges and at depriving his opponents of water, he now found himself in that very unenviable position. However, not to be daunted, and well aware that veins of fresh water are often to be found on limestone headlands, he set his troops digging in the palace grounds. Water was soon discovered, and his legionaries were comforted by the knowledge that their leader's cleverness equalled his

171

known bravery. Quite early in the course of the war, Cleopatra's younger half-sister Arsinoë managed to escape from the palace in company with her tutor, the eunuch Ganymedes, another court intriguer of the same stamp as the dead Pothinus. Arsinoë now took the place of Ptolemy XIII, still a prisoner in the palace, as the centre of the popular revolt to evict the Romans, and shortly afterwards, Achillas, whose protégé was Ptolemy, was murdered at the instigation of Ganymedes and Arsinoë. With the young girl as his figurehead, the eunuch tutor now became the leader of the revolt.

The war in Alexandria, although it was petty compared with those other wars and battlefields in which Caesar was engaged, was nevertheless a highly dangerous one, and in its small circumference he is seen at his best as a man of action and infinite resource. Ganymedes now not only mounted a land attack on the palace quarter but threatened the seaward side by bringing up a large part of the Egyptian fleet: a grave threat to Caesar's communications as he was expecting troops from Asia Minor by sea. Making one of those lightning attacks which were the hallmark of so many of his successes, he managed to capture the Egyptian fleet and set it on fire. The flames spread to the quayside and, in the general conflagration and confusion, part of the world-famous library of Alexandria went up in flames. Antony would make some amends for this some years later by giving the great library of Pergamum to Cleopatra.

In another passage of the Alexandrian war Caesar took charge of the Roman ships that lay off the palace and went out to escort the vessels carrying the 37th Legion. This had arrived from Asia Minor, but was unable to enter harbour because of the Egyptian ships patrolling off the coast. Caesar embarked aboard his small galley fleet, manned only by Rhodian sailors since he had to leave his legionaries to garrison the beleaguered palace, and in the ensuing action soundly defeated the Egyptians, allowing the convoy to enter harbour safely. His attempt to capture the Pharos, Alexandria's great lighthouse and one of the Wonders of the World, even though it ended in failure and he nearly lost his life, showed the same spirit and audacity in the forefront of the action which never failed to endear him to his troops. On this occasion, an uncharacteristically bold move by the Egyptians had the Romans under Caesar trapped on the great dyke that led between the city of Alexandria and the island on which the Pharos stood. When they were forced to embark in small boats in order to escape, many men were lost through the boats being sunk or overturning under their weight. Caesar himself only managed to get clear of his craft by swimming for it (holding, so legend has it, important despatches in one hand so as to keep them out of the water). Even his purple general's cloak, upon which he set great store, had to be abandoned: it was later displayed over a trophy which Ganymedes and the Egyptians erected in memory of the Roman defeat.

It almost seems as if Caesar treated this early phase of the Alexandrian war in a lighthearted fashion, as some sort of escapade. But the loss of four hundred legionaries in the struggle for the Pharos, as well as a great many sailors, reminded him that he must play for time, and he reverted to his earlier policy of holding the palace position and waiting. In due course the land and sea forces which he had sent for from Syria and Asia Minor would arrive, capture Pelusium and take the Egyptian army in the back.

The politician in Caesar now took over. Hearing that the Egyptian army, unhappy with the combination of Arsinoë and her tutor Ganymedes, was still clamouring for Ptolemy to be restored to them, he decided to accede to their demands. This youth, the technical husband of Cleopatra, was no more than a nuisance to Caesar, since it had long been clear that the Egyptian people would not respect any commands he gave while he was in Roman hands. The two youngest children could remain in the palace as hostages, Cleopatra herself staying with Caesar of her own accord, but it seemed good tactics to restore Ptolemy XIII to the Alexandrians and the army. With his adviser Pothinus dead he was no more than a figurehead in any case, and as such, when the relief army came down and the Egyptians had to stand and fight, Ptolemy would be forced either to fly or to lead his troops in battle. In either case he was doomed. On being told that Caesar intended to restore him to his people the young Ptolemy is said to have burst into tears, saying that he did not want to leave Caesar and the palace. Clearly he saw his future prospects much as the Roman did, but he insisted on sending the Egyptian back to the embrace of his enthusiastic subjects – who promptly relieved Arsinoë and Ganymedes of the command of the army.

Mithridates of Pergamum, the son of a Galatian princess and the man whom Caesar had entrusted with the task of raising the relief army, finally appeared off Pelusium and quickly captured this important fortress. His troops, from Asia, Syria and Arabia, were powerfully reinforced by a Jewish contingent under Antipater (father of Herod the Great), who was the minister of the High Priest of the Jews. A forceful character, it was Antipater who was largely responsible for securing the help of other eastern princes, as well as bringing over to Caesar's side the many Jews resident in Alexandria. Mithridates, after an easy victory over the Egyptians as he advanced towards Memphis, then crossed to the western bank of the Nile and prepared to march on Alexandria.

Ptolemy and his advisers moved out from Alexandria with their army to give battle, while Caesar embarked his troops and sailed off as if in the direction of Pelusium. Overnight the fleet was reversed, and Caesar sailed back west of Alexandria, where the troops disembarked and proceeded by forced marches through the desert to join up with the army of Mithridates near Memphis. Their combined forces now marched north to meet the Egyptians under Ptolemy. The battle, when it came, was hard-fought, lasting two days, but in the end the Egyptian army was practically annihilated. Those who fled by small boats across the Nile were mostly drowned, among them Cleopatra's brother Ptolemy XIII, whose body was only identified by the gold royal corselet that he wore. Caesar had it sent back to Alexandria as proof to the citizens that the King was indeed dead – and that the struggle was over. On 27 March 47, he entered the city in triumph, the citizens sending a deputation to him in mourning, begging forgiveness for their part in the recent events. He was prepared to be clement, for he could be confident that he would have no more trouble in Egypt. Cleopatra was installed as Queen with her young brother as co-regent. Egypt was pacified and Caesar could have made it a Roman province without any real difficulty; that he did not do so was most probably due to his very real affection for Cleopatra. Cyprus was added to her kingdom and, to avoid any further potential trouble in the royal family, Cleopatra's sister Arsinoë was sent away to Rome to grace his later triumph. Cleopatra was pregnant by Caesar – a fact which could no longer be concealed from the court, but which necessitated some clever propaganda among the Egyptian people. Cleopatra, in her capacity as Queen of Egypt, was equated with the goddess Isis, and a goddess could not conceive by a mere mortal (hence the royal incest). Now Caesar had already been hailed at Ephesus as 'Descendant of Ares and Aphrodite, God Incarnate, and Saviour of Mankind', so the story was circulated for the benefit of the superstitious Egyptians that he was an incarnation of the god Amon (more or less equivalent to Zeus or Jupiter). Bas-reliefs have been found near Thebes showing Cleopatra as Isis in conversation with Amon, as well as depicting the birth of the divine child, who would be formally named Ptolemy Caesar but popularly known as Caesarion, 'Little Caesar'. An epitaph dating from the last years of the Queen's reign is inscribed 'in the twentieth year after the union of Cleopatra and Amon'.

Caesar, in effect, now joined the divine royal family – which he will not have found difficult. He had in any case a good precedent, for Alexander the Great, after his visit to the famous temple of Amon at Siwah in the Libyan desert, had become known as the son of Amon. Coin portraits depict him with the ram's horns of the god projecting from his head. Whether Alexander the Great or Caesar credited the identification is irrelevant, the fact was that it became widely believed among their subject peoples (whatever the sophisticated may have thought and said). It has already been suggested that something of

Caesar's apparent nonchalance and indifference to danger may have been due to some belief, however irrational, in a divine ancestry. This characteristic, as well as his will to power, was to become even more marked in his later years.

For the moment, the intricate and savage five-month-long Alexandrian war being over, Caesar intended to relax. Commentators then, and indeed ever since, have found it difficult to accept his behaviour at a time when so many grave problems were pressing upon him. The empire and particularly Italy itself was in a state of confusion; the Pompeians had a strong fleet and army at Dyrrhachium and Corfu; a considerable army supporting the Pompeian cause was still in Africa; yet Caesar apparently chose to idle away his time in Egypt. Cicero, writing in June 47, states that, since December the previous year, not a letter from Caesar had been received in Rome – perhaps not so surprising if one considers the circumstances of the war in Alexandria.

It was now, in the spring of 47, that Caesar embarked on his famous boat trip (in the magnificent Ptolemaic state barge) up the Nile, in company with Cleopatra and with an enormous concourse of attendant barges, together with Roman troops keeping pace with the assembly along the river banks. A strong military escort was certainly necessary, not only for security reasons but to demonstrate to the whole of Egypt the might of Rome. Caesar was merely repeating what Alexander and then the Ptolemies had done – impressing the people, upon whom ultimately the wealth of Egypt depended, with the power and the protecting arm afforded to them by divine-style monarchs. The secret of monarchy in the East rested on the fact that, as was evident to even the simplest peasant, the rulers were more able to affect their lives, living conditions, and even the crops, through their actions – whether for peace or war – than the remote gods in the temples. It was understandable, therefore, that the powers of the gods should be seen incarnated in these rulers and – even as in modern parades and presidential or royal processions – it was essential that this power and splendour should be visibly displayed.

There was also a human factor for his staying on in Egypt after the war. At his age, month upon month of unremitting warfare, Pharsalus following upon Dyrrhachium, and the Alexandrian war upon that, had taxed Caesar to the hilt. He was entitled to some rest in the company of his young mistress – about to bear his child – and also to look with the eye of both a traveller and an administrator on this new land which he had, in effect, just added to the territories of Rome. Affairs of state, trouble in Asia Minor, subduing the last of the Pompeians, all these problems would soon enough call him away. Before he left, however, he was determined to see Egypt secure and Cleopatra secure in charge of Egypt. He had decided to leave three legions in the country, the command of which would normally have devolved upon a senator, but Caesar rightly did not trust any senator with the power of so many troops as well as the wealth of Egypt. He entrusted the legions to a man whom he knew to be a completely reliable officer, Rufio, neither an aristocrat nor one of his own set, but the son of a freed slave. It was an intelligent choice and later, after the annexation of Egypt, Augustus was to make such a type of appointment a basic part of imperial policy. Early in June Caesar left Egypt for Syria, and not long afterwards Cleopatra gave birth to his only son.

CHAPTER THIRTY

Pharnaces and Pompey's Sons

Caesar had felt, as had many others, that the war should have ended after Pharsalus, and certainly the death of Pompey would seem to have been its logical conclusion. But the Roman civil war was far more than just a contest between two men. It was the struggle between two completely different concepts of government: on the one hand the old powerful families, calling themselves the *Optimates* and clinging to the concept of government by the senate; on the other Caesar, who envisaged a centralized form of government, a cabinet but under a dictator such as himself, with the senate acting as little more than a rubber stamp. Although in his last years Caesar seems to have been struggling towards the idea of empire under an emperor which Augustus (by 'hastening slowly') was to achieve, he was still too close to the violence that marked the birth of this concept to be able to understand it fully. Some of his opponents, such as Cato, seem to have grasped what was happening, and to have foreseen the decline of their class and of 'the republic' (that ideal which their famous ancestors had served but which no longer existed). For these *Optimates* Pompey had been no more than the figurehead, and the fact that he was dead did not end their resistance: their war was against 'Caesarism'.

Conscious of the troubles that awaited him in Italy, Africa and now Spain (where his generals had gravely mishandled the people), Caesar was determined that he would at least leave the East secure behind him, and serious trouble had broken out in Asia Minor. His legate in Asia, weakened by the fact that he had sent two legions to Caesar in Egypt, had been defeated by Pharnaces, son of Mithridates the Great. Pharnaces hoped to revive his father's empire and throw the Romans out of Asia, taking advantage of their distraction in the civil war and then of Caesar's absence in Egypt. He was already marching through Bithynia on his way to the province of Asia when a revolt behind his back by some of his followers brought him to a temporary halt. Caesar left Egypt accompanied by only one legion, rewarding as he went all those peoples and princes in the Near East who had assisted in the recent war, particularly the Jews, who he allowed to rebuild the walls of Jerusalem as well as giving Antipater Roman citizenship. Hyrcanus II, their High Priest and prince, was officially recognized as such, and the territory of the Jews was not only freed from contributions but from that often costly operation, the billeting of Roman soldiers.

Settling the affairs of Syria and Cilicia as he moved north towards Pharnaces, Caesar also saw fit to receive a number of distinguished Pompeians who came to seek for mercy and, as usual, granted it. He had found that this policy of reconciliation was generally successful, and there can be no doubt that it reinforced among the troops who had fought against him the warm respect which he sought. Everywhere that Caesar moved through Asia and the East it was as Imperator and Dictator, not as consul or provincial governor, that he dispensed justice and mercy. Hailed with wreaths of gold like any god-monarch of those countries, he now had behind him the two assets which he had said were the only essentials for a ruler – soldiers and money. The conquest of Gaul had already proved his point – that the general in command of a victorious army, backed by the wealth resulting from his conquest, does not need the dispensation of the senate.

Pharnaces, preoccupied with the rebellion in the Crimea, had withdrawn from any further advance into Asia. He was resting with his army in the northern district known as Pontus near the town of Zela. This was a name well enough known to Romans, since it was there that a Roman army had been heavily defeated by Mithridates the Great. But Pharnaces had no wish to confront the conqueror of Pompey, and he knew well enough that Caesar was eager to attend to all the other affairs that needed his attention in Rome and the West. He reckoned that if he adopted a conciliatory policy Caesar would happily leave Asia and while he was busily engaged in Africa or Spain, he himself could then set about rebuilding his father's empire. As soon as he heard that Caesar had crossed the frontier into Pontus, he sent envoys carrying golden wreaths and begging him to halt his advance, while giving him every assurance that Pharnaces had never lent any assistance to Pompey and would accede to any demands the Roman might make. Caesar was waiting for further troops to join him, for he had with him only the one legion weakened by the Alexandrian war and the remnants of the two which had already suffered defeat at the hands of Pharnaces. Until he was reinforced he was prepared to keep the negotiations going, listening with apparent interest to what Pharnaces' emissaries had to say. When he was ready to move he sent back the unacceptable demand that Pharnaces should leave Pontus altogether, pointing out at the same time that not to have assisted Pompey did not excuse him, nor did his subsequent treatment of Roman citizens.

The battle of Zela somewhat resembled the one against the Nervii at the Sambre, when the enemy had attacked while his troops were still engaged in fortifying their position. Caesar had occupied a hill facing the one on which Pharnaces was encamped. Thinking he had the Romans at a disadvantage, Pharnaces ordered his troops down into the valley that separated the two armies. Their aim was to assault the hill while the Roman legionaries were still busy with their stakes and spades. Amazed at his audacity, and to see war-chariots (which had caused him such concern in Britain) in action once more, Caesar made no immediate response to the threat. He could hardly believe that such an attack, up a hill, could ever succeed. It was far from a one-sided action, however; the front ranks of the legionaries were thrown back in confusion by the chariots, and it was not until the Sixth Legion (from Alexandria) commanded by Caesar himself threw the enemy down the side of the hill that the outcome was certain. The rout was later completed by his left wing and centre which drove back the main body of Pharnaces' army, seizing and sacking his camp. Pharnaces himself escaped, only to be killed later by his own rebels in the Crimea.

To his victories over Pompey in Greece and over Ptolemy in Egypt, Caesar now added a further one that would keep the peace in Asia Minor. He was well aware that, though their arms may have been as good or better, the fighting spirit of these people was not comparable with that of the Gauls, the Belgae or the Germans. He remarked sarcastically that it was little wonder Pompey had been regarded as a great general, if such was the calibre of his enemies. Writing to a friend in Rome, he coined the neat phrase: 'Veni, Vidi, Vici: I came, I saw, I conquered.'

After dealing with some outstanding administrative matters, and leaving his officers to supervise and his soldiers to enjoy the fruits of this recent victory, Caesar sailed for Athens and then made his way to Tarentum (Taranto). It was September, nearly a year and a half since he had set out in pursuit of Pompey, and in that time the affairs of Italy had lapsed into anarchical confusion. The hand of Antony, his Master of the Horse, had not been the right, steady one to administer affairs in his absence. Hastening to Rome, Caesar met Cicero on the road to Brundisium – who was hurrying to meet him. Cicero was another who considered that the civil war should have ended at Pharsalus, and he had done everything he could during the subsequent months to disassociate himself from the Pompeians. Caesar was not surprised to see him, for he had received offers of support from him while still in Asia; but Cicero's goodwill, his oratorical abilities and his consular prestige were no longer of the value to him that they might formerly have been. But he was tactful enough to spare this former Pompeian from any further humiliation, gave him leave to go to Rome if he wished (something forbidden by Antony), and no doubt learned from him some more about the state of affairs there. Cicero, for his part, however he might dissemble, could never bring himself to like Caesar. He would never write after his death as he had after Pompey's: 'I cannot help being sorry about his fate: in my experience, he was an honest, clean and upright man . . .'

Antony was a fine soldier but no administrator, and during Caesar's absence he had thoroughly mishandled the affairs of Rome. A woman-iser, a heavy drinker and a spendthrift, Antony had not failed to profit from Caesar's instruction to liquidate the affairs of the Pompeian party. This meant the confiscation and sale of the houses and estates of Pompey's supporters, and of similar property of those Pompeians who had remained in Italy or who attempted to return from the wreckage of Pharsalus. Antony was foremost among those to bid for the properties of dispossessed *Optimates* as they became available for sale by auction, and property speculation was rife among the rich. One notable specu-lator was Dolabella, a spendthrift crooked son-in-law of Cicero who bore a certain resemblance to Clodius. He sought to gain favour with the masses by such wild proposals for the cancellation of debts and rents that even Antony had to curtail his gangster-like operations by bringing in troops against a Dolabella-inspired mob – an operation which cost the lives of 800 Roman citizens. This over-reaction brought Antony, and therefore Caesar, into grave discredit. Among the people themselves there was general dissatisfaction, for Caesar's decree during his first dictatorship to reduce debts by one quarter had not gone far enough. The vast army of debtors was clamouring for a moratorium, a cancellation of debts on unpaid rents and reductions in the future. For the moment Caesar rejected all these demands, but he also showed his displeasure towards not only Dolabella but Antony, compelling both to pay the proper price to the treasury for properties for which they had bid thinking that they would never have to produce the full amount. Antony, whose dissolute way of life was offensive even by the standards of Rome (and would ultimately lead to the decline that would end in his suicide in Alexandria), fell from favour and was removed from any public position for two years.

Caesar's worst trouble was with the army. There was mutiny among the legions stationed in the Campagna, men who had served him faithfully in the past demanding their release from military service and the payment, both in land and money, of the rewards long promised them. He had known how to deal with the previous mutiny at Placentia but that was small compared with this, which involved even such units as his favourite Tenth Legion. There can be little doubt that there were some concealed Pompeians among the officers, and among them was the military tribune of the Tenth, who had formerly been a close associate of Labienus. Although all the legions had had their pay doubled, it was only those who had served in Gaul who had really profited in Caesar's campaigns; Greece and the East had yielded relatively little in terms of slaves and plunder. The news that the veterans were to be transferred to Sicily – which meant Africa, with a further war against other Roman legionaries – produced an explosion. Sallust, the future historian and one of Caesar's most reliable men, was sent to talk to the mutineers with a promise of a further 1,000 denarii per head over and above the money already owed to them. He was forced to flee for his life. The legionaries shouted that they were tired of promises and wanted ready money. They began a march on the city, looting and pillaging as they went, and Caesar debated whether to send the one legion that he had in Rome against them, but decided against it on considering that these men might also join the rebels.

When the veterans reached Rome, messengers were sent asking what they wanted, to which they replied that they would tell Caesar, and they then assembled in the Campus Martius. Rough from barracks and foreign campaigns, awed by the city, they were thoroughly taken aback when Caesar himself, accompanied by only a few of his intimates, suddenly appeared and addressed them. He seized the initiative and asked them bluntly what they wanted. Their spokesmen laboured their complaints, their long service and their long-expected rewards, and then (their trump card, as they thought) demanded to be released from military service. Caesar had expected this, for, short of mindless violence, they could only threaten him by refusing to accompany him on the next campaign in Africa.

He opened his reply by addressing them as 'Citizens', not 'Fellow Soldiers' as was his custom – thus automatically demoting them to the ranks of despised civilians. Then to their stupefaction he granted them their discharge, saying that he would give them everything else that had been promised when he returned in triumph *with other soldiers*. They could hardly believe that in a flash their roles had been reversed, and it was now they who were begging him to keep them in his service. Caesar pretended to a grave reluctance, made as if to leave, hesitated, and then said that no one would be punished, but that the Tenth Legion would be disbanded – since he was so outraged to find them guilty of insubordination. At this the Tenth even asked that they should be decimated rather than disbanded. Caesar finally extended his pardon to all, and told them his plans for their settlement in accordance with his previously expressed ideas on agrarian grants. The mutiny was over, but he had taken careful note of the ringleaders: they could be expended in the future.

The year was already drawing to a close, but before he could attend to Africa Caesar made appointments to ensure that some stability was restored to the constitution while he was away. Two of his followers were rewarded with the consulships for the rest of the year, while he and his close colleague Marcus Lepidus were to be the consuls for the year 46. (Election for the consulship had already become a mere formality.) The numbers of praetors and priesthoods were now increased, the appointments – like those to the senate – being filled by Caesarians. Centurions were elevated to the rank of knights, as were reliable followers from Spain and even Gaul. Having ensured that the instruments of government would be faithful to him, he resigned the dictatorship, thus leaving the impression that when this war was finally concluded a free constitution might well be restored.

Pompey's sons, Cnaeus and Sextus, had now gathered round them in North Africa those other Roman leaders who had determined to resist Caesar to the end. They included his former colleague Labienus, Pompey's lieutenants Afranius and Petreius, Metellus Scipio, Pompey's father-in-law, and inevitably Cato. Allied with Juba, the Numidian King, they could field an army of about fourteen legions, 15,000 cavalry, and over 100 elephants, and presented a most serious challenge to Caesar. When he sailed from Sicily in December he had only six legions and 2,000 cavalry, five of the legions being composed of recruits, while four legions of veterans from Campania had not yet arrived. Caesar was determined as usual not to delay but to strike as soon as possible, believing that postponement was something that always benefitted the waiting enemy and reduced the morale of the attacking force. However, as he was soon to find out, the conditions in Africa were such that delay was inevitable, and circumstances were against him from the start.

The galleys set out from Lilybaeum (Marsala) in Sicily 'under sealed orders', none of the ships' captains knowing their destination – their only instructions being to follow Caesar's galley. His destination in fact was Hadrumetum on the east coast of the Cape Bon peninsula, in the south of the province and far removed from the main body of the Pompeians at Utica. Hadrumetum itself, however, turned out to be heavily garrisoned and he was forced to move farther south. Capturing the township of Leptis Minor, he then took up his position on a nearby coastal plateau. The omens had been unfavourable before they left Sicily; during the crossing a number of his ships had lost contact and for the time being were lost, while, on landing in Africa, he stumbled and fell. This was something that he managed to make the most of by calling out, as he grasped the earth, 'I hold you, Africa!' As Pontifex Maximus, High Priest of the state religion of Rome, he had shown throughout his life that he held little if any regard for auguries and omens, save – as now – when they could be turned to his own advantage. He believed in Luck. In Africa he was certainly to need all the help from his chosen Goddess that he could find.

In the first days of January 46 the missing ships of the convoy arrived, and when, in due course, the troops had all assembled, Caesar moved out on a requisitioning expedition throughout the surrounding country. The unknown author of the *African War*, probably one of Caesar's officers to judge by his detailed and careful military account, shows how Caesar, at first at a grave disadvantage, gradually adapted his strategy to a campaign in a large territory unfamiliar to him, defeating an enemy whose advantages should have enabled him to crush Caesar in the first stages. On this first occasion Caesar's scouting and foraging party met with a strong force of Labienus' men, consisting mainly of Numidian cavalry, archers and slingers. Outnumbered, Caesar's troops were quickly surrounded and it was more by luck than by design that he managed to cut his way clear of the knot of horsemen. He had come near to reversing the situation by cutting off one section of Labienus' troops from the other, when the arrival of a second force under Petreius put him in peril once more. The battle was turning into a rout and Caesar himself, as Appian tells it, at one moment was forced to seize a fleeing standard bearer, catching him by the shoulder and turning him round as he cried out: 'That is where the enemy are!' Caesar and his troops managed to escape under cover of darkness, but there could be no doubt that this first encounter on African soil had been a defeat – the first since Dyrrhachium. Pompey might be dead, but the spirit and the enmity of the *Optimates* lived on.

'This defeat,' wrote Dio Cassius, 'was a savage blow to Caesar. The realization that he had been beaten by comparatively small forces, coupled with the knowledge that Juba and Scipio must soon be expected with all their troops, threw him into confusion and he hardly knew what to do.' The historian errs, for what Caesar did was – contrary to his usual tactics – to play for time. As he had done before on occasion during the wars in Gaul, he allowed the internal dissensions and rivalries among his enemies to work to his advantage. For his part he could not in any case move far from the sea, since he was still waiting for his veteran legions (the more so since his young recruits had shown themselves unreliable) as well as being dependent on the water for his supplies.

Politics and propaganda now prepared the way for the final contest. Bocchus, King of Mauretania, who had been recognized as such by Caesar at the same time that he had declared Juba an enemy of the Roman people, took advantage of Juba's involvement with the Pompeian Romans to open an attack on his kingdom of Numidia, in which he was aided and abetted by Sittius, a Roman adventurer who had become a captain in his army. The result was that Juba had to concentrate on the defence of his own kingdom, abandoning the Pompeians and taking away from them the cavalry which had given them such an advantage. The native chiefs to the south of Juba's kingdom of Numidia were also drawn into the conflict, being reminded that Caesar was the nephew of Marius, their former benefactor, and that the Pompeians had done nothing for them. Among the Roman soldiers who served under Scipio much scandal was made of their leader's dependence upon, and even subservience to, a 'barbarian' such as Juba, while Caesar for his part promised them honour and fortune and equal treatment with his own soldiers. If they joined him they would then be Romans among Romans, and not Romans serving under an African king. In the weeks that followed, while Caesar waited for his forces from Sicily, the effects of his propaganda were seen in the thousands of native tribesmen, as well as legionaries from the Pompeians, and even whole cities, that came over to Caesar's cause.

By the end of January two veteran legions at last arrived from Sicily, together with 800 Celtic cavalry and 1,000 archers and slingers. Caesar still awaited two further legions, the Ninth and the Tenth (so conspicuous during the recent troubles in Italy), but he felt that he could now at least try to provoke Scipio to battle. The latter was, understandably, a cautious general when confronted by one of Caesar's reputation, and in any case was unwilling to put things to the test when Juba, his legions and his invaluable cavalry were distracted by the Mauretanian attacks. Caesar moved south from the plateau where he had been encamped towards the town of Uzita, a main storage depot for Scipio's army, and prepared to besiege it if Scipio was unwilling to give battle in its defence.

The weeks went by. Spring came to North Africa, and still the positional war dragged on. There was bad news from the East where there had been a mutiny among the legions in Syria. Urgent messages went to Sicily for the missing legions to cross to Africa – whatever the weather conditions. Scipio sent word to Juba that he must leave the fight for his own kingdom against his Mauretanian enemy, and promised him something that was in no way his to give – all the Roman possessions in Africa in return for victory. If Caesar won, he said, there would be nothing for any of them.

CHAPTER THIRTY-ONE

Thapsus and Triumph

As soon as he heard the unprecedented terms on which his help for securing victory would be repaid, Juba left his own affairs in Numidia and joined Scipio. He brought with him three legions, light infantry, a host of cavalry, and thirty elephants. Now was the moment when Scipio might well have accepted any challenge that Caesar offered for a setpiece battle but, cautious to the last, he refused to take the offensive and continued to hope that Caesar's manpower and supplies would be worn away by the passage of time. He was right in one estimation, for it was the shortage of provisions that finally caused Caesar to make a major move. In the meantime he had at last received his two extra legions from Sicily, the Ninth and the Tenth. This in itself brought its problems, for Caesar knew that among these legions were disaffected officers, against whom he had taken no action at the time of the mutiny, but who were the last men he wanted in positions of command against the Pompeians. Fortunately for him they made the problem of their disposal comparatively easy.

When the two legions landed they were exhausted after a bad crossing, almost dying of hunger and thirst, and generally in a poor state of morale. However their senior officer, the tribune Avienus and his staff, arrived in great comfort, in a vessel appointed for their exclusive use. This in itself was enough to infuriate Caesar, who never spared himself when on campaign, and owed no little of his popularity with the rank and file to the fact that he always shared their discomforts and privations. He did not hesitate to make an example of the tribune, using the occasion also to get rid of the other officers known to have favoured the mutiny and to be secret Pompeians. They were denounced in front of a general assembly of all officers and centurions and sent back to Italy under armed guard.

This increase in Caesar's forces inevitably led to further problems in provisioning, and the fact that Avienus, perhaps deliberately, had not brought any corn ships with him to feed the two new legions added to the difficulties. He knew too that the arrival of Juba and his forces had already caused something approaching panic among his troops. He had put heart into them by deliberately and mockingly overstating the extent of the danger that these reinforcements represented, but he knew that now was the moment when, if ever, he must force an action. To the south-east of him lay the maritime city of Thapsus (Ras Dimas). Although it was not a natural harbour (rare enough in that part of North Africa) it was used because of the shelter that was afforded by an offshore island. Thapsus was well-garrisoned and a major depot for Scipio's forces – indeed, Caesar's ships had long been blockading it. The threat to the garrison, the stores, and the sheltered access to the sea, was something that not even Scipio could ignore. Caesar had now been in Africa for more than four months: his original intention to force an immediate battle and destroy the Pompeians had developed into a war of attrition. It was time to make an end.

'Realizing,' as Dio Cassius puts it, 'that he could not get the enemy to engage him, Caesar marched on Thapsus, intending to give battle if they came to the aid of the town or to capture it if they would not come to its protection.' He calculated that, in view of his increased numbers, he must have a secure base, and one that could be revictualled and reinforced from the sea if need be. Thapsus would provide him with this – if Scipio and Juba did not elect to come to its rescue. But the Pompeians obliged, unwilling to see so strategically important a town together with all its stores fall to Caesar, and Scipio with all his available forces began to march towards the coast. Caesar, as usual, out-distanced his enemy and reached Thapsus first.

The town stood on a small rocky headland, protected offshore to the north by a long sickle-shaped island and from the west by a marshy lake, the only approaches to the town being through gaps a mile wide or less between this lake and the coastline. It was easily defensible then, but open to blockade from the sea, which, if backed by a strong attacking force ashore, must lead to its ultimate fall. By bringing up his army into the comparatively narrow area between lake and shoreline Caesar was apparently allowing himself to be caught like a fish in a net. And this, in effect, was the impression he intended to give; for only by inducing Scipio and Juba to come up and seal the ends of this net could he provoke that open battle which he so badly needed. (It is unlikely that he ever considered capturing Thapsus, withdrawing inside its walls and withstanding a long siege while being dependent on sea supplies. It would have been contrary to his character, and quite useless for ending the war in Africa swiftly.)

Jubilant at having trapped Caesar on the isthmus – as he thought – Scipio moved up the main body of the army to the north, blocking off the entrance near the town, while Juba and Pompey's former lieutenant

Afranius did the same to the south. This division of their forces proved fatal, and on the morning of 6 April Caesar moved out from his camp opposite the walls of Thapsus and his troops formed up facing Scipio, the nearest of his enemies. He had already instructed his blockading fleet to make a diversion on the side of Scipio's camp (which seems to have caused some kind of panic amongst his men just as they were establishing their lines), and his troops now waited for the order to advance. They were drawn up in their usual three-line formation, with a fourth oblique line stationed behind on each wing to deal with the elephants that Scipio had deployed on the wings of his army. It was a crucial moment in the civil war. As at Pharsalus, as in Alexandria, as indeed even at Zela, one defeat would have meant the end for Caesar – and yet it seems that he failed to seize that essential flashing minute when everything called for action. It was left to the army itself, a trumpeter sounding the advance, to set all the cohorts in motion and precipitate an attack which proved fatal to the already disorganized Pompeians.

The anonymous author of the *African War* reports that the centurions attempted to prevent the men from advancing until their commander had given the order, but that they would not be restrained until finally, 'Caesar realized that it was impossible to resist his soldiers' impetuosity. He gave the battle-cry "Felicitas" – "Good Luck" – and galloped forward against the enemy front line.' The slingers and archers on Caesar's right wing – to seaward – created havoc among the elephants, which, as so often happened if insufficiently-trained elephants were used in battle, turned and became far more danger to their own side than to their enemy. As Scipio's left wing collapsed his native cavalry took flight, and soon the whole of his army was fleeing round the shore of the lake in the direction of Juba's camp. Juba and Afranius had escaped as soon as they saw the collapse of Scipio's army, and their camp was now seized by the soldiers whom Caesar had left behind to guard his own camp when the attack began. The defeated who were left upon the field laid down their arms and surrendered in the usual manner – only to be met with a brutality that had not been seen in any of Caesar's previous campaigns. The legionaries, in some curious kind of rage that they had never displayed before, proceeded to massacre their opponents. Caesar, who had had no part in starting the battle, seems to have had no influence over his soldiers once it was clearly at an end. Indeed, his legionaries even singled out for death members of their own camp whom they said were traitors, not sparing a number of knights and even senators. 'After so resounding a victory they thought that anything was permitted to them.'

That may be so, but the behaviour of Caesar's troops after Thapsus marks a great moment of change in the whole history of Rome. Caesar's legionaries may well have been, as the author of the *African War* tells us, so poor that 'to secure foodstuffs they had been compelled to spend all that they had, only a few having tents made of hides, the others making shelters with their tattered clothes.' It was possibly their sheer desperation and desire for loot that drove them to butcher the Pompeians when they yielded after the battle. But a more significant factor had now emerged, something demonstrated by their murder of political figures and even senior officers on their own side – the legionaries had at last learned who wielded power. They had been used before for many decades, by Caesar and others, as the instruments of policy. By attacking without orders, by killing their surrendered opponents without orders, and finally by storming through their own lines, murdering people whom they considered traitors or opposed to their own interests, they demonstrated that power lay in the sword and the arm of the legionary. Once acquired, such knowledge could never be forgotten. In the centuries to come the legions would often determine the course of the empire, and make or unmake emperors at will.

The most curious circumstance of the battle of Thapsus was Caesar's apparent reluctance to give the order to advance, when the moment was opportune and his troops were begging for the signal. But was it reluctance or inability? Plutarch reports that 'Some people say that he was not in the action, but that he was taken with his usual distemper just as he was setting his army in order. He perceived the approaches of it, and before it had disordered his senses, when he was already beginning to shake under its influence, withdrew into a neighbouring fort, where he reposed himself.'

This reference to his 'usual' malady confirms something that Suetonius also tells us, that 'he twice had epileptic fits while on campaign'. Epilepsy was clearly something with which he was familiar, if this account is correct, for Caesar perceived the 'warning' or *aura*, as it is called, which often precedes epileptic fits, and had time to have himself carried out of sight. It would explain his failure to give the order to charge, although it belies the statement that he led on his horse into battle. The epileptic is invariably left prostrate and comatose for a time after an attack. The 'divine malady', as it has been called, has often been found in men of extreme intelligence. The strangeness of its manifestations has led to sufferers in many countries being associated with occupation by a god. It may well have contributed to Caesar's view of his own divine origin.

The aftermath of Thapsus was the disintegration of the Pompeian forces, the death of many of their leaders and the suicide of Cato in the city of Utica. Cato had not been present at the battle because he was in command of this, the greatest city in Africa after Carthage, where the bulk of the Pompeian senators and the rich property owners who supported their cause had made their capital and base. When the news from Thapsus reached them, nearly all except Cato accepted that everything was lost and made their preparations for coming to terms with Caesar. Cato was willing to fight, but could find no supporters.

Leaving a strong force behind to clear up whatever pockets of Pompeians were left in the area of Thapsus, Caesar hastened across country to reach Utica, hoping to catch up with the fleeing Pompeian leaders and also to capture Cato alive. No doubt he would have pardoned him – it would have been a fine gesture. But the latter, true to his republican principles to the last, had already made his statement on that score: 'I am not willing to be indebted to the tyrant for his illegal actions. He is acting contrary to the laws when he pardons men as if he were their master, when he has no sovereignty over them.' The death of Cato foreshadowed that of Caesar. As a republican martyr he had far more influence over those who became the conspirators dead than alive. Of the other leading Pompeians, the Numidian King Juba and Petreius died in a death-pact duel, Scipio was killed in a sea-battle and Afranius was killed on Caesar's orders. On the other hand, the two sons of Pompey, Gnaeus and Sextus, managed to escape to Spain, as did Caesar's unremitting enemy and former lieutenant, Labienus. The rich state of Numidia was turned into another province, New Africa, Sallust becoming its governor, while all the towns that had sided with Caesar's enemies had to pay heavy penalties in money, grain and oil. The African campaign had concluded successfully for him, but it had been ill-conducted throughout by both sides, and Thapsus was a victory for his legionaries rather than for Caesar. It only remained for him now to return to Rome, celebrate his triumph and begin the work of restoration, except – that one cloud on the horizon – there still remained the threat posed by the sons of Pompey who had escaped to Spain.

The defeat at Thapsus, and above all the death of Cato, brought a kind of despair to all those, Cicero for example, who in their heart of hearts had continued to dream of the restoration of the republic. Despite Pharsalus, despite Caesar's triumphs in the East, they had continued to hope that Africa would see the end of him, and that the victorious fleet of the Pompeians would sail north to Italy to announce the tyrant dead, the republic restored and the continuation of *Optimate* rule in the senate. Caesar sailed from Africa in June, but instead of proceeding directly to Rome called in at Sardinia ('the only one of his properties he has not yet visited' wrote Cicero sarcastically), where he promptly raised the annual tax. He did not arrive in Rome until late July, thus giving his friends time to put the capital into some kind of order and his enemies to compose the smiles upon their faces.

The fact that Caesar had been away from Rome for over eleven of the past twelve years had given him a completely different perspective from that of the senators and others who inherited their attitudes from the old days of the republic. To them Rome was still the world, but Caesar's viewpoint had changed considerably during his absence and his acquaintanceship with the countries that now constituted the empire. From his youth, as has been seen, he had always been careful to keep in touch by constant correspondence with friends and informants in the city. This had now been reinforced by an exchange between himself and his associates all over the empire, especially in Gaul where he had been the undisputed ruler for nearly twelve years.

Caesar's close associates (his *familiares* Cicero called them) whether senators, knights, practical men of business or soldiers, all had one thing in common – they were Caesar's men first and foremost. Thus, paralleling or overshadowing the official posts of the state, Caesar had his own administrative machine working within the framework of the empire. It had served him well so far throughout the civil war, but the very fact of its existence inevitably increased his contempt for the Roman constitution, and indeed for everything associated with republican institutions. The *Optimates*, who formed the ruling Party in the senate, had done all that they could to oppose him, and it was they who had finally forced him into the illegal act of crossing the Rubicon (although he was always at great pains to stress that all his actions had been constitutional). The same men who had opposed him in the senate had formed the hard core of the Pompeians, and he was well aware that those who had never even left Rome hated him no less. The total eclipse of republican institutions during the civil war had demonstrated – to Caesar at least – that they could be dispensed with, except as some kind of decorative façade. But it was not yet time to say it openly, although Suetonius, admittedly quoting a Pompeian witness, has Caesar maintaining 'that the republic was nothing – a mere name without form or substance. As for Sulla, he proved himself a fool by resigning the dictatorship.'

There was nothing left for the leaders of the old senatorial party to do but come to terms with Caesar. They must now show him unconditional loyalty and the best way to begin was with thanksgiving festivities that would exceed anything that Rome had ever known. On the first occasion that the City had showed its gratitude Caesar had been accorded ten days, on the second fifteen; now as a thanksgiving for his cumulative victories they voted him forty. He was made dictator for ten years and, as visible evidence of his authority, the number of lictors assigned him (to mark the fact that this was his third dictatorship) was increased to seventy-two. A new office was even invented for him – Prefect of Morals. It was equivalent to the office of censor, but with enlarged powers that gave him control over almost every aspect of public or private life for three years. The name of the great Sullan, Catulus, was erased from the Capitoline Temple and Caesar's replaced it, while inside the temple a triumphal chariot was installed, bearing a statue of Caesar with the globe at his feet. An inscription recalled his descent from Venus and described him as a demigod. The honour of giving the signal to open all the circus games was his. In the senate he had the right to sit between the two consuls in a curule chair and always to speak first during their deliberations. There was little more, it seemed as yet, that they could do for him. But all these honours were tainted with the smell of fear.

CHAPTER THIRTY-TWO

Imperious Caesar

In those first weeks, while all the preparations were being made for the celebration of his triumphs in September, Caesar did his best to reassure both the senate and the people that his policy remained one of reconciliation. While accepting the power and the honours that they accorded him, he pointed out that he had pardoned all those who had fought against him at least once and some more. He had no taste for despotism, and did not wish to emulate either Sulla (arch-enemy of his family) or Marius and Cinna (his uncle and his former father-in-law). He was careful to reassure the rich that he had no designs upon their property or intentions to introduce any new taxes and, as for the immense riches that had been gathered in recent years, he had kept none for himself but all would go to adorn and administer the city. 'Although he may have succeeded in calming the general fears,' writes Dio Cassius, with more than an element of understatement, 'he was unable to put all minds entirely at rest.' There was a very good reason for this. Although Caesar, whenever there was occasion to mention him, spoke of the dead Pompey only with respect, he had never had any respect for his judgement. When, all those years ago, Pompey had burst upon Italy victorious out of the East, he had immediately disbanded his legions, and Caesar had watched him rapidly dwindle in stature. Caesar had not disbanded his legions. They thronged the city – in theory at least, as Caesar put it to the people, 'as the guardians of my authority and of yours'.

All ancient triumphs were a massive act of propaganda, on a scale that is difficult to envisage in a more sophisticated and literate age. Just as the coinage, with the head of the ruler on one side and some object associated with his prowess or his power on the other, conveyed a clear message to hundreds of thousands of illiterates, so a Roman triumph was something of a massive advertising campaign. It was combined with a visual display like a circus, followed by free food and wine, the distribution of money that for some would almost constitute a year's income, and ended with the favourite Roman spectator-sport – the vivid and violent games. The subjects of Caesar's four triumphs, which were celebrated between 20 September and 1 October, old calendar (actually 20 to 30 July), were the victories over Gaul, Egypt, Pontus and Africa. Pharsalus must be tactfully forgotten, since it was a victory of Romans over Romans, and on this score Africa too was to prove something of a problem. Each triumph was given its own distinctive characteristic – for example, different woods and inlays associated with the countries concerned were used in the elaborate carpentry and cabinetwork in which representative treasures, jewels and precious metals were transported and housed. Statues depicting the great rivers of the various lands, scenes from the actions, and a huge replica of the famed Pharos of Alexandria – all these had kept painters, sculptors, carpenters, cabinetmakers, and theatrical designers busy for many weeks. Some of the effects must have been prepared months before in anticipation. The first triumph, brilliant with Gallic weapons, enamels, statues and innumerable objects taken from temples or the homes of private citizens, display-cabinets full of gold and silver, was interspersed with great signs proclaiming the names of battles and towns hitherto unknown in the Latin tongue. The Ocean in chains represented, for all those thousands who did not know the truth, the conquest of Britain by Caesar. The living chained figure of Vercingetorix represented the reality of conquered Gaul. As a rebel against Rome, he was destined for death.

Cleopatra herself, together with her eleven-year-old brother Ptolemy XIV, had been summoned to Rome to witness the Egyptian triumph. It had been deemed impolitic to leave the young Pharaoh behind, in case – in accordance with family tradition – he and his advisers should make a bid for the throne during her absence. Prominent among Cleopatra's entourage was the child Caesarion, believed to be Caesar's son. Cleopatra's sister, the unfortunate Arsinoë, together with Ganymedes and others who had taken part in the rebellion, walked among the prisoners in the triumph. She was later granted her liberty, but Ganymedes disappears from history, so he may have shared the same fate as Vercingetorix. Elephants and exotic animals hitherto unknown to Romans, such as the giraffe, added to the rich curiosity of the Egyptian procession.

Whereas the wealth and grandeur of the defeated had been the main theme of the Gallic and Egyptian triumphs, the third, the Eastern one celebrating the victory over Pharnaces, introduced a satirical note – Pharnaces being depicted in full flight before Caesar's army. This was untrue, for Pharnaces' army had fought well at Zela, and the King had not been put to flight but had died later at the hands of his own rebels. The point was taken, however, that the kings of the East (over whom

Pompey had secured his triumphs) were slightly comic figures. Before Caesar's triumphal chariot came a large panel inscribed with the three words: VENI, VIDI, VICI.

Africa presented a rather difficult problem, for the victory had been gained over fellow Roman citizens and soldiers. This fact was obscured, however, by making it seem that the African war had been against King Juba, that the triumph was being celebrated over his defeat, and that the Pompeians who had fought in it were merely serving under him (Romans under an African king – thus further demeaning them). Since Juba was dead his place among the captives was taken by his five-year-old son, whom Caesar had brought back to Rome. (He was brought up in the city, became one of the most famous scholars of his day, was reinstated in Numidia and later married the daughter of Antony and Cleopatra.) The representations of the Pompeians however struck a discordant note. Scipio, Petreius and Cato were depicted in gory detail, committing suicide in different ways but, as Appian records from some contemporary account: 'The people, although repressed by fear, could not control their cries of pain and disapproval . . .'

After the triumphal procession came the animals destined for sacrifice at the Capitol, conspicuous among them the white oxen with their gilded horns. Musicians and men bearing incense-burners accompanied that visible reminder of the dictator's power: the seventy-two lictors in their red military cloaks, bearing the laurel-crowned fasces from which projected shining axe heads, symbolic of the power over life and death of the old Roman kings. At last came the victorious dictator, Caius Julius Caesar, in the triumphal chariot drawn by four horses. Dressed in purple and gold, with the ornaments of divinity like Capitoline Jupiter to whom he was going to dedicate the symbols of victory, he held a laurel branch in his right hand and in his left an ivory sceptre surmounted by an eagle. Above his laurel-bound head a slave held the gold crown of Jupiter, too great for him to bear and a reminder that even in the midst of glory he was a mortal man. Last, in their cohorts and centuries, came the men who had made his victories possible, the legionaries in their parade dress, crowned and wearing their medals of gold and silver. As they marched, refreshed no doubt by countless drinks from the crowd, their songs commemorated their achievements and battles, celebrated their leader and, their verses growing steadily broader, his sexual prowess:

> Home we bring the bald adulterer,
>   Romans, lock your wives away.
> Gold he spent on Gallic women,
>   Which you Romans helped to pay.

Caesar was at home with their simple bawdy; so many of his years had been spent in camp that the sensitive young aristocrat had long been buried under the soldier's skin – or had he? Certainly he seems to have accepted without any visible concern verses which plainly alluded to his regal aspirations although others, referring to that time more than thirty years ago when the rumour was that he had been King Nicomedes' catamite, are said to have irritated him profoundly.

Even more disturbing than this old allusion was that, nearing the temple of Fortune (the one goddess whom he respected), the axle of his chariot broke and Caesar was brought to the floor and forced to summon another one. It was an ill omen indeed, and would have caused most Romans of the time to abandon the ceremony. (It is just possible that this had been the intention of some unknown enemy.) Conscious of the need to defer to superstition, instead of mounting the steps of the Capitol like the triumphant conqueror, he ascended them on his knees, making his abasement to Fate.

The historians who recorded Caesar in triumph all wrote with the benefit of hindsight, yet there can be no doubt that the unfortunate impression made by the African triumph, the soldiers' verses recording an old scandal, and the incident of the breaking axle-tree, all cast a shadow over these days of triumphant festivities. Superficially, it was soon dispelled by the enormous public banquet that followed, with 22,000 tables designed for 200,000 guests, and the distribution of lavish sums of money to the veterans. Private soldiers received 5,000 denarii, centurions twice as much, and senior officers four times as much again. All the poor (those entitled in Rome to free corn) received 100 denarii apiece, as well as a further gift of grain and oil, those staples of the Latin diet.

Yet the distribution of money to the legions did not escape that ever-pervasive shadow of bitterness and discontent. From one account, many of the veterans complained that they would rather have had more money than see so much spent on people who did not deserve it, and on such sumptuous displays. According to Dio Cassius (writing two centuries after the events) on one occasion at a public performance Caesar in person led off one of these vociferous complainants for execution, while two others were formally turned over to the pontiffs and sacrificed to Mars, their heads being displayed outside the basilica of the god. Such sacrifices were rare indeed at that time in Rome's history, and indicate that only serious trouble could have called for such severe measures. To keep the Roman crowd happy, many thousands of condemned prisoners and prisoners-of-war fought in the gladiatorial contests; theatrical performances were given in various parts of the city; and the whole of Rome was for days turned into a vast amusement park. There were wild-beast hunts featuring animals from

Africa, chariot races in which young noblemen drove four-horse and two-horse chariots, athletic contests, a battle between two 'armies' of 500 infantry a side together with cavalry and elephants. On an artifical lake, specially constructed for the occasion, a naval battle was fought between biremes, triremes and quadriremes, representing the fleets of Egypt and Tyre. Satiated with food and drink, over-indulged with spectacles, some of the populace like the disillusioned legionaries at last began to murmur at such extravagance, but their complaints were in a very low key. So the splendour of the victory celebrations, while they undoubtedly had the desired effect of cementing most veterans and Romans to Caesar, did not pass without their detractors and without arousing some feeling of resentment against such regal munificence. The Etruscans were said to have been the first to hold triumphs and games – and the Etruscans were ruled by kings.

As part of the victory celebrations Julius Caesar dedicated a whole new forum, the Forum Julium. As early as 54, while he was in Gaul, he had asked his friend Oppius and some other rich associates to buy a large area east of the forum with a view to building this new addition in honour of his clan. It contained as centrepiece a temple which he intended to dedicate to Venus Victrix, Venus the conquering Goddess. He had vowed this dedication before the battle of Pharsalus, but he now changed it to Venus Genetrix, the Mother-Goddess (the mother of his clan). Venus the Mother-Goddess had also another association for him, and one which would be readily understood by the people, for he Julius Caesar had only one child, and that a son, whose mother was Cleopatra Queen of Egypt. She was living with all her court in a sumptuous villa surrounded by gardens on the far side of the Tiber, where Caesar had established her. The entertainments given by the Egyptian Queen, the presence of Caesarion, and the sophisticated luxury of the Ptolemies which made Rome seem almost provincial, were a major feature of that Roman season in the year of triumphs. Cicero, who clearly met her at this time, recorded with dislike 'her pride and haughtiness' – distasteful no doubt to an old republican, but natural enough in one who was 'the descendant of so many kings'. In an age when statues, like the emblems on coins, played so important a part in propaganda it was not without considerable political significance that on inauguration of the Forum Julium on 26 September the temple was found to contain not only the image of Venus Genetrix but a golden statue of the Egyptian queen. The symbolism must have been plain enough to Caesar's contemporaries, although a great many scholars subsequently have turned a blind eye to it:

In the temple of Venus the Mother-Goddess, ancestress of the Julian clan, stands equally a golden statue of the Queen Cleopatra, the mother of Caesar's son.

As Queen of Egypt Cleopatra was seen by her countrymen as an incarnation of the goddess Isis; Caesar claimed divine ancestry; and Caesarion was their child. The intention was clear enough, but the policy which it implied was never to be carried out because of Caesar's premature death. It has been argued that monogamy was the custom among Romans and that Caesar was married to Calpurnia. But divorce, as has been seen, was neither uncommon nor difficult, and Calpurnia was childless. Rome recognized Cleopatra as Caesar's mistress – her boy-husband was of no consequence – and Caesarion as their illegitimate son. Marriage to this Egyptian Queen, even though she was of Greek blood, would have been highly unpopular with the upper classes perhaps, but certainly possible. Caesarion would have been legitimized; and in any case there was every likelihood of Cleopatra bearing him more children (as she did to Antony).

The idea of establishing a dynasty may well have been in Caesar's mind. But a royal dynasty implied kingship, and Caesar, although he was soon to be made dictator for life, was not king and the very title *Rex* inspired fear and hatred among Romans. Any suggestion that he desired that title was enough to inflame the republicans and provide them with propaganda to inspire almost anything – even the murder of a sacrosanct dictator. It has been maintained that Caesar's relationship with Cleopatra was no more to him than 'a brief chapter in his amours, comparable to Eunoë the wife of the Prince of Mauretania' (Sir Ronald Syme), but this is to contradict the evidence. She was specially brought to Rome for this season of triumphal thanksgiving when only the presence of her sister as a prisoner was required; she was marked out by Caesar with special favour, and she brought with her their son. It was only later, under Augustus, that it was deemed politic to deny that this child was Caesar's (it was unlikely to have been anyone else's); at the time no one queried Caesar's paternity.

After Caesar's death, when Caesarion was a grown boy, people were to comment on his resemblance to his father; and the speed with which Octavian/Augustus had him murdered after the deaths of Antony and Cleopatra is as good an argument as any for Caesar's paternity. The placing of Cleopatra's statue next to that of the goddess in the new temple of Venus Genetrix openly associated her with the mother of the Julian clan. But the title *Rex* eluded Caesar, although he would try in the near future to see whether the Roman public would accept it.

CHAPTER THIRTY-THREE

Administrator and General

In the aftermath of this designed extravagance Caesar rapidly turned to the reorganization of Roman administration. As a first step to tackling the immense problems in Rome and Italy, he had a census taken of the inhabitants of the city. The sight of thousands of unemployed eating at the banquets and festivities must have served as a visual reminder of the number in Rome who were living at the republic's expense, contributing little or nothing to its welfare. A revision of the list of citizens entitled to free corn was drawn up as the result of this census, and the number was cut drastically – from 320,000 to 150,000. Aware that those who were now the recipients of this bounty would be his firm supporters, he was also well aware that the dispossessed would be equally a danger to him. Something must be done to remove from the capital the burden of useless mouths and hands, and the sensible answer was emigration. To deal with unemployment he arranged for the despatch of some 80,000 settlers to two new colonies, Carthage and Corinth (both of them once famous cities which had been destroyed by Romans a century earlier and which, because of their geographical position, were ripe for resettlement), as well as to Hispalis (Seville) in Spain. Another source of discontent and, worse, revolutionary intrigues, were the workmen's clubs and mutual aid societies which had been turned by men such as Caesar's agent Clodius into political clubs that determined elections by bribery and violence. With the exception of religious associations they were all suppressed, and a special dispensation was made for the Jewish synagogues, for Caesar wished to recognize the help that the Jews had given him during his Egyptian campaign.

To lessen the danger of slave revolts, and to ensure that native-born Italians were not forced to leave the soil by the pressure of slave-labour, a law was passed requiring large landowners to employ one-third freemen among their labourers. While encouraging the urban proletariat to emigrate, Caesar did not want to see a drain of the educated bourgeoisie into the new territories of the empire. No Roman citizen, therefore, between twenty and forty, unless on military duties, was to be absent from the city for more than three years. This gave the young citizen a chance to complete his education in Greece, or the middle-aged merchant to trade in the empire, but ensured that the fruits of his learning and earning came back to the capital. At the same time, to attract brains and talent to the new Rome that he was busy creating and which he hoped to see a centre of art and learning (like Alexandria), citizenship would automatically be granted to doctors and artists. As Prefect of Morals he attempted to regulate the ostentatious display of wealth by a sumptuary law regulating everything from the usage of litters (the Roman sedan-chair) to jewellery and even the dishes at table, but these measures proved unenforceable. The criminal code was also tightened up, sentences for murder were increased, and the penalties for other crimes, which the wealthy had been largely able to escape, were made more severe – even to the confiscation of half or more of the criminal's property. Apart from this revision of the criminal code, a new codification of all the laws was begun. At the same time, to obviate future dangers from ambitious provincial governors, no consuls at the end of their term of office should govern a province for more than two years, and praetors for no more than one. The plebs, too, were curtailed in their political power by excluding their representatives – who formerly had sat on equal terms with knights and senators – from the tribunals. Caesar had thus, by various measures, blocked the roads to power which he himself had used.

If the proletariat had been curbed and encouraged to emigrate, the bourgeoisie to deploy their talents in the city, and foreign skilled professionals to immigrate, the senate still remained to be dealt with. Caesar's office of Prefect of Morals allowed him to make radical changes in its composition, which he did by increasing the number of senators until, at the time of his death, there were nine hundred of them. The new members were naturally adherents of his, many of them from the provinces and some even former non-commissioned officers in the army. The feelings of the old *Optimate* aristocrats can be imagined! Before all else the settlement of his soldiers engaged his attention, and they had been assigned land in the provinces as well as Italy. Caesar's view was a global one, and all his measures to improve Rome were at the same time intended to make it the heart from which ran improved arteries to the provincial limbs.

As evidence of this grand design he planned a canal to link the Tiber with the river Anio, which would then run down to Tarracina on the coast, facilitating traffic between the city and the sea. The Pontine marshes were to be drained (not, in fact, achieved until the dictatorship of Mussolini), and a road was contemplated that would run from Rome across the Appenines to the Adriatic. Envisaging that Corinth would one day become a prosperous commercial city (as it had been before the Roman devastation) he proposed to drive a canal through the isthmus, linking the Aegean sea with the Gulf of Patras and the Ionian. (The Emperor Nero was later to attempt this, but the rocky nature of the terrain proved too hard for the tools of the time, and it was not achieved until the late nineteenth century.) The port of Ostia was to be improved and expanded, as were others throughout the empire, and the city of Rome was to be transformed. He had already given it the magnificent new Forum Julium with its temple of Venus Genetrix, and he now proposed the erection on the Campus Martius of a great temple to the God of War as well as a large theatre at the foot of the Tarpeian rock, similar to that at Athens. Public libraries were to be established in Rome that would rival those of Alexandria. Again and again in these new schemes and projects the influence of Alexandria, its scholars and its buildings, its libraries, the Mouseion, and the magnificent canal systems of Egypt can be detected. It seems clear that, after his experience of the gleaming marble town-planned city of Alexander and his architect Deinocrates, Caesar was uncomfortably aware of the muddled provincialism of Rome.

Another area of confusion which Caesar was determined to have cleared up was the all-important one of the calendar. The Roman calendar, which at this time was some two months ahead of the solar seasons, had been based on the lunar year of 355 days instead of the solar 365¼. To correct this, it had been customary to insert an intercalary month as necessary but, with the failure of so many institutions during the recent years of chaos, this had been neglected. The year 46 had already received one additional month. Now, by the insertion of two extra months, this unique year was extended to 445 days. From then on, the solar year of 365 days was followed, the institution of a 'leap year' giving an extra day in February every fourth year. The astronomical calculations to perform this very necessary regulation of the calendar were performed by the Greek astronomer and mathematician Sosigenes from Alexandria. Caesar may well have met him in that city when talking with the *savants* in the Mouseion, or he may even have been recommended by Cleopatra. In any case, this new Julian calendar was now promulgated throughout the whole empire. One month, our modern July, was named Julius in honour of Caesar. Even this most beneficial reform found its detractors among the embittered *Optimates*, eager to disparage every new measure of Caesar's, and when a companion remarked that the constellation Lyra would rise next morning Cicero replied: 'Yes, in accordance with the edict.'

In the midst of all these preoccupations Caesar was still not free from the shadow of war. The Pompeian faction was like the Hydra – as soon as one head was cut off another grew in its place. It was the worst of misfortunes for Caesar that Labienus and Pompey's two sons had escaped after Thapsus. Moreover he had chosen his governors of the province badly, and the native Spaniards along with many Roman legionaries and fugitives from North Africa had gathered round the elder son, Cnaeus. They held the Balearic islands and almost all of southern Spain (the part known as Baetica south of the Guadalquivir river). It was from this area that Hannibal had first launched the assault that led him to the very walls of Rome, and the Pompeians still had an efficient fleet, something that the great Carthaginian had lacked. By now Cnaeus Pompeius had thirteen legions and six thousand horse behind him.

The legates to whom Caesar had entrusted the command by land against the Pompeians seemed unable to make any headway, and he saw that once again he must go in person to settle the affairs of the empire. He left Rome in November 46, taking with him his great-nephew and adopted son, Octavius, anxious that this seventeen-year-old should see something of warfare and administration at first hand. With them also in Caesar's carriage went one of his most trusted generals, Decimus Brutus, named by Caesar in his will as one of Octavius's guardians. As regards troops, Caesar's position was little better than it had been in North Africa. Most of the legions were in the provinces, and he had only the Tenth and the Fifth of his veterans with him; apart from them he must make do with such troops as were available in Spain. Despite all the triumphs and festivities, titles and honours conferred upon him in Rome, he could still lose everything in one battle.

After his arrival in Spain he soon found that the winter conditions which usually suited him (since his enemies did not expect attack during the hard months) were of no benefit here. Pompey and Labienus, well-established in the country, had the benefit of sheltering their men in the towns, while Caesar and his forces were compelled to live under canvas. Although he very much wanted a quick decision, so that he could return to attend to all the other matters that awaited him, the Pompeians, as in Africa, were inclined to play a waiting game. Since Thapsus the mood of the contestants had changed, the change of mood most marked in Caesar, whose early policy had always been towards clemency; but now both sides adopted the practice of instantly executing any prisoners taken. There was no longer any room for sentiment or the courtesies of war. The Pompeians knew that there was no hope for them if they were defeated, and the Caesarians were weary and embittered at the protraction of the war. The battle finally came at Munda, a place south of the Guadalquivir and within sight of Corduba.

It was the most furious and savage of the whole civil war – eclipsing Pharsalus and Thapsus in the number of men killed, and leaving behind it such a taste of fratricidal bloodshed that thereafter the legions and their leaders desired nothing more than peace. It had been preceded by Caesar's successful siege of the town of Ategua and a further engagement in which the Pompeians suffered so badly that Cnaeus Pompey feared largescale desertions and even the defection of whole Spanish communities from his arms. Thus provoked to a battle which must be decisive, he finally settled on Munda, standing on a hill that formed the centre of his lines, and here on 17 March 45, the armies finally engaged. It was a bitter hand-to-hand battle. The Pompeians having the advantage of the terrain but Caesar's men the better discipline, the sides were more or less evenly matched, and the struggle went on with charge and counter-charge throughout the day. At one moment, seeing his whole life's work in the balance, Caesar forced his way through the ranks of his soldiers, calling out to them 'Were they not ashamed to deliver him into the hands of boys?' (He later told his friends that he had often fought for victory, but Munda was the first time he fought for his life.) 'The battle was won,' says Plutarch, 'on the feast of Bacchus, the very day on which Pompey, four years before, had set out for the war.' It had been a harsh four years fought from one end of the Mediterranean to the other, and the convulsions were not yet at an end.

The routed Pompeians fled first within the walls of Munda, and then into Corduba – but there was no quarter; 30,000 are said to have fallen on the battlefield itself, among them many of those young aristocrats who had escaped from Pharsalus, as well as survivors from Thapsus. Labienus, one-time friend and fellow-general and later most bitter enemy, was among the slain, together with Attius Varus, former governor of Africa and friend of King Juba. The eagles of the thirteen legions that had fought for Pompey's son were all taken, but he himself and his younger brother both managed to escape. Cnaeus survived only to meet his death while trying to flee to North Africa, and his head was brought to Caesar in Hispalis. There were no tears this time for a Pompey. Sextus Pompeius, the younger son, outlived the war, outlived Caesar, and was finally killed in the reign of Augustus, having first made himself master of Sicily and emulated his father as Sea King of the Mediterranean. But the Pompeian cause, militarily, was ended on the bloodstained field of Munda.

Before leaving Spain Caesar spent many weeks reorganizing the province, founding new citizen colonies and designing the administration in such a way that inland towns and important harbours on the Mediterranean and Atlantic coasts (including Lisbon) became new centres for Roman emigrants. Matthias Gelzer in *Caesar: Politician and*

Statesman has pointed out the importance of the measures that he took in Spain after his victory at Munda:

> This radical transplanting of communities of Roman citizens to territories with no geographical connection with Rome dealt a death blow to the character of the Roman republic as a city state and symbolises the monarchic imperial policy beside which the assemblies of the sovereign people were merely decorative formalities.

This victory in Spain signalled the final defeat of the old senatorial system and the beginning of the imperial.

While still in Spain Caesar, as usual, did not spare the cities and communities that had fought against him. Most of the towns in the rich province of Baetica found themselves compelled to pay fines and to hand over the treasures from their temples and the houses of the rich who had been rash enough to embrace the Pompeian cause. Greece and Asia Minor had yielded little (for political reasons) to the conqueror and his soldiers, but Egypt had paid highly for the privilege of being saved from the family struggle of the Ptolemies and Africa for being the base for Scipio, King Juba, and the other Pompeians. Now those districts of Spain which had been the last stronghold of the sons of Pompey must pay for that doubtful privilege. The unknown author of the *Spanish War* details the reprisals inflicted by Caesar upon the Spanish cities, noting that not even Gades was spared. Yet it was here, in a city always favoured by Caesar and in the time-hallowed temple of Hercules that, as a young man on his first major overseas appointment as quaestor, he is said to have wept before the statue of Alexander and envied him his glory. The temple was plundered of its treasures none the less. He was now master of an empire eclipsing that which the great Macedonian had carved out of the East. Only Parthia, where Crassus had met his fate, Parthia and the lands beyond that led to India, still eluded him. If he redeemed the ineptitude and incompetence of Crassus and made himself master of that kingdom and the road to India and the Far East, his empire would be greater by far than that of Alexander.

CHAPTER THIRTY-FOUR

Dictator Perpetual

On his return journey to Italy Caesar stopped for a while in Narbonese Gaul, that province with which he was so familiar from earlier years and which had helped him greatly during the Gallic war. He strengthened the colony by settling a number of his veterans in it, thus paying off debts to his soldiers and at the same time founding Arelate (Arles) and Forum Julii (Fréjus). During this period, while he was applying the same principles to Narbonese Gaul as he had just done to Spain, young Octavius was with him throughout, a spectator of the tasks of administration – something at which he was later to prove himself a master. They were joined by Mark Antony, to whom Caesar promised the consulship for the following year, regarding his earlier quarrel with him as over and done with. Caesar, from his lonely height of power, was always willing to forgive previous lapses by his appointees or even the downright hostility of his opponents, but he was perhaps unable to realize that those to whom this almost regal pardon was extended sometimes felt, like Cato, that he had no right to bestow it. Such was certainly the case with Gaius Trebonius who, among other petitioners, had come to see Caesar while he was in the province. Trebonius, who had been the governor of Farther Spain, was in considerable disgrace for his conduct of that province and, an embittered man, seems to have been plotting Caesar's assassination. This perhaps is not so surprising, but what does seem almost incredible is that he even tried to involve Antony in the conspiracy. That Caesar's supposedly most devoted lieutenant should have been party to a murder plot at this moment in Caesar's career and not have revealed it, doing no more than turn down the offer, requires some explanation. If Cicero is to be believed Antony had, in fact, been privy to a previous conspiracy against his friend, and his behaviour now goes some way towards explaining his curious inaction immediately after Caesar's death. In the pursuit of power, loyalty is almost as rare as the phoenix. In the event, Trebonius abandoned his design, finding the moment inopportune, but he was later to play a most curious and sinister part in the final and successful conspiracy. Antony's behaviour, both now and later on the Ides of March, must be seen in the context of a man who was not above involvement in the assassination of Caesar.

Another trusted friend who travelled back with Caesar to Rome was Decimus Brutus, governor of Transalpine Gaul, while among those who had come to visit him was Marcus Brutus, Servilia's son. Men like these were quite prepared to work with Caesar so long as it served their political ends, but they would not brook subservience to autocratic power. If such were the feelings of men who had risen to power because of him, those of his opponents can well be imagined.

Marcus Brutus had recently married Porcia, the daughter of Cato and the widow of Caesar's great enemy Bibulus. At his request Cicero had dedicated his encomium of the republican virtues to Brutus' dead father-in-law. Cicero's *Cato*, which Caesar will have read towards the end of 46, provoked him to such anger that he even – rashly – wrote an *Anti-Cato* in refutation. Cato, 'the hero of Utica', as he was seen by old republicans, was extolled by Cicero as a model of all the ancient Roman virtues, representing that dream of an *Optimate* republic which Cicero had never discarded. Caesar's angry and intemperate response to Cicero's work, portraying Cato as a drunkard and a miser, did no damage to this republican image. If anything, the bitter nature of the *Anti-Cato* increased the circulation of Cicero's encomium, for something that so annoyed the great dictator must be presumed to contain more than an element of truth. Cato dead became a far greater force than Cato alive.

As soon as the news of the battle of Munda reached Rome the obsequious senate and the pleasure-loving people vied with one another to overwhelm Caesar with fresh honours. Nothing less than fifty days of thanksgiving for his victory would suffice for the dictator, also named 'Liberator', and to whom the title of Imperator was now given as a hereditary name. The triumphal dress, normally reserved for the occasion of a triumph only, might be worn by Caesar on every occasion, while he was also granted the honour of always wearing a laurel wreath (something designed to gratify the vanity of a balding man). A temple was to be built to the new Concord that Caesar had restored to the people, as well as a palace for him on the Quirinal and another temple to Liberty. In the temple of Quirinus (Romulus after his elevation to a deity) a statue of Caesar was to be erected, with the inscription: *To the Invincible God*. The latter provoked Cicero to the witticism that he would rather see Caesar sharing the temple of Quirinus (Romulus had allegedly been assassinated before his deification as Quirinus) than that of Salus (goddess of Health and Prosperity). But Rome was to be inundated with statues to Caesar, one in the

Capitol next to those of the ancient kings, and two more in the Forum, until finally it was decreed that a statue of Caesar should stand in every temple of Rome and of the republic. Thus the cult of the ruler and of the divine monarch, so familiar to all those in the East, was brought to the capital and was ultimately to spread throughout the whole of the Roman empire. After the personal outward signs and symbols of his glory, and after the statues and the temples, came the celebrations. All the anniversaries of his victories were to be celebrated every year, and every five years a special celebration was to be held in his honour as hero and demigod. But even full divinity did not long elude him, for all the ceremonial trappings which the Romans bestowed upon their deities were soon accorded to him. His statue carved in ivory was to be carried on its special carriage, along with those of the other gods, during the formal processions that heralded the opening of the games at the Circus.

It must certainly be suspected that his enemies, quite as much as his friends, were eager to inundate him with honours to an excessive degree, and in this connection Plutarch has a revealing passage:

> . . . his countrymen, conceding all to his fortune, and accepting the bit, in the hope that the government of a single person would give them time to breathe after so many civil wars and calamities, made him dictator for life. This was indeed a tyranny avowed, since his power now was not only absolute, but perpetual too. *Cicero made the first proposals* [my italics] to the senate for conferring honours upon him, which might in some sort be said not to exceed the limits of ordinary human moderation. But others, striving which should deserve most, carried them so excessively high, that they made Caesar odious to the most indifferent and moderate sort of men, by the pretension and the extravagance of the titles which they decreed him. His enemies, too, are thought to have had some share in this, as well as his flatterers. It gave them advantage against him, and would be their justification for any attempt they should make upon him; for since the civil wars were ended, he had nothing else that he could be charged with.

Caesar's triumph for his victory in Spain was not celebrated until October and, although he was in Italy by July, he does not seem to have spent much if any time in Rome. At first this seems surprising, but not so perhaps if one considers his age and his state of health, and that he had just fought a major campaign, won a decisive victory and completed an arduous round of lawgiving and administration. He was fifty-five years old; intellectually and physically he had subjected himself constantly to almost superhuman strains; his health was failing; he was subject to epileptic fits, and (according to Suetonius) 'sudden comas and a tendency to nightmares'. Coins depicting him at this time in his life show an elderly man with a lean and wrinkled neck, furrows around the eyes and a deeply-lined face. He badly needed a rest, and it was hardly surprising that not long after his arrival back in Italy he made his way to his estate at Lavicum, south-east of Rome. It is clear that his thoughts were turning towards the future, when he would no longer be present to direct the destiny of Rome – had he not already said to the senate in a tired and bitter mood: 'I have lived long enough'?

In September 45, there in the country far from the endless petitioners, the confusions and complexities of Rome, he wrote his will. Three-quarters of the inheritance went to Octavius, the remaining quarter to two other grand-nephews. The formal adoption of Octavius into the Caesar family was confirmed, but a clause provided for the possibility of a son being born to himself – and in this event several of those who were to be his assassins were appointed as the boy's guardians. Decimus Brutus even figured among his potential heirs, in the case of any of the three heirs in the first degree dying or refusing to accept the legacy. His gardens on the banks of the Tiber were to be left to the commons, as well as three gold pieces a man. Provision for the future having been made, his health presumably somewhat restored, he left for Rome where the celebration of his Spanish triumph was due to take place in October.

If it had been difficult to justify the African triumph, and the reason for it had been masked under the defeat of King Juba and the exhibition of his small son among the captives, it was impossible to find any pretence of a foreign enemy for the celebration of the victory in Spain. The battle of Munda had been fought by Romans against Romans, both the generals and the legionaries, and if Pharsalus had been tacitly omitted from Caesar's triumphs so should Munda have been. It was evidence of blindness on his part, and perhaps some deliberate blindness on the part of advisers, that the Spanish campaign and victory was celebrated. It was not popular. A single incident which occurred during the procession of the conqueror is indicative of much of the suppressed bitterness and impotent rage of many of the people. As Caesar in his triumphal chariot was passing the bench reserved for the tribunes of the people, one of them, Pontius Aquila, ostentatiously failed to rise to his feet. Caesar was so incensed at this deliberate discourtesy that he called out to him: 'Hey there, Aquila the tribune! Do you want me then to restore the republic!' The incident clearly rankled and, for several days afterwards, he is reported as having added to every undertaking that he gave: 'Provided that Pontius Aquila gives me permission.' Perhaps it was because he felt the growing resentment, and wished to placate the people in the simple manner that had served so often in the past, that he declared the entertainment provided for them after the procession had not been up to standard and ordered another public banquet to take place a few days later.

But his arrogance now seems to have known no bounds. 'One day,' as Suetonius recounts, 'when the entire senate, armed with an imposing list of honours which had just been voted him, came to where he was sitting in front of the temple of Venus Genetrix, he did not rise to greet them.' This deliberate affront was the kind of action that more than almost any other led to his death. (It is noticeable how careful Augustus always was, even though the senate was no less a rubber stamp in his day, to treat its members with formal courtesy, and to keep up the pretence that he was no more than first man among them.) During the triumphal festivities Caesar summoned an old and famous writer of mimes, Laberius, personally to direct one of his own plays. Laberius, feeling that the command was insulting both in view of his age and his rank (he was over sixty and a knight), took his revenge. He inserted into the known script a number of lines which indicated the feelings of the people towards Caesar. Among them were these:

He must many people fear
Whom many people fear.

According to the grammarian Macrobius, reporting the occasion: 'Everyone fixed their eyes on Caesar at these words, and were pleased to see that the import of them had not escaped him.' Plutarch confirms the unfortunate impression made by the triumph and its accompanying celebrations: 'For he had not defeated foreign generals, or barbarian kings, but had destroyed the children and family of one of the greatest men of Rome, though unfortunate; and it did not look well to lead a procession in celebration of the calamities of his country . . .' As if to increase the magnitude of his folly, Caesar even allowed his two legates in Spain, Fabius and Pedius (whose failure against the Pompeians had caused him to come to their assistance) to celebrate individual triumphs. This was quite contrary to all accepted Roman tradition and, if it was designed to humiliate the opposition even further, did no more than increase their hatred of him.

It is significant that throughout all this time, and indeed right up to his death, Queen Cleopatra of Egypt continued to reside in Rome in the villa which Caesar had allocated to her. It is understandable, perhaps, that her presence might have been required during the Egyptian triumph (though not necessary), and certainly comprehensible that in the mantis-like Ptolemaic style she might have wished to witness the humiliation of her sister Arsinoë, but her continued stay in the Roman capital requires more explanation than most historians have been willing to accord it. She openly held court (to Cicero's great disgust), she openly proclaimed Caesar as the father of her son, and she presented to the many Romans who daily flocked to her presence the spectacle of a woman who was, in the eyes of her subjects, both a Queen and a Goddess. It is significant that, according to Suetonius; 'Mark Antony informed the senate that Caesar had acknowledged Caesarion's paternity and that other friends of Caesar's . . . were aware of this.' (The fact that one of them, Oppius, later wrote a book to 'prove' that the boy was not his at all can be readily understood in the light of Caesarion's murder on Octavius' orders.) Even more significant perhaps is that, again according to Suetonius: 'Helvius Cinna, a tribune of the people, told a number of people that, in accordance with instructions, he had drawn up a bill for the commons to pass during Caesar's absence from Rome [on his Parthian campaign] which would allow him to have as many wives as he pleased – for the purpose of having children.' Such a bill, in fact, would have legitimized his bigamy as well as Caesarion and any other children. Its relevance in the case of Cleopatra can hardly be over-emphasized. The presence of the Egyptian Queen, however much her court was sought after by the Roman *monde*, was infuriating to the *Optimates* (though men like Cicero called on her, and he was even offered some literary position by her – possibly at the Mouseion in Alexandria). The people most probably regarded her presence in their capital with indulgence; as no more than another of his foreign mistresses.

All this does not explain Cleopatra's continued presence in Rome, nor Caesar's determination to depart almost at once for Parthia. Yet his desire for a glory beyond that of Alexander is comprehensible, and the subjugation of the Parthians would provide this, as well as effacing the bitter memory of Crassus' defeat. Furthermore, his distaste for the atmosphere of Rome and the feeling that he was surrounded by an invisible wall of hatred may well have made him long for the simplicity of the life of action. In Rome the torrent of measures, the appointments and elections, continued under his dictatorship, but always on the understood basis that even consulships were no longer any more than posts which he could give to his supporters as a return for their services. Thus, when a consul died on the last day of 45, Caesar had one of his adherents elected to the vacant consulship – even though it lasted less than twenty-four hours. Cicero commented sarcastically that during this consulship no one had lunch, and that such was the consul's vigilance that he never slept a minute during his term of office.

Incidents which showed that nothing would satisfy Caesar but the title of king continued to multiply. As has been suggested, it may well be that some of them were deliberately instigated not by his supporters but by men who wished to see him destroyed. One day, for instance, his gold statue on the *rostra* was discovered to be crowned with the white fillet that was the traditional symbol of monarchy. Two tribunes of the people ordered it to be torn down and thrown away, declaring that Caesar had no need of such embellishments. His head appeared on the coins used in metropolitan Rome, an honour never before accorded to a living man but redolent of the East, where the heads of divine monarchs were normal features of the coinage. It certainly seems that he was earnestly seeking that short and unambiguous title, even to the extent of wearing the tall red boots which had been part of the garb of the ancient kings. Since the senate had already accepted that he was entitled to the royal purple toga, and since he had all the power of a king, such minor details can have only served further to inflame those who already hated him. All the senators had taken an oath to protect his life, and early in the next year (44) he was to dismiss his Spanish bodyguard as if to indicate to the senate and the people that he required no protection save that of Romans.

As if a further test was being made of the willingness of the Romans to accept the title of king, a claque – clearly organized in advance – hailed him as *Rex* during a festival in late January 44. On this occasion Caesar was entering Rome on horseback (another regal prerogative) in his purple toga and red boots, when the prearranged cries assailed him from various quarters. The test, if such it was, was conclusive, for a murmur of opposition grew to a roar of dissent, and Caesar, sensing the real feelings of the people, halted and called out: 'I am Caesar, and not Rex!' The two tribunes, who had previously removed the fillet from his statue, proceeded to arrest the ringleader of the demonstration on the grounds that hailing Caesar as king was an attack on the republic. The whole affair assumed ominous proportions when Caesar's supporters proposed to take action against the two tribunes, the senate meekly assenting. This was only averted by Caesar's magnanimously intervening on their behalf – by having them expelled from the senate and their office. This second test of public opinion seems to have shown quite conclusively that Caesar might have all the power and the titles that he wanted, but not the one that obsessed him, for it bore a deep and ancient tabu. Caesarism had triumphed, and the foundations had been laid of the system that would henceforth rule Rome and the empire, but against the irrational not even Caesar could succeed.

The third and last test of public opinion was by far the most carefully prepared, and designed to be carried out at a moment when the people might be expected to be in affable and generous mood. This was on the occasion of the festival of the Lupercalia, held annually in Rome on 15 February. The whole city was *en fête* in celebration of this ancient fertility rite, whose origins were obscure but which almost certainly dated from Etruscan times. Caesar on his return from Africa had made a donation to the college of the priests of Lupercus for an additional college to be known as the Julian designed to celebrate his cult, and Mark Antony had been made its high priest. Lupercus, who was identified in later Roman eyes with the nature god Faunus, or Pan, represented the return of the spring and, by natural identification, the growth of plants, the mating of animals and fecundity in human beings. After the sacrifice of a goat and a dog, two young nobles who belonged to the Order of Lupercus cut the skins of these animals into strips known as *februa* (hence February) and, using them as whips, ran through the streets at the head of two bands of Luperci, striking out at every woman that they passed. The belief was that any woman so touched would become pregnant before the year was out and there was great competition between women who wanted to bear a child to be struck by the *februa*. On this occasion Caesar, as president of the ceremonies, was seated on his golden throne in the Forum, surrounded by all the notables of Rome, and Antony by chance (or by arrangement) was one of the leading Luperci. As custom decreed, he was wearing only a goatskin as, at the head of the dense crowd that always followed the 'Faun-men', he bounded into the Forum and hailed Caesar as Lupercus himself. He then ran forward and, mounting the rostrum, placed a crown on Caesar's head. At this dramatic moment a claque of Caesar's supporters, stationed throughout the Forum, shouted out and urged him to accept it. Caesar made a gesture of protest, but for a brief while the crown stayed upon his head. Then, the silence of those around him and the failure of the crowd to respond to the isolated cries of his supporters told him that the time was still not yet ripe. Caesar removed the crown, and the crowd burst into loud cheers. Concealing his disappointment (which must have been deep indeed) he gave orders that the crown should be placed upon the head of Jupiter's statue in the Capitol, and that an entry should be made in the public records to the effect that: 'On this day, acting on the wishes of people, Mark Antony offered Caesar the royal crown, but the Dictator refused to accept it.'

CHAPTER THIRTY-FIVE

The Desired Death

The weeks of February and early March were largely occupied with the preparations for the Parthian campaign. When so much still remained to be done in Rome and Italy, and when the various measures he had set in train all needed supervision, and when the line of petitioners at his house was such that even a former consul like Cicero had to wait a long time for admission, it might seem that the dictator's time would be occupied for many months or even years in administration alone. This was probably what Caesar was eager to avoid. He wanted the simplicities of camp and campaign, where command was followed by obedience, orders by the sound of the trumpet and the disciplined manoeuvres of trained men. In Rome all was plot and confusion, dissimulation and uncertainty and, as he now knew, above all the smell of fear and hatred. He who had always known that power could only be grasped in Rome and, since a young man, had always kept his eye on that objective, had now attained it in an almost immeasurable degree. In distant Britain, in Gaul, in Spain and Greece, Asia Minor and Egypt, he had never lost sight of his aim – Rome and power. Had he dreamed of the city?

The drip of water from the aqueduct that passed over the gate from which the dusty, squalid Appian Way stretched through its long suburb; the garret under the tiles where, just as now, the pigeons sleeked themselves in the sun and the rain drummed on the roof; the narrow, crowded streets, half choked with the builders' carts, and the pavements ringing under the heavy military boots of guardsmen; the tavern waiters trotting along with a pyramid of hot dishes on their heads; the flower-pots falling from high window ledges; night, with the shuttered shops, the silence broken by some street brawl, the darkness shaken by a flare of torches as some great man, wrapped in his scarlet cloak, passes along from a dinner-party with his long train of clients and slaves . . .

(J. W. Mackail)

That was Rome: violence, brutality, squalor and beauty – and power. And he had attained it to a degree such as no man in Rome before him had known; his head was on the city's coinage; a queen who had borne his son waited with her court in his villa on the banks of the Tiber; and his legions waited for his further orders.

Six legions with their accompanying auxiliaries had already crossed the Adriatic and were ready at Apollonia. A further ten legions and ten thousand cavalry were assembling in the eastern provinces, for Caesar had no intention of having to fight on this great campaign with hastily improvised forces, as had so often been the case in the past. His aim was first to restore order to Macedonia, where the King of Dacia (Rumania and Hungary) had been advancing his borders, and then, after settling the frontier, to march through Asia Minor and attack Parthia via Armenia. The conquest of Parthia might well afford the extension of Roman rule to the Persian Gulf and even to India. He planned to return through the Caucasus and southern Russia and then, following the Danube, to annex further vast territories on his way back into Gaul.

The range and scope of this immense design was more suited to a giant or a demigod than any ordinary man, but Caesar had transcended mortal limits – and, in any case, can hardly have considered that he would ever return from a campaign of such limitless aggression. At his age, and in his state of health, he would be lucky indeed if he completed his conquest of Parthia. But then, perhaps the rumours that were circulating in Rome were true? It was being said that

> . . . Caesar intended to move the seat of government to Troy or Alexandria, taking with him all the national resources, drafting every man in Italy of military age for service with the army, and leaving his friends to govern what was left of the city.
>
> (Suetonius)

The idea of Troy as capital city of the empire (based solely on his claimed descent from Aeneas) can be dismissed, but Alexandria retains an element of probability. After the conclusion of the campaign against Parthia, it would offer a suitable base for administering the new territories in the East, and it was in many ways far better designed to be a capital than Rome. It was nearer to the richest provinces of the empire for one thing, and for another it had been specifically intended by Alexander and his architect as a capital, whereas Rome had just grown over the centuries, unplanned and in many respects provincial. In Alexandria, a god-king and a goddess-queen would not only be accepted but expected. A Julian-Ptolemaic dynasty, ruling out of Egypt over all the known world, and backed by the immense riches of the East (immeasurably increased by recent conquests), would have nothing to fear from the almost tribal squabbles of a few dissident families in Rome. That city, like Athens and Antioch, Gades and Corduba, Narbo and Gergovia, would take its place among the great administrative capitals of the empire. Such was indeed a possibility, and though it may not ever have been carefully formulated by Caesar (like so much else) as a master-plan, the very idea of it – spread by rumour – was enough to arouse feelings of the most utmost hatred.

One rumour which probably contributed to the decision of his assassins to act swiftly was that a consultation of the Sibylline Books had revealed that the Roman armies could only be victorious over the Parthians if commanded by a king. These prophetic books, most of the originals of which had long since been lost or destroyed (and suitably replaced), were consulted in emergencies by order of the senate. In charge of them were the *quindecemvirs* (a college of fifteen priests), at the head of whom, as of all Roman religious institutions, was the Pontifex Maximus. Since Caesar had long held this office, it was not difficult to arrange for the Books to be consulted – nor for the desired answer to a question to be found. The Parthian disclosure, so it was said, would be officially made by Lucius Cotta, a member of the college which kept the Books who was also a relative of Caesar (his mother's cousin). The announcement of the prophecy, followed by a speech proposing that the title of Rex should be immediately conferred upon Caesar to secure the success of Roman arms in Parthia, would be made at the next meeting of the senate on 15 March. This was three days before Caesar was due to leave Rome.

Once Caesar was away in the East with his legions, Rome being administered by consuls and other officials whom he had appointed to take charge during the next two years, there would be no redress. The *Optimates* and many of a genuine republican persuasion, as well as those who simply detested Caesar, were conscious that time was running out. If the tyrant (as they now saw him) was to be removed, they must act at once, and the meeting of the senate on the Ides of March would present the ideal opportunity – not only for the murder but to involve the whole senate in the action. They could be confident that Caesar would be present, for it was then that he expected to hear from that august body (which he too openly despised) the confirmation of his kingship. Their oath to protect him meant little to them now that they had decided that in every respect he fulfilled the role of tyrant. From the moment that he had accepted the dictatorship for life, thus depriving all future consuls and indeed all officers of state of any real significance, he had stood openly revealed. Romulus, it was remembered, had moved from the position of constitutional monarch to absolute ruler – and had been put to death by his senators. After the death of the last King of Rome, Tarquinius Superbus, the Roman people had taken a solemn oath never again to have a king. Junius Brutus, from whom Marcus Junius Brutus claimed descent, was the hero of many legends about the expulsion of the last king of Rome. Tyrannicide was a virtue.

Chief instigator of the conspiracy was Gaius Cassius, an able general who had also been one of Pompey's admirals, was married to a sister of Brutus and had fought against Caesar at Pharsalus – subsequently being pardoned in the amnesty. Long an ardent republican, he had headed the few senators who had voted against the accordance of honours to Caesar after the battle of Munda. An embittered man, who felt that he had been unfairly set aside by Caesar for one of the more coveted offices of state, he was to win over his brother-in-law Marcus Brutus to the conspiracy, although Brutus seems to have had some reservations about its morality. Caesar had been suspicious of Cassius for some time and had once remarked that he mistrusted him: 'Cassius looks so pale. What can he be up to?'

Marcus Brutus was a very different kind of man. Young, scholarly, an intellectual, he was treated by Caesar like the son that he may well have been. His pride lay in his legal father, husband of Caesar's much-loved Servilia and descendant of the Roman hero. Caesar had given special orders that if Brutus was captured at Pharsalus (he was not, in fact, present) he should be spared. He had pardoned him for his adherence to Pompey and had given him high office: he was praetor at the time, along with Cassius, and expected to become consul in 41. Like his father-in-law Cato he was high-minded, something of a prig, and his inclination to moralize when speaking in the senate had once caused Caesar to say: 'I don't know what the young man means, but whatever it is, he means it vehemently.'

Decimus Brutus, favoured by Caesar since he was a young man, one of his best generals and consul-designate for 42, was another leading conspirator, along with Gaius Trebonius the unsuccessful governor of Farther Spain who had been consul in 45; he was another of Caesar's men, but had already tried to involve Antony in an assassination plot. The leaders of the conspiracy, then, were all successful politicians, and came from both sides in the civil war. Many had enjoyed his friendship, and admired and been charmed by his intelligence and wit. Among the lesser conspirators (Suetonius says there were sixty in all) there was to be found a mixture of idealism, personal hatred of the dictator, self-seeking and a confused desire to return to the days of the republic. After the death of Caesar they hoped that normal government by the senate would once more be resumed.

Caesar was well enough aware of the hatred by which he was surrounded, but he counted upon his enemies possessing something that they did not have – foresight. With his intimate knowledge of home politics as well as the affairs of the empire, he saw quite clearly that his death would bring such chaos to the state that the confusion from which he had just rescued it would be as nothing. As usual, he was more prescient and astute than everyone else, and his accurate assessment that his death would cause 'a new civil war far worse than the last' did not deter the conspirators. He failed to understand just how strong was the republican ideal, nor how much the image of Cato, as an embodiment of the old principles which had saved and governed Rome in times past, meant to his opponents. They for their part did not understand – or did not wish to understand – that the immense changes brought about by Caesar could never be eradicated. An assembly of noble Roman families – the *Optimates* – could no longer dominate the senate, let alone deal with the complexities of running a vast empire.

At the same time, obsessed as they were with pride of rank and position, they were more than unwilling to become mere officials in the dictator's bureaucracy. In the appointment of consuls and other officials who were merely executors of his designs, Caesar had removed all hope and ambition from the whole ruling class of Romans. He had cynically used the plebeians against them to gain his way, and yet he had no more use for them than they! His exaltation of the Julian clan, as if it were above all others, offended men whose families over the centuries had been just as distinguished and rendered even more service to the state. Quite apart from any personal reasons (Tullius Cimber, for instance, had an exiled brother whom Caesar refused to pardon), this hatred for what Caesar represented was the main motive for his assassination.

There is little reason to doubt that in the weeks before his death the atmosphere of Rome was sombre in the extreme. The legions were about to march against the dreaded Parthians. Small groups of men were known to be meeting behind closed doors in private houses, and the air was full of rumours. The murder of Caesar made such an impression upon ancient historians that it was natural that, with the benefit of hindsight, they should describe innumerable portents foretelling his end. It was said that the horses which Caesar had consecrated to the gods on crossing the Rubicon had declined to eat, and had shed vast tears. Spurinna, a renowned soothsayer, of whom there were many in Rome (who naturally kept themselves well-informed for their 'magic' information), had come to him and warned him to beware of the Ides of March. Caesar paid no more attention to him than he did at any time to auguries, religious rituals or diviners. A sacrifice before the battle of Munda had proved unfavourable, but he had merely dismissed it, saying that everything would turn out well since such was his wish. Similarly, in the days before his death, and even right up to the last morning, he paid no attention to ill omens. As head of the established religion of Rome he had never had any use for it, except where he could turn it to his advantage for political ends. Unlike many of his contemporaries he had no use for philosophers either – he believed in Luck. Fortuna, that was his goddess, and always had been. She was not always inclined in your favour, but you could assist her – and if Luck turned against you, then there was nothing you could do about it. As for death, he had made his feelings quite clear on a number of occasions. On the very evening of 14 March he had dined with Lepidus, his Master of the Horse, and a few friends. The conversation had taken a philosophical turn and among other things the guests had expressed their opinions as to what manner of death they would prefer. Caesar had no doubt: he desired an end, he said, that was both sudden and unexpected.

That night, so Plutarch tells us, as Caesar was lying next to Culpurnia, all the doors and windows of the room suddenly burst open as if struck with a great gale of wind. At the same time the ceremonial armour of Mars, which Caesar as Pontifex Maximus kept in his house, fell with a crash from the wall. Calpurnia is said to have had terrible visions and nightmares, to have lain moaning in her sleep and, on Caesar's awaking her, to have said that she had dreamed he was murdered. She implored him not to leave the house that day. Calpurnia, the childless wife who had seen very little of her husband since she had married him in 59, who had organized his household like any Roman matron of her standing, dutifully accepted his affairs with other women – including this Egyptian Queen who now held court in Rome – who had seen him depart for many a campaign and battlefield, seems to have been distraught at the dark image of her dream.

Troubled by the strange events of the night and by his wife's entreaties, Caesar, who may have been genuinely indisposed, sent for Antony in the morning with the intention of postponing his visit to the senate. His doctors advised him to stay at home, and the augurs reported that the sacrifices for the day were inauspicious. As the time went by, and the dictator failed to make an appearance, the conspirators were on tenterhooks. An agony of fear possessed them as they imagined that perhaps the plot had leaked out, and that Caesar was even now on his way with his legionaries to surround Pompey's Theatre where they were assembled. In their terrified quandary they sent Decimus Brutus as an emissary to persuade him of the importance of his personal attendance, no doubt urging upon him his necessary acceptance of the title *Rex* before he left for Parthia with the legions. This Brutus, the Judas of the story, who owed his whole career to Caesar (like Labienus before him), was destined like most of the others to die in the civil war that followed his death.

Persuaded against his will to attend the meeting, Caesar was being borne in his litter through the streets of Rome when a man ran after him waving a message. This was Artemidorus, a Greek rhetorician, who had long ago been Greek tutor to Marcus Brutus and who had accompanied Caesar as a secretary during his passage through Asia Minor after his victory at Pharsalus. As Caesar prepared to enter the portico to Pompey's Theatre, brushing aside petitioners and referring them to his officers, he recognized Artemidorus and acknowledged the urgency of his request to read the note. Caesar took it, but was prevented from reading it by another petitioner who claimed his attention. Undoubtedly Artemidorus had discovered the details of the plot and his note would have saved the dictator; it is said that it was still with him when he died. Spurinna, too, was waiting for him at the entrance, where it was customary to take the auspices. To Caesar's ironical remark that the Ides of March had come and here he was, Spurinna replied: 'They have come, but they are not yet gone.'

The auguries were inauspicious, the beast's entrails defective, and another victim was tried – with the same result. Impatient of this antiquated ritual, remembering so many other occasions when he had confidently disregarded such superstitions, Caesar entered the portico and made his way towards the assembly. The senators were awaiting him, although it was curious perhaps that Antony should be deeply engaged in conversation with Trebonius in the anteroom. Apparently Trebonius had distracted Antony sufficiently to prevent his being present at this all-important meeting, which Caesar had reluctantly agreed to attend . . .

The whole senate rose to its feet as he entered the building, walked over to his throne and took his place. While the senate as a body was paying the dictator its usual formal tribute, the conspirators, as if to ask him questions or favours, gathered round in a half circle so as to,screen him from the others. One of the foremost was Tullius Cimber, petitioning Caesar to recall his brother from exile and, when the latter refused his request, stretching out his hand towards Caesar's robe in a gesture of supplication. When he drew back, Cimber, as if turning from pleading to indignation, laid his hand on the dictator's purple robe and pulled it down from his shoulder. It was the signal. The other conspirators crowded round him as he stood there, clad only in the simple Roman tunic. They had stripped him of his emperorship, and Caesar, as if divining the symbolism of the act as well as their hostility, cried out: 'But this is violence!' At this, Casca, who was standing behind him, struck the first blow at the victim's neck but, missing, pierced only his shoulder. Caesar wheeled round, caught Casca's arm and ran it through with the stylus that he used for writing, crying out, 'You villain, Casca! What are you about?'

He was moving away when another stabbed him in the side and

Cassius pierced him full in the face with his dagger. Now they were all on to him like a pack of wolves, one striking him in the thigh, another in the back. Caesar, says Appian, fought for his life like a wild animal. Inflamed with hatred and blood-lust, the conspirators were like madmen, striking out so wildly that they wounded several of their own number. Fighting to the last, defending himself to left and right with his stylus, Caesar slowly sank to the ground in the Theatre of Pompey at the foot of the statue of his old enemy. It was at this moment, so tradition has it, that he saw Brutus coming towards him with his dagger in his hand. His last words, spoken in Greek, were to Brutus: 'And you too, my child!'

Covering his head with his toga, he slid to the floor and died. Twenty-three dagger wounds were later counted upon his body, but it was so mangled that there may well have been more. They were wounds that would be paid for terribly, and over and over again, in the body of Italy and the empire.

CHAPTER THIRTY-SIX

Apotheosis

If the death of Cato had strengthened the forces that opposed Caesar, his assassination unleashed a hurricane that devastated the Roman world. Far from ensuring the triumph of republicanism, the death of Caesar ended the republic for ever, and provided Octavius with the opportunity to erect the military monarchy of the Roman imperial period. Far from the senate immediately taking over the government, a panic-stricken fear gripped every member who had not taken part in the plot, while even those who had participated in the murder seemed at a loss once the deed was done. Rome itself was paralysed.

Caesar had well known what a vacuum his death would cause, and the city and the senate now experienced it. The power, as Caesar had known for so many years, lay in the hands of the general who could command the legionaries. Antony was the only man who had their trust and, since he had access to all Caesar's papers as well as his will, was in a position within a few days to take command. The conspirators, Brutus and Cassius and their fellows, were faced with the fact that they had no control over the real source of power – the legions. The accuracy of Caesar's assessment of the situation was made abundantly clear. 'If Caesar,' as Gaius Matius, one of his friends remarked, 'with all his genius could not find a way out, who will find one now?'

It took thirteen years of further civil war before Octavius finally resolved the legacy of Caesar. The military monarchy which the dead dictator had all but established was confirmed by his successor, who had the opportunity to judge what mistakes Caesar had made and to apply a superficially more amiable dominion over senate and people. Augustus (as he became) inherited a world in which the desire, above all, was for peace; in which the foundation stones of empire were laid; and in which his natural characteristic of 'hastening slowly' suited the times. In due course it would present a unified Near-Eastern, Mediterranean and European world where, as Gibbon wrote:

The frontiers of that extensive monarchy were guarded by ancient renown and disciplined valour. The gentle but powerful influence of laws and manners had gradually cemented the union of the provinces . . . The image of a free constitution was preserved with decent reverence: the Roman senate appeared to possess the sovereign authority, and devolved on the emperors all the executive powers of government.

Such a unity, which Caesar had sought to achieve, has not been known again since the fifth century AD.

The immediate effect of the murder was that the streets were full of panic and confusion, most of the senators fleeing to their homes, while Cicero, who had not been invited to take part in the plot 'because of his age', misunderstanding events as usual, hastened to the Capitol to congratulate the conspirators. He soon learned that nothing was as expected. The senate had not by some miraculous means regained its old republican glory, and had meekly and fearfully assembled when summoned by Antony as consul. Furthermore, Lepidus, Caesar's Master of the Horse, occupied the city with his troops. As it had begun, so it would continue. Caesar's funeral, and the moment when the people learned the dead dictator's legacy to them, would merely confirm the feelings that had already taken possession of Rome. Some time or other, early in the days after the assassination, Queen Cleopatra left the city. She sailed back for Alexandria, where one future day she would again attempt the empire – by the side of Antony. Her son Caesarion was not mentioned in the will, for testamentary bequests were not allowed from Romans to foreigners. If Caesar had established a second capital in Alexandria, Caesarion would no doubt in due course have become Ptolemy – King of the East. But as it was, it seems that Caesar had chosen well enough in Octavius.

As a general, Caesar was lucky – and he would have been the first to admit it. Time and again he might have been killed; he never scrupled to hazard himself; and he often plunged into actions which most generals, however brave, would have considered foolhardy. That same aristocratic nonchalance, that insouciance which had distinguished him all his days never failed him. That he was an excellent general cannot be doubted, although he was again lucky to find ready waiting for him the form and pattern of the legions which Marius had prepared. Very many of his actions, although hard-fought, were against brave but undisciplined barbarians, unfamiliar with organized warfare, Roman weapons or siege engines. In North Africa he enjoyed less success, and the culminating battle of Thapsus seems almost to have been won by his soldiers alone. Zela, which he made a mock of in his triumph, was a 'close-run' thing – although it suited him to pretend otherwise.

Pharsalus was a brilliant victory, but his last battle at Munda in Spain was probably the hardest of his whole career. The Alexandrian campaign, fought throughout a palace, a city and a disaffected people, showed his mastery of tactics and his understanding of politics – as when, for instance, he sent the young Pharaoh back to his army. The rapidity of his movements was what always impressed and startled his enemies: at sea, indeed, as well as on land. He relied very greatly on the courage of his soldiers, and it must perhaps be doubted whether he would have been the equal of Hannibal given the latter's tenuous supply lines and mercenary army. Both had one thing in common – they were aristocrats.

Oratory has relatively little standing nowadays – probably because those who are called upon to speak are insufficiently literate – but Caesar, even before he had attained any great fame, had a reputation second only to Cicero; and time and time again, both in formal speeches or in battlefield addresses to his troops, he reveals his ability to convince and move his listeners. As a prose writer he has been recognized throughout the ages for his commentaries on the Gallic wars, which (though necessarily biased at times) have remained one of the monuments of Roman literature. His other writings are lost; one or two juvenilia, it is believed, having been destroyed by Augustus as either unworthy of or unsuitable to the Divine Julius.

Certainly he became divine – within a day or so of his murder. The foreign communities mourned him deeply, particularly the Jews, who remembered how much he had done for them, and a cousin of his built an altar on the funeral pyre where his body had lain. This was later replaced by a marble column in the Forum, with the inscription 'To the Father of his Country'. But, quite apart from the supernatural signs which had presaged his death, a comet traced itself across the sky for the six nights following. People believed that it was Caesar's spirit being translated to the heavens and that was why, on his posthumous coinage, he is shown with a star above his head.

It was as a politician that Caesar proved himself supreme. From the beginning of his career he had followed the popular, Marian alignment of his family. He had greatly restored the power of the people, as a means of reducing the power of the *Optimate* senate. At the same time he was no liberal democrat and he bought whatever votes he needed with complete cynicism, while his attitude to the masses was that of a stern but indulgent master. As a true aristocrat he was completely at home with the ordinary people, being so far removed from them by breeding and nature that, although – again like Hannibal – legendary for 'living rough' along with his men, he was untouched by the daily life of camp or barracks – though never forgetful of the needs of the men who furnished his power. As a conqueror in a civil war and as dictator, he showed himself completely unlike Sulla by his policy of conciliation towards his enemies. Time and again he displayed a far wider vision than the old-style *Optimates*, who tried always to cling to the narrow prerogatives of their rank. Middle-class men such as Cicero, who idolized the old institutions, and men of similar stock like Pompey, could not understand that their talents were used by the *Optimates* as tools – no more. Caesar, as aristocratic as any of his opponents, knew them through and through – and was not deceived. His folly was to allow the senators to see that he despised them, and to allow the Caesar cult to reach absurd proportions. 'We have killed the king,' cried Cicero bitterly, 'but the kingdom is still with us. We have removed the tyrant, but the tyranny still survives.'

All men are mad who devote themselves to the pursuit of politics and power when they could be harmoniously engaged in cultivating a garden or fishing, or in a myriad activities both harmless and fruitful. At the same time, since history is made by the mad, it must be conceded that de Tocqueville's description of Napoleon is even more relevant to Caesar: 'He was as great as a man can be without morality.'

19 April 1983

Chronology of Caesar's Life

BC

100   Born on July 12.

84   Marries Cornelia, the daughter of Cinna, mother of his daughter Julia.

81   Endangered by victory of Sulla. Is pardoned but refuses to divorce Cornelia.

80   Military service in Asia. Involved in scandal with King of Bithynia. Wins Civic Crown at Mitylene.

78   Military service in Cilicia. Returns to Rome on death of Sulla.

77   Achieves fame by prosecution of Dolabella.

75   Visits Rhodes and is captured by pirates.

74   Involved in Mithridatic War.

72   Military tribune.

69   Death of his wife Cornelia. Quaestor in Farther Spain.

67   Marries Pompeia.

65   Curule Aedile.

63   Pontifex Maximus. Consulship of Cicero. Conspiracy of Catiline.

62   Praetor. Clodius scandal and divorce of Pompeia.

61   Proconsul of Farther Spain.

60   With the help of Pompey and Crassus stands for consulship. The Triumvirate.

59   Consul. Marries Calpurnia. Pompey marries his daughter Julia. Secures provinces of Cisalpine Gaul and Illyricum, and finally Transalpine Gaul.

58   Proconsul. Campaigns against Helvetii and Ariovistus successful.

57   Campaign against the Belgae.

56   Further campaigns in Brittany and Normandy. The Triumvirate renewed.

55   Proconsulship renewed for five years. Successful campaigns

against German tribes and crossing of the Rhine. First expedition to Britain.

54   Invasion of Britain. Rising under Ambiorix against Romans in Gaul. Death of Julia.

53   Risings in Gaul suppressed. Second crossing of the Rhine. Death of Crassus in Mesopotamia.

52   Outbreak of the rebellion of Vercingetorix in Gaul. Finally surrounded in Alesia, Vercingetorix surrenders. Disturbances in Rome. Clodius is murdered and Pompey is elected sole consul.

51   Gaul pacified. Publication of Caesar's *Commentaries* on the Gallic war. His enemies in Rome attempt to get him recalled.

50   Continued attempts by the Optimates in Rome to bring Caesar to trial.

49   Caesar ordered to dismiss his army. Pompey granted dictatorial powers.
January 10 Caesar crosses Rubicon. Pompey crosses Adriatic to Greece in March. Pompeian forces surrender in Spain in August. Caesar is elected dictator.

48   Caesar's second consulship. After inconclusive struggle at Dyrrhachium, Pompey is defeated at Pharsalus on 9 August. Pompey is murdered in Egypt and Caesar occupies Alexandria.

47   Conclusion of the Alexandrian war. Cleopatra is installed as queen. Caesar defeats Pharnaces in Asia Minor on 1 August. Returns to Rome in October and lands in Africa in December.

46   Victorious over Pompeian forces at Thapsus on 6 April. Third consulship. Returns to Rome and is made dictator for ten years. Leaves Rome for Spain in November.

45   Victorious at Munda on 17 March. Fourth consulship. Returns to Rome to receive dictatorship for life. Divine honours.

44   Fifth consulship. Attempts made to crown Caesar as king. Preparations for Parthian expedition. Caesar is murdered on 15 March.

Further Reading

Balsdon, J. P. Y. D.:	*Julius Caesar & Rome*, 1967
Bradford, E.:	*Cleopatra*, 1971
Cambridge Ancient History:	Vol. IX, 1932
Clare, J. S.:	*Caesar and Roman Politics*, 1971
Connolly, P.:	*Greece and Rome at War*, 1981
Ellis, P. Beresford	*Caesar's Invasion of Britain*, 1978
Froude, J. A.:	*Caesar – a Sketch*, 1886
Gelzer, M., trans. P. Needham:	*Caesar – Politician and Statesman*, 1968
Grant, M.:	*Caesar*, 1972
Holmes, T. R.:	*Caesar's Conquest of Gaul*, 1911
Syme, Sir R.:	*The Roman Revolution*, 1939
Taylor, L. R.:	*Party Politics in the Age of Caesar*, 1949.
Walter, G.:	*Caesar*

Ancient Sources:

Anon:	Accounts of the *Alexandrian*, *African* and *Spanish* Wars
Appian:	*Civil Wars*
Caesar:	*Commentaries, Gallic War Books I–VII*; *Civil War Books I–III*
Cicero:	Extensive writings, especially the *Letters*
Dio Cassius:	*The Histories*
Hirtius, Aulus:	*Gallic War Book VIII*
Lucan:	*The Civil War* (Pharsalia)
Plutarch:	*Caesar*
Sallust:	*Catiline*
Suetonius:	*Caesar*

Index

life of – *cont.*

attempts reconciliation with Cicero 60; checks advance of Helvetii 62–3; defeats Helvetii 69–72; negotiates with Ariovistus 74, 76–7; quells incipient mutiny 75–6; drives Ariovistus and Suebi from Gaul, 58 BC 77–8; settles troops for winter among Sequani 78; returns to supervise Cisalpine Gaul 78; moves against Belgae, 57 BC 82–3; early successes 83; hard fighting against Nervii 83–5; destroys Atuatuci 85; lays down framework for government of Gaul 85–6, 87; proposal for public thanksgiving in Rome 86; campaigns against Veneti, 56 BC 89–91; fails to penetrate marshes of Flanders 91; his legions help Crassus and Pompey wins consulships for 55 BC 91–2; powers prolonged for four years 92; drives Usipetes and Tencteri over Rhine, 55 BC 92–3; makes pre-emptive strike against Germans across Rhine 95–6; first invasion of Britain, 55 BC 97–9; deals with trouble in Illyricum 101; second invasion of Britain, 54 BC 101, 102–7; sends troops to winter quarters, 54 BC 109; relieves besieged Q. Cicero at Amiens 109; defeats Belgic tribes 109; crushes Nervii 110; calls meeting of Gallic chieftains, 53 BC 110; defeats all revolts 110; spends heavily on building and entertainment for people 114–15; doubles soldiers' pay 115; actions to deal with Gallic revolt, 52 BC 116–21; successful siege of Alesia, 52 BC 122–5; moves against Belgae, 51 BC 126; captures Uxellodunum 126–7; achieves Gallic power base 129–30; tours Narbonese Gaul, 51 BC 130; gives Gaul its constitution 130–1; faces legal proceedings when proconsulship ends 131, 132; detaches two 'Trojan Horse' legions to Pompey 133–4; tours Cisalpine Gaul, 50 BC 135; prepares for war with Pompey 137–8; crosses the Rubicon 138; successful invasion of Italy, 49 BC 139–43; fails to gain legal justification for invasion 144, 145; seizes Roman treasury 145; besieges Massilia 146; defeats Pompeians in Spain 146–7; puts down mutiny of Ninth Legion 148; nominated dictator 148; deals with problem of debtors 148–9; takes measures to restore economic stability 149; named consul for 48 BC 149; takes army across Adriatic into Greece, 48 BC 150–1; proposes peace to Pompey 151–2; fails in attempt to return to Italy for reinforcements 152–3; defeated by Pompey at Dyrrachium 154–5; moves army deep into Greece 156; sacks town of Gomphi 157; reaches plain of Pharsalus 157; defeats Pompey at Pharsalus 158–61; pursuit of Pompey 163; narrow escape in Hellespont 163; visits Troy 164; sails to Alexandria 165–6; discovers Pompey is dead 166; decides to collect Egyptian debt to Rome 166, 167; moves into royal palace in Alexandria 166; first meeting with Cleopatra 168; becomes Cleopatra's lover 169; confirms Ptolemy XIII and Cleopatra as rulers of Egypt 170; besieged in palace in Alexandria 171–2; attacks Pharos 172–3; returns Ptolemy XIII to Egyptian army 173; defeats

Egyptians in battle, 47 BC 173–4; installs Cleopatra as Queen of Egypt 174; becomes an Egyptian god 174–5; makes journey up Nile 175; leaves Egypt, 47 BC 176; settles affairs in East 177–8; defeats Pharnaces at Zela 178–9; returns to Rome, 47 BC 179–80; settles affairs in Rome 180; deals with army mutiny 180–1; moves against Pompeians in Africa 182–3; suffers early defeat 183; receives reinforcements 184; defeats Pompeians at Thapsus, 46 BC 186–8; returns to Rome 189; becomes Prefect of Morals 190; becomes dictator 190; honours granted to 190–1; celebrates triumphs, 46 BC 192–6; dedicates Forum Julium 196; dedicates temple of Venus Genetrix 196; arranges emigration of Rome proletariat 198; bans workmen's clubs 198; controls agricultural labour 198; plans to attract talent to Rome 199; tightens up criminal code 199; reforms senate 199; actions as Prefect of Morals 199; plans better access to Rome 199; plans new building in Rome 200; reforms calendar 200; crushes Pompeians in Spain, 46–45 BC 200–2; settles veterans in Narbonese Gaul 204; writes *Anti-Cato* 205; honours accorded to after battle of Munda 205–6; writes will 207; celebrates unpopular triumph 207–8; question of kingship arises 209–11; refuses crown from Antony 211; prepares invasion of Parthia 212, 213; development of conspiracy against 214–16; portents before death of 216–17; assassination of, 44 BC 218–19

opinion of Rome 190
oratorical ability 13–14, 222
origin of name Caesar 2
physical descriptions 3
political ability 222–3
possible idea of founding dynasty 197
possible plan to move capital to Alexandria 213–14
qualities as general 221–2
quest for fame 80–1
riches received from Gallic conquests 114
statues of 205–6
writing ability 222

Caesarion 174, 193, 196, 197, 221
  birth 176
  murdered by Octavius 197
Calendar
  reformed by Caesar 200
Calpurnia (Caesar's third wife) 55, 112, 197
  fears for Caesar's death, 44 BC 217
Calvus, Licinius 12
Carnutes, the 109, 110: rise against Rome, 52 BC 115; Romans defeat 117–18
Carrhae, battle of 111
Carthage
  conquered by Rome 4
  Roman colonisation 198
Casca
  part in Caesar's assassination 218
Cassius Longinus, Caius 220: leads conspiracy against Caesar 215; suspected by Caesar 215; part in Caesar's assassination 219
Cassius Longinus, Quintus 137, 145
  at battle of Pharsalus 159
Cassivellaunus 108
  opposes Caesar's second invasion of Britain 103–7 *passim*
Catiline (Lucius Sergius Catilina) 33, 36, 135: offers social programme in bid for consulship 37; conspires against state 37–8; death 42

239